IMAGE TRANSFORMATION THERAPY®

CW01095861

A

ImTT Press, publisher

B

ImTT Press, publisher

Dedication

This book is dedicated to my wife, Janet.

Her ideas and spirit influenced the development
of Image Transformation Therapy.

Fire and Water Unite.

C

ImTT Press, publisher

Image Transformation Therapy®, ImTT®, The Feeling-State Addiction Protocol®, FSAP®,
The Feeling-State Image Protocol®, FSIP®, and Enter A New Dimension®, are
registered trademarks by Robert Miller and are to be used
only with express written permission of Robert Miller.

Cover photo courtesy of: Hubble Space Telescope, Photo Credit: STScI

Image Transformation Therapy, Third edition

Enter A New Dimension

ImTT Press, publisher

Table of Contents

ImTT Press, publisher

H

Introduction

What has made this book so hard to write is that the consistent experiences of the clients guided through the ImTT protocol are frankly unbelievable. The therapists who are using ImTT are astonished as their clients' experiences are profoundly different from what both clients and therapists expect. ImTT has made psychotherapy for the therapist a fun, exciting, intellectual, psychological adventure.

Image Transformation Therapy was developed as the result of clinical experience. New processing protocols were developed, and a new model of psychological dynamics was conceptualized in order to explain that clinical experience. This model, called the Survival Model of Psychological Dynamics, provides new insights into the underlying dynamics of dysfunctional behaviors profoundly different from current psychological theories. The results of those insights is a therapy that makes psychological and behavioral changes faster, easier, and gentler than current psychological treatments are capable of.

As of yet, there is no scientific evidence supporting ImTT treatment—this book is the first full explanation of the ImTT process. Hopefully, this book will stimulate the needed research. For now, the best indication of the effectiveness of Image Transformation Therapy is my experience and that of my clients, as well as the experiences of the therapists who have begun using ImTT in their practices.

The ImTT book is divided into eleven chapters. Chapter One provides the current understanding of the ImTT process and the psychological dynamics involved. Chapter Two gives a general overview of the three techniques that compose the ImTT protocol and describes the changes patients may experience following treatment. Chapter Three provides a detailed description of the stages of change and the dynamic transformational changes. Chapter Four lays out the Survival Model of Psychological Dynamics. Chapter Five provides a detailed account of how to identify pain, terror, and their associated images so that one can use ImTT to treat the psychological dynamics generated by pain or terror.

Chapter Six describes the ImTT treatment for trauma. Chapter Seven lays out ImTT's treatment of issues that have pain or terror as their energizing force— issues ranging from depression and anxiety to PTSD and OCD—and more. Chapter Eight describes the dynamics of OCD and how to identify images for processing. Chapter Nine sweeps up and illustrates ImTT used for a variety of additional issues that do not fit neatly into a category.

Chapter Ten illustrates the use of ImTT with children. Two case studies are presented. Chapter Eleven consists of actual transcripts of ImTT sessions to further illustrate the hands-on utilization of ImTT to treat a variety of mental issues. The appendix contains the instructions for the processing protocols.

In addition to this book that explicates ImTT, there is also a companion book for therapists: *Image Transformation Therapy Scripts for Therapists*. The book has a brief introduction to ImTT treatment and a discussion of the ImTT approach for each disorder. To help make the learning curve of ImTT easier, every section has a script that can be read in session.

L

Chapter 1

Image Transformation Therapy

Image Transformation Therapy (ImTT) is a total revolution in psychological treatment.   The most intense emotional pain or terror can be released gently and easily without the person having to experience the feeling. Guilt and shame can also be released with the same gentleness and ease.   ImTT utilizes a breathing-visualization protocol to release the feeling. The result is that traumatic memories can be processed quickly and completely with fewer complications and with less resistance to treatment.

In addition to the new protocols for gently releasing intense feelings, ImTT proposes an entirely new theory of psychological dynamics called the Survival Model of Psychological Dynamics.   This new model provides a new approach to psychological treatment that introduces change in dysfunctional behaviors without any behavioral management.

With ImTT treatment, the transformation of images changes the psychological dynamics, which alters the dysfunctional behaviors.

In fact, people's behaviors may change without any self-awareness of the difference in their behaviors. Transforming images transforms behavior. Awareness of the change in their behavior is not required.

Richard's Story: Gently Releasing Terror

ImTT challenges the conventional wisdom that feelings have to be experienced intensely in order to be released.

Gentle treatment, while always desired, is especially crucial while treating the elderly. Richard, a 90-year-old gentleman, is a good example of the importance of being able to release an intense feeling without having to experience it.

Richard's wife insisted he begin treatment because he was making her take him to the emergency room two to three times a week. Richard was terrified he was dying every time. After six months, his wife had had enough. Richard's terror of dying was caused by his having had a heart attack at age 52. Whenever he experienced a physical symptom, Richard's terror of dying was triggered.

During Richard's first session, his anxiety about dying was traced to his experience of a heart attack when he was 52 years old. Richard was able to identify that his terror of dying was related to his "heart attack" experience.

Whenever he experienced a physical symptom, Richard's extreme terror of dying, created at the time of the heart attack, was triggered. His anxiety was so intense each time, he would insist on being taken to the emergency room.

Releasing Richard's terror of dying posed a particular challenge. As a 90-year-old man, Richard was frail. Having Richard experience the feeling of terror in order to release it posed a medical risk in the session; the intensity of his terror might be too much for his body to handle. Clinical experience indicated that a purely cognitive approach was unlikely to succeed as it would be difficult to overcome an intense feeling of terror by challenging and replacing fear-producing cognitions. Instead of either of these approaches, Richard's terror was released utilizing the Pain/Terror Release Protocol of ImTT. He reported at the end of the session that he felt better about his physical situation.

Richard's next session was two weeks later. His wife reported that Richard's behavior had drastically changed; although he had had some physical problems that required visits to the doctor, he did not ask to go immediately to the ER. He was able to wait and make a regular appointment to see the doctor.

Richard's story illustrates an important component of the ImTT process: keeping a distance from the feeling. Clients are specifically instructed to *not* experience feelings intensely during ImTT. As part of the protocol, Richard was asked to identify the color of his terror. Once the color of terror had been identified, Richard no longer focused his attention on the original event or his feelings about the event. Richard focused solely on releasing the color. Only after the color had been completely released was Richard asked to reevaluate the feelings present at the beginning of his treatment.

As Richard's story illustrates, ImTT's gentle processing of emotionally disturbing feelings and memories occurs even when the event is severely traumatizing.

With ImTT, it is not necessary to re-experience intense feelings associated with an event. The person need only identify them. This means that ImTT treatment is significantly easier and faster than traditional treatments. No one wants to re-experience intense negative feelings; sometimes the feelings are just too intense. *With ImTT treatment, the person does not have to.*

Image Transformation Theory

ImTT postulates that images formed in the mind determine feelings and behavior. Imagine a person is watching a TV, reacting to the images on the screen. Sad images create sad feelings, happy images create happy feelings, horrifying images create fearful feelings, and so on. If a person "sees" an image of people calling him stupid, he may be able to fight off the feeling of shame, but so long as the image is on the "TV," he will always have to contend with the image. If he sees an image of himself hurting someone, he will continue to react with feelings of guilt for as long as the image is present. Whatever the images on the TV are, he will react.

Now imagine that the TV is actually inside his mind. Imagine that the images are like a collection of paintings in a museum—all present at once. There is also a light shining on each painting. Some paintings are more brightly lit than others. The brighter the light, the more intensely the painting shines. Sometimes the person will focus on a specific image/painting, but most of the time, the images/paintings exist in the mind, influencing day-to-day feelings and behaviors.

Developing the metaphor of a gallery of paintings in the mind, the paintings are lit by different intensities of light. This light is the energy the person gives to that painting/image. The more intense the light, the more Intensely the image affects a person's life.

The goal of Image Transformation Therapy is to change feelings and behaviors by transforming the images in the mind.

A basic tenet of ImTT is that images are viewed as the primary source of feelings, behaviors, and cognitions.

What follows from that tenet is that

1. Negative cognitions (e.g., "I'm stupid"), negative feelings (e.g., shame), dysfunctional behaviors (e.g., co-dependence), addictions (e.g., cocaine addiction) result from images.

2. Releasing a person from the influence and constraints of the images allows new, healthier cognitions, feelings, and behaviors to emerge.

ImTT Press, publisher

There are three psychological dynamics that energize the painting/images:

The first dynamic occurs as a result of traumatic or painful events. The pain and terror experienced during the event energizes the associated memories or images of the traumatic or painful event. This pain-and/or-terror-energized image, in turn, creates more pain and terror, which then energizes the image—a vicious cycle.

The second psychological dynamic that energizes images arises when the images are linked with positive feelings. An image of graduating from college may be linked with the feeling of pride. The more intensely the feeling of pride, the more energized the image. As has been described by Miller (2010, 2012), addictive behavior is the result of positive feelings becoming linked with behavior.

A person who smokes, for example, may have linked an image of the feeling of acceptance with the behavior of smoking. Thus, whenever he needs to experience the feeling of acceptance, he smokes. The image is powered by his desire for acceptance.

A third psychological dynamic which can energize an image is a person's belief in the image.

A boy may have accepted the image of the "Marlboro Man" as the image of manliness. A woman may have accepted the image of a supermodel as the ideal woman. For better or worse, culturally accepted images influence a person's feelings and behaviors. Once created, an image will continue to exist until it is deconstructed.

The images do not just go away because a person no longer believes in them. Even when a person "changes" his or her mind or adopts new images, the old images remain in the "museum of the mind" and continue to influence behavior.

The previous discussion describes the different ways in which images are energized. Images are normally defined as mental representations. For example, (2 + 2 = 4) is a mental representation. ImTT, however, defines the word "images" differently. In ImTT, images are defined as **_energized_** mental representations—energized by pain, terror, desire, or belief. In ImTT, the term "image" refers to these energized mental representations.

ImTT Press, publisher

ImTT Definition of "Image"

An Image is a psychologically energized Mental Representation

Psychologically energized by:

1. **Pain or terror:** caused by a painful or terrifying event.

2. **Desire:** a link between a desired feeling and a behavior called a Feeling-State.

3. **Belief:** a culturally accepted idea (e.g., the culturally accepted image of what it means to be a man or woman.)

Stories of Image Transformation Therapy

David's Suicidal Thoughts

For six months prior to treatment, David, a 40 year-old professional, had been having increasing thoughts of killing himself since his wife left him for another man. David stated that he never had problems with depression or thoughts of harming himself before his wife's departure. However, the pain of his loss and her betrayal had become worse over time; he reported that his pain had become increasingly more difficult to live with. After David released the pain with ImTT, all his thoughts of suicide disappeared and were no longer a factor in treatment.

Jeanette's Guilt

One morning Jeanette found her fiancé's body hanging in the garage; he had committed suicide. Her fiancé, Jeffrey, had been having some problems related to his deployments in Afghanistan, but nothing had suggested that he was suicidal. The previous night Jeanette and Jeffrey had had a good evening playing pool with friends. She left him playing pool with their friends and walked home. The next morning she found his body.

Since Jeffrey's suicide, Jeanette had been experiencing depression and severe guilt. She felt guilty even though her friends tried to reassure her that his death was not her fault. Drinking alcohol had become a significant problem for her. With ImTT treatment, Jeanette released the pain of Jeffery's death and eliminated her feelings of guilt.

Pain of fiancé's death ➡ Guilt

ImTT Press, publisher

Ron's Angry Behavior

When Ron was a boy, his father would call him stupid for not knowing whatever his father thought he should know. Even though he became an electrical engineer, Ron was afraid of being thought of as stupid. As an adult, he had difficulty working with people because, whenever anyone would criticize his work, he would become extremely angry and either attack the person or become depressed and the depression could go on for days.

Utilizing ImTT, Ron was able to release the image and the pain of his father calling him stupid. Once Ron released the painful image, his attitude immediately changed. Ron was able to perceive that his previous behavior had been inappropriate; he also realized that he had created many of the problems he had been experiencing.

In Ron's case, the pain of being told he was stupid was kept alive or energized by the image that he was stupid. When Ron released this pain, it de-energized the negative image of being stupid; consequently, he no longer had to suppress that thought by becoming angry. He did not have to process the memory further or try to change the image.

The only reason the thought of being stupid continued to bother him many years later was because that image created in his childhood was energized by the pain. Once the pain was gone, there was nothing to maintain the power of the negative image. Then the image could be easily deconstructed.

Pain + Image of Being Stupid ➡ Depression or Anger

Sexual Assault: Mary

Mary's treatment for a sexual assault that occurred a year earlier is a good example of the effectiveness and efficiency of ImTT treatment. Mary had tried previous therapies that had not been successful. She could not talk about what happened with anyone. Whenever she began to even think about the assault, Mary would be flooded with feeling. Previous EMDR treatment was unsuccessful because she was so easily overwhelmed with feelings of terror.

In the session, Mary appeared terrified. Even though we had not begun to talk about the assault, both of her legs were intensely shaking. Rather than focusing on the assault, the treatment began by targeting the intense terror Mary was experiencing in the office at that moment.

After releasing the terror with the Pain/Terror Release Protocol, Mary's legs stopped shaking. Then, without Mary having to experience the shame of the assault, the shame was released. Once the shame was released, Mary was able to talk about the assault. The memory of the assault was then processed with the Image De-Construction Protocol.

At the end of that session, Mary no longer had any problem talking about the assault. Over the next few weeks, Mary reported that she had been able to talk about the assault with her husband and a friend without emotional discomfort.

Flow Chart of Mary's Treatment

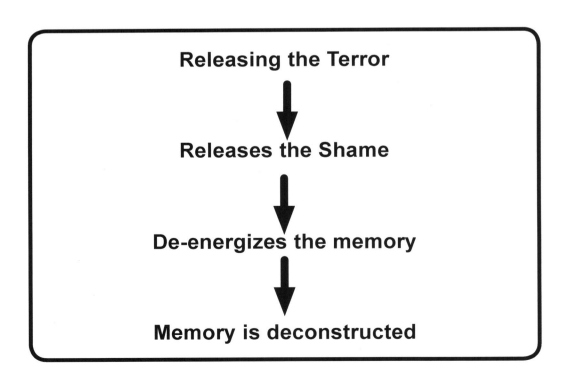

Releasing the Terror

↓

Releases the Shame

↓

De-energizes the memory

↓

Memory is deconstructed

　　　　　　　8

Sue's Pain of Not Being Loved and Problems with Boundaries

Sue reported that she had difficulty setting boundaries with her mother. At times, she tried to help her mother, but the situation would leave her exhausted and feeling crazy. She often developed a "game plan" ahead of time, but the plan usually fell apart.

When Sue was growing up, her mother was often abusive to her. As a child, Sue had wanted her mother to love her, respect her, and make her feel cared for. Because Sue's mother did not make her feel this way, Sue was in a lot of pain from not having the relationship with her mother that she wanted. In order to reduce the feeling of pain, Sue continued to help her mother even when she still was not getting the feelings that she wanted.

Sue felt responsible for her mother's situation because of the dynamic "If I'm good, mother will love me." So if her mother is hurting, she is not "being good." If she is not being good, that means she has done something wrong. Hence, Sue's feeling guilty.

The solution to Sue's problem was for Sue to release the childhood pain of not getting what she wanted from her mother. Once that pain was released, Sue could assert and maintain appropriate boundaries with her mother. Previously, her need to overcome the pain from childhood would keep her interacting with her mother in order to finally get the love she had needed.

It is important to note that, even if Sue could have finally received the love from her mother that she had always wanted, the old pain would still be in her psychological system. In other words, she would still be attempting to overcome the old childhood pain. Receiving the love she had always needed would not have made the pain go away; only releasing the pain makes the pain go away.

ImTT Press, publisher

Chapter 2

PROTOCOLS AND PROCESS

ImTT created three protocols to free a person from negative and destructive behavior. This chapter provides a general overview of each ImTT protocol and describes the changes one can expect after treatment.

The ImTT Protocols

1. **Pain/Terror Release Protocol**: releases the pain and terror linked with an image;

2. **Image De-Construction Protocol**: releases the image;

3. **Changing Patterns Protocol**: alters the psychological patterns stemming from the negative image.

Together, these three protocols deconstruct negative or limiting images and allow new, more positive and healthy images to be created.

The Pain/Terror Release Protocol

What makes the Pain/Terror Release Protocol (P/TRP) a major advance in the treatment of trauma and other negative memories is that a person can release the most intense pain or terror without having to experience the feelings. In addition, because pain and terror underlie other feelings such as guilt and shame, those feelings can also be released without having to experience the feelings. This revolutionary development makes psychological treatment of even the most difficult memories easier to release and much more tolerable for the person seeking treatment.

The Pain/Terror Release Protocol utilizes a form of breathing and guided visualization to release the pain or terror (P/T). (In this book the terms "pain" and "terror" will often be referred to by the acronym "P/T.") In the protocol, the therapist helps the client to:

1. Identify a memory,
2. Indicate whether that memory is painful or terrifying,
3. State the "color" of the pain or terror,
4. Identify where the P/T is located in the body.
5. The client visualizes the color leaving his body.

Many different types of psychological and spiritual practices use some form of a breathing/visualization exercise. The breathing/visualization technique is not what makes the use of the P/TRP in ImTT different. What sets ImTT apart from both other psychological approaches and spiritual practices is the theory that guides how this technique is used. This process will be explained further in the book.

The script for the full P/TRP is in the Appendix.

A basic overview of the P/TRP, using Ron as an example:

1. **Ron remembers the event in which his father told him he was stupid.**

2. **Ron identifies the image that was created during that event: "I am stupid."**

3. **Ron identifies either pain or terror linked with that image.**

4. **Ron identifies the color of the P/T.**

5. **Ron identifies the location of the P/T in his body.**

6. **Ron visualizes the color as being composed of tiny, tiny particles of color.**

7. **Ron breathes into the color and visualizes the color particles leaving his body.**

8. **Ron re-evaluates the intensity of the image of his father calling him stupid.**

ImTT Press, publisher

Don't Feel the P/T – Release the Color

ImTT treatment de-energizes the image that creates the negative feelings and cognitions. What makes ImTT so gentle for the client is that the memory, the feeling, and the P/T have only to be identified, not experienced. In fact, intensely experiencing the feelings will make the release of the P/T more difficult.

The goal of ImTT treatment is to release—not to feel.

Identify the color of the P/T – NOT the color of the emotion

In ImTT theory, pain and terror are primary reactions to all negative events. All negative emotions and thoughts are created and maintained only because of the pain and terror energizing them. The practical effect of this dynamic is that, if the pain or terror energizing a negative emotion or cognition is released, the emotion and cognition will also be eliminated.

To restate: releasing the pain or terror linked with the emotion or cognition will automatically eliminate the emotion or cognition.

For example, if the pain underlying the feeling of guilt is released, the person will no longer feel the guilt. If the terror underlying shame is released, the person will no longer feel the shame. The dynamics of emotions will be further explained later.

In ImTT treatment, because pain and terror are primary reactions, all negative emotions are traced back to either pain or terror. Then the color of the pain or terror is identified. Once the color is identified, the color is released using the P/TRP.

It is important to note that the color of the pain or terror is identified, NOT the emotion. An easy mistake for people to make is to ask the color of the emotion. ONLY the color of the pain or terror is identified and then released using the P/TRP.

Do *NOT* feel the pain or terror

Release the Particles of Color linked with the P/T that underlie the emotion

Fear of Pain is not Terror; Terror is not Fear of Pain

When a person goes to the dentist, he may be fearful of getting a shot of painkiller in his sensitive gums. That fear of pain is not the terror that is targeted with the P/TRP. The target in that situation is his anticipated pain and his image of that event. A person's anxiety about failing a test may be his fear of looking ridiculous, which may be a painful prospect. Terror is something totally different.

Terror is a reaction to a threat to a person's survival. Terror is part of the fight/flight/freeze response of the person's reaction to physical threat—and only to a physical threat. Being abandoned, shunned, or exiled from the group that the person needs for survival doesn't just create an emotional reaction but a real sense of danger to a person's physical survival. That danger creates the terror that is the focus for release with the P/TRP.

> **Don't confuse fear of pain with terror of dying.**
>
> **Fear of pain is not the same as terror of dying.**
>
> **Terror always involves the perception of being endangered.**

Changing Colors of the P/T and the Tiny, Tiny Particles

P/Ts come in a variety of colors. Pain or terror can be green, blue, orange, or any other color. The specific color probably means something, but currently the meaning is not understood. Sometimes the person just sees a darkness. Whatever the color turns out to be, it is important to identify the color and release it.

During the release process, the color of the P/T may change. This means that another emotion is surfacing and may have to be released after the first process is complete. After the original color has been released, the clinician should ask the client to identify the feeling linked with the new color and then release the P/T linked with the new feeling.

The Tiny, Tiny, Tiny Particles of Color

When doing the P/TRP, the client visualizes the color as being composed of very tiny particles of color. This visualization appears to make the release of the color (and the P/T) much easier. When guiding a client through the technique, emphasize each time that the color is composed of very tiny particles. This approach reinforces the visualization and makes the release more complete.

Resolving Resistance to Releasing Pain/Terror

There are times when people will have difficulty releasing the particles of color. Such difficulty arises when the color will either not release or begins to release and then returns to the person. When this occurs, the person is resisting the release of the P/T. Understanding the psychological dynamic creating the resistance is important to resolving the resistance. Resistance to releasing the color of the P/T arises for one of the following four reasons:

1   The pain is a reaction to the loss of a loved one,

2. The person that caused the client's pain is a person the client wants to be close to,

3. The client feels guilt or shame, or

4. The client does not want to admit that they lost.

The first type (#1 above) of resistance arises when the client's pain is a reaction to the loss of a loved one. The person may feel that the pain keeps him connected to the person who died. The fear is that, if the pain is released, the connection to the loved one will also be released.

The resistance to releasing the pain can often be resolved by reassuring the person that they will have an even stronger connection by being connected through the good memories, the fun and loving times of being with him or her. Explaining to the client that pain blocks positive memories will help the client overcome his/her resistance. After discussing this, the clinician should try doing the P/TRP again.

The second type (#2 above) of resistance to releasing pain may exist when the person that caused the P/T is someone the patient wants to have a close attachment with. This can occur, for example, when the abuse is from a parent. Releasing the P/T may feel to your patient that s/he is losing a very intense connection with the parent. Once the patient understands that releasing the P/T will allow the good memories to surface, s/he will usually allow the P/T to be released.

The third type (#3 above) of resistance occurs in the context of guilt or shame. The person may feel guilt or shame about his behavior and not want to release the pain. If this is the situation, use the P/TRP on the guilt or shame first. Then do the P/TRP on that painful memory.

The last type (#4 above) of resistance arises when releasing the pain means that the person has to admit that they lost. Such a dynamic is indicated when there is intense anger and rage about the event. The person resists releasing the P/T because that would release the rage. As long as the rage exists, there is a feeling that they can do something about what happened. The person feels that releasing the rage would mean that he would not be able to change the outcome of the event.

The solution to this resistance is to confront the client with the truthful fact that he did lose and that no amount of rage will change that. Loss is normalized by noting to the client that sometimes people win and sometimes people lose. "That's life."

The fact that the person lost is a painful truth. Acknowledging and releasing that pain allows people to move on instead of being stuck in one past event.

Once the person has acknowledged the pain of losing, ask him what color the pain is. Most of the time, the anger/rage will disappear with the release of the P/T. The anger was just a way of not feeling the P/T of the loss.

Summary of Reasons for Resisting Releasing the P/T

1. **Feeling that releasing the P/T will lose the connection to a loved one.**

2. **The person who caused the P/T is also the person the client wanted to have a connection with; e.g., a parent.**

3. **Feelings of guilt or shame block the release of the P/T.**

4. **Not willing to admit losing because of the pain.**

The Image De-Construction Protocol

Images are the "facts" of the mind. People experience images as facts. The more intense the image, the more people feel the image is true and, therefore, believe the image is true. In ImTT treatment, an interesting experience occurs when a P/T is released from an image yet the image remains.

After releasing the P/T that energizes the image "I'm stupid," a person may feel that the image is no longer painful but still true. However, once the IDP is performed on the image, the person not only recognizes but feels that what he accepted as a fact was actually only an image—an image that can be easily deconstructed.

Since images are the "facts" of the mind, identifying images is clearly important. However, the images that people have formed in their minds may only have a loose connection with reality.

For example, the traumatic "memory" of being ridiculed by a large group of children for not being able to answer a question may not be factually true. The "truth" of the memory is not relevant. What is relevant is the image of the event that the person holds in his mind. The monsters under the bed may never have been there, but the person may still be reacting as if they were.

Identifying the actual image the person has in his mind is important. Memory is inherently unstable. We're always adding to or subtracting from our memories of events. So the focus of ImTT treatment is the image—no matter how unrealistic the image may be.

The script for the full IDP is in the Appendix.

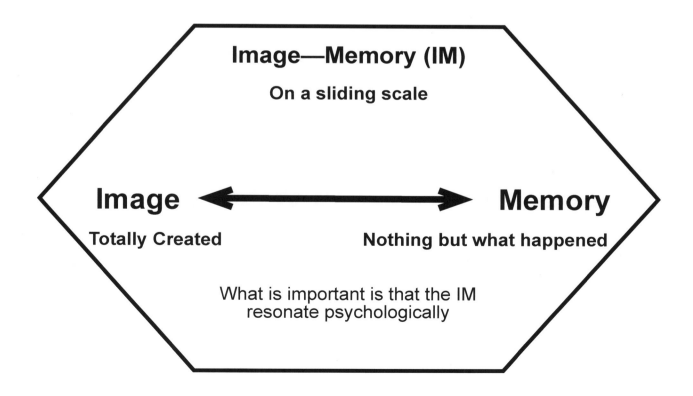

IMAGE TRANSFORMATION THERAPY®

Identifying Images for Processing

The Imaginary Scenario Technique

Identifying the image can sometimes be difficult. A person can have an intense feeling but no memory linked with it. He may not be able to articulate the feeling in a way that an image can be identified; maybe the event was pre-verbal. Trying to release the P/T of a poorly defined feeling will not work well. There may be some relief, but the underlying psychological pattern and the behavior linked with it will not change.

When the feeling cannot be articulated, creating an imagined scenario that resonates with the feeling brings together all the affective elements and allows the feelings, P/T, and image to be articulated. That the imaginary event never happened is not important. What is important is that the imaginary event resonates with the feeling. An imaginary scenario that resonates with the feeling will link the person with the P/T and an image that represents the psychological pattern. Then the complete psychological and behavioral pattern can be released by releasing the P/T and deconstructing the image.

Suzanne: Identifying and processing a feeling with the Imaginary Scenario Technique

Suzanne's story illustrates the use of the Imaginary Scenario Technique for a person who has difficulty identifying an image. Suzanne had a history of forming relationships with men with whom she was unlikely to form any lasting relationship. She experienced a lot of pain about her inability to form a lasting relationship because she kept trying to have relationships and the relationships would not work out.

She had progressed in therapy to the point where she was dating someone with whom she might be able to form a real relationship. However, she noticed that she was beginning to experience a feeling inside that usually preceded her finding a reason to end her current relationship.

Because Suzanne was unable to identify the feeling, she was asked to imagine a scenario that would resonate with the feeling.

Suzanne imagined a scenario where she had brought her boyfriend to a dinner with her mother, father, brother, and various friends. When asked to choose the person whose judgment was the most bothersome to her, she picked her mother. In the scenario, her mother said, "Great pick," with a strongly sarcastic tone. This imagined statement made Suzanne feel as if she did not belong in the family. She then experienced the feeling of shame and the terror underlying it. Suzanne identified the color of the terror as black and proceeded to release it.

At the end of the release, Suzanne's reaction to her mother having said, "Great pick" was, "You're really judgmental. You'll get to like him."

Copyright 2017 by Robert Miller, PhD

18

Thus, as Suzanne's experience illustrates, when a patient is initially unable to articulate the feeling or understand where the feeling comes from, the Imaginary Scenario Technique makes it possible to identify the feeling and the underlying P/T and image.

Similar to dreams, the Imaginary Scenario Technique provides a window into the psyche, linking the conscious mind with affect. The specific memory is less important than the link to the affect. Processing the image linked with the affect changes the psychological patterns.

Images of the Future

Therapy normally focuses on the past–namely, past trauma and events that have changed our behavior and feelings. However, the future orientation of negative images is often the underlying cause of anxiety-, depression-, and avoidance-type behaviors. So, in addition to helping formulate images of psychological dynamics that the person has difficulty either articulating or identifying, the Imaginary Scenario Technique is useful for identifying images the person has created regarding what may or may not occur.

For example, a person who has an image of his future self being alone in the world may experience depression and anxiety. That image of the future may cause intense emotional pain that then leads to depression; the anxiety may be caused by his fear that the future of "being alone" will occur. While past events may have contributed to the creation of these images, once these images are created, they have a life of their own.

Processing past events may not alter images of the future; processing the images with IDP will.

An example of this is a woman named Rose who had been sexually assaulted two years before seeking treatment. At the beginning of treatment, Rose could not talk about the assault. Utilizing ImTT treatment to process the sexual assault memory and its accompanying PTSD symptoms allowed Rose to easily talk about the assault without anxiety or depression.

Rose, however, continued to have problems with anxiety. Rose identified the source of her anxiety as her fear that, since she couldn't protect herself, she wouldn't be able to protect her child either. Rose's nightmare image was of her child being kidnapped while she stood frozen, unable to protect her child. Resolving this image of the future eliminated her anxiety.

19   ImTT Press, publisher

Unconscious Images

Just as we have beliefs and feelings that we are not aware of, our minds create imaginary scenarios that we are not aware of. A child's "monster under the bed" is identified by the child because the child allows his imagination free play. It would not occur to a child to suppress thoughts or images simply because they are not real or are ridiculous. This mind play allows the child to become aware of the images of his mind.

Adults, on the other hand, suppress images that don't fit their version of reality. The problem is that, though the images are suppressed, the images do not just go away. Rather, the images exist within the mind, shaping feelings and behaviors. The consequence of these unconscious imaginary scenarios is that these images are why we do what we do.

While the past informs our images of the future, the images of the future are creations that can include more fanciful elements, either positive or negative. Current behavior is a reaction to these images of the future.

The fact that future scenarios influence current behavior has therapeutic implications: It means that people will resist changing behaviors as long as their future scenarios motivate the behavior. For example, a heroin addict will not want to give up heroin if his image of being without heroin is that his life will be empty and without meaning. The Imaginary Scenario Technique can be a good method for identifying the unconscious images of the future.

Different Types of Images

The word "image" is often associated with a particular type of image—the visual image. In ImTT, the definition of the word "image" is a psychologically energized mental representation. The mental representation does not have to be visual. The sensory modalities of auditory, tactile, and olfactory can also be ImTT types.

As defined, an image is a psychological energized mental representation. The image can take on any sensory form such as visual, auditory, or tactile. The image can be represented in any sensory format. For those therapists who are not visual, a person imaging the pixelation and deconstruction of an auditory image may be quite baffling. For a visual person, how a person represents an image as auditory or tactile may not make a lot of sense. What is important, however, is that the process makes sense to the person doing the

protocol.

A person who uses auditory or tactile modes of representation will be able to figure out on their own how to turn the image into tiny units and then deconstruct the image. In this situation you can depend on the person to creatively find a method that works for them.

A broader view of the concept of image is that an image is psychologically energized information. This means that no sensory modality is required for the image. Rather, the image can take the form of psychologically energized thought. For example, the cognition, "nothing I do is any good" when energized by pain is an ImTT image.

When people have a non-sensory modality image, they can usually sense or feel the image. This "sensed" image is processed in the same way as a visual image except that instead of "seeing" what they are doing to the image, they "sense" what they are doing to the image. For example, the person with the image "nothing I do is any good" would sense the image as being composed of tiny little particles; the image would then be deconstructed.

Whatever form of mental representation the image takes, the ImTT protocol can be adapted to deconstruct it.

Overview of the Image De-Construction Protocol (IDP)

After the P/T linked with an image has been released, the image still remains. The image might consist of a visual memory of the event or, if the P/T was linked to a negative belief such as "I'm stupid," an image of the person as stupid.

The Image De-Construction Protocol (IDP) provides a means to easily release these images.

The IDP consists of five basic procedures

3. **Visualize the image as intensely as possible.**

4. **Visualize the image as being composed of tiny little particles.**

5. **Deconstruct the image.**

6. **Repeat steps 1, 2, and 3 until the image can no longer be visualized.**

7. **Release the particles of the image from the body.**

When to use the P/TRP before the IDP

The ultimate target in order to change feelings and behaviors is the image. When images are energized by pain or terror, however, the pain or terror should be released first. Once the pain or terror has been eliminated, the image can be deconstructed. When an image involves reactions of pain or terror, the clinician should use the P/TRP to release the pain or terror first and then deconstruct the image with the IDP.

The Changing Patterns Protocol

Once the person releases the P/T and deconstructs the image, the image ceases to drive his/her psychological and behavioral patterns.

However, their old expectations and images of how they will react in a given situation will still linger. For example, after a person deconstructs an image related to food, they may find grocery shopping a little confusing. Such confusion may arise when they visit their usual aisles, only to find that their customary food purchases no longer interest them. Or, if they are in a hurry, they may not notice their reactions and buy the food, only to realize, when they get home, that they are not interested in the food.

The more formative the event, the greater the variance between the old patterns and the new emerging ones.

Adjusting to one's new emerging patterns takes time; the person learns about their new self as they go about their daily living.

The purpose of the Changing Patterns Protocol (CPP) is to speed up the adaptation process. The CPP is very simple. The person merely focuses for a short time (20 seconds or so) on different aspects of their life, such as their job or a relationship. Focusing the mind on an aspect of life will automatically activate the mind to transform the old patterns and begin to create new ones. Performing this technique at the end of a session will make the transition to the new patterns easier and less disorientating.

A script for the CPP is in the Appendix.

Summarizing the Image Transformation Therapy

ImTT can be summarized in five points as follows:

1. Pain and terror (P/T) underlie and energize all negative memories, feelings, self-beliefs, and dysfunctional behaviors.

2. Releasing the P/T releases the negative thoughts and feelings, and changes the dysfunctional behavior.

3. The Pain/Terror Release Protocol (P/TRP) directly releases the P/T, de-energizing the image, beginning the process of altering feelings and behavior.

4. The Image De-Construction Protocol (IDP) deconstructs the image.

5. Once the P/T and the image are released, the mind will immediately begin to change the psychological patterns related to the P/T and create more positive, adaptive patterns. Performing the Changing Patterns Protocol (CPP) expedites this process.

Miller, R. M. (2010). The Feeling-State Theory of Impulse-Control Disorders and the Impulse-Control Protocol. *Traumatology, 16*(3), pp. 2-10.

Miller, R. M. (2012). Treatment of Behavioral Addictions utilizing the Feeling-State Addiction Protocol: A Multiple Baseline Study, *Journal of EMDR Practice and Research, 6*(4) pp. 159-169.

Chapter 3

The Psychological Dynamics of ImTT THERAPY

The "ImTT effect" names the transformational effect that people experience when an image has been released. Releasing an image, in effect, releases the force underlying the psychological patterns supported by the image.

An image related to the belief, "I'm stupid," for example, may have created psychological patterns causing test anxiety behaviors. The behavior patterns may include many different behaviors: what the person does before the test to prepare for taking the test, coping skills used during the test, interactions with other people during the test, and self-image patterns that influence other types of behaviors. Once the image underlying the psychological patterns is deconstructed, the patterns underlying the test anxiety will begin to disappear. As the person realizes that they do not have test anxiety, their expectations about taking tests will change. In addition, pre-test behavior will change as will self-image and other patterns related to a person's self-image.

Stages of Change

After a person releases a negative image, he will experience relief. He may also experience a feeling of emptiness. The emptiness occurs because the old patterns are no longer energized by the power of the old image. After completing the P/TRP, some people report an odd sensation that the thoughts are still there but that there is no energy in them. These thoughts are a shadow of what they once were. Once the clinician performs IDP, the "ghost" of the thoughts also disappears.

The result is that people have a new attitude toward themselves, the event, and the people involved.

The amount of change that a person experiences after doing ImTT depends on how much the image has influenced behavior. For a person who has suffered a recent loss of a job or relationship, the change will likely be small and affect only how the current pain has changed his behavior since the loss occurred. On the other hand, if the image-creating event occurred many years earlier or if the event caused a significant change in behavior, then releasing the image may result in significant changes in feelings and behavior.

The change in such a formative image can cause disorientation, confusion, and a loss of a sense of self while the old patterns fade and the new ones emerge. The person may feel de-motivated for a few days. The previous motivation had been energized by the underlying image. So a feeling of tiredness and of no desire to do anything may occur. There can also be a feeling of sadness, grief, or regret about the choices made and the years lost. Without the pain and the psychological patterns driven by the image, the person sees his behavior and the events of his life through a more realistic lens.

Sometimes people experience anxiety during this time because they are not sure what is happening. This stage can last from a few days to a week.

The effect of the pattern changes is that a person's sense of self begins to change. Our sense of self is partially the result of knowing how we typically act and react. Releasing images changes a person's actions and reactions. The change in patterns makes a person feel uncertain about how s/he feels or will behave. The result can be some confusion and disorientation about who the self is.

In the midst of all this change, the person will also experience what can be described as a greater expansiveness. No longer constrained by the painful/terrifying image or its accompanying thoughts and behaviors, the person eases into a life free of the limitations created by the P/T-energized images. A new, deeper sense of self begins to emerge, accompanied by a new understanding of what the person feels and wants. Awareness of this experience is most acute in the first few weeks. After a few weeks, the most obvious changes have taken place, and the person may no longer be aware of the changes. The person then senses himself in this new way as if it were the most natural way to be.

ImTT Press, publisher

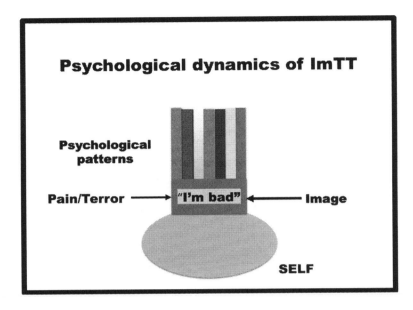

Figure 1 shows that painful and terrifying images create negative psychological patterns, interactions, and behavior.

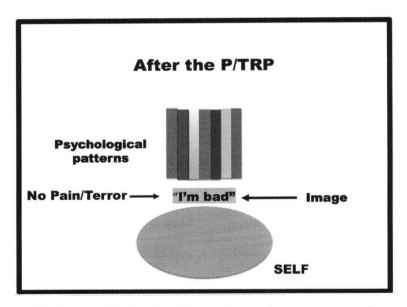

Figure 2 shows that after the pain and terror are released, the image is no longer powered by the pain and terror.

ImTT Press, publisher

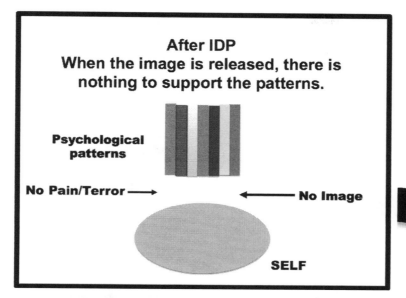

Figure 3 shows that, once the old psychological patterns are not energized by the image, there is no foundation to support the old patterns.

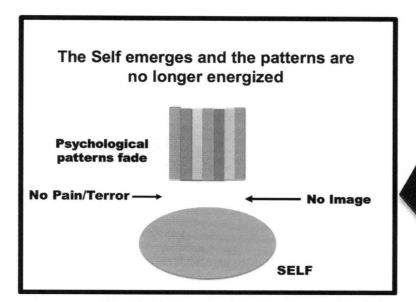

Figure 4 shows the psychological patterns–the behaviors, feelings, and expectations–that were created by the negative image are now fading.

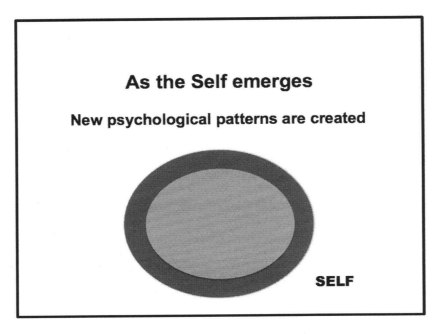

Figure 5 shows the emergence of the self that had been suppressed by the negative image and the new psychological patterns that are beginning to form.

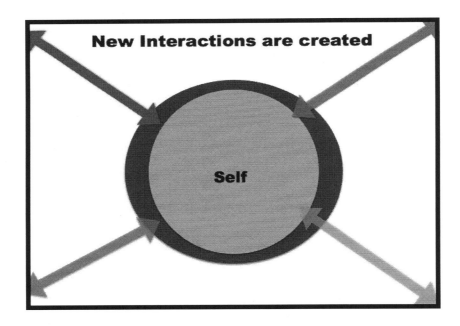

Figure 6 shows that the self is now making new interactions, new patterns, new behaviors, feelings, and expectations.

Dynamic Transformational Change

Releasing negative images transforms the personality. As a result, a new, energized self emerges after ImTT. Specifically, it is worth noting the following two dynamic transformational changes: First, the person will develop positive thoughts and feelings almost effortlessly, without any clinical intervention; and, second, their self-consciousness will decrease.

The Emergence of Positive Thoughts and Feelings

With ImTT, positive thoughts and feelings emerge almost automatically, with little conscious effort.

Pain/Terror (P/T) blocks thoughts and change.

No one wants to think a thought or experience a feeling that triggers pain or terror. The problem is that, if a person cannot think the thought or experience the feeling, they cannot release the thought and feeling. This is because changing a thought or feeling requires one to re-experience the thought or feeling. Any person's natural response is to avoid linking with anything that triggers the P/T. Thus the P/T makes it difficult to change thoughts and feelings.

Once the P/T underlying the thoughts and feelings is released, however, those same thoughts and feelings will automatically begin to change. For example, Jeff was ridiculed in high school because he did poorly on an oral presentation. From that point on, he thought of himself as stupid, even though, as an adult, he had been successful academically. The thought of being "stupid" influenced Jeff's behavior, causing him to become angry or depressed whenever others criticized his work.

Because of the P/T associated with the thought "stupid," Jeff was unable to change the thought, and it persisted, despite many positive professional experiences. When the blocking P/T was released, Jeff's mind automatically began to change. He was able to hold in his mind the thought "I am stupid" and evaluate it in light of his memories of academic successes. This transformation of his thinking allowed Jeff to change his image of himself.

Releasing the image linked with the thought of being stupid did not result in new thoughts such as "I am intelligent." Jeff no longer became defensive when criticized. Jeff was able to interact calmly with a presence of mind that allowed him to utilize his intelligence in situations that previously would have made him angry and depressed.

The Emerging Positive State

The "need" to "think positive" or install positive thoughts is an attempt to overcome the negative effect of an image. For example, people need to feel "special" because they believe there is something wrong with them. People need to feel important because they feel unimportant. People need to feel competent because they feel incompetent. Without the negative image, people do not need to feel special, important, or competent. Their inherent worth is taken for granted. Without an image blocking action, the person just acts un-selfconsciously.

The natural emergence of new positive psychological patterns means that installing positive beliefs is contraindicated in ImTT. Once the image is released, new positive feelings and beliefs will emerge automatically as appropriate.

The positive beliefs/feelings that are often used in therapy are actually chosen to counter the image that underlies the negative feeling/behavior. This is not necessary in ImTT because ImTT eliminates the negative image which is the obstacle to changing thoughts and feelings.

For this reason, after releasing an image with ImTT, positive thoughts and feelings emerge automatically, with little effort.

ImTT Press, publisher

Living in the Zone: No Self-Consciousness

In addition to blocking thoughts and change, negative images also cause a person to be self-conscious. When a person fears personal pain or terror, they must focus on themselves simply for survival reasons. Because people are wired for survival, any threat to survival requires immediate attention. Memories of pain, terror of dying, and anticipated pain or terror of dying will all require a person to fixate their attention on survival needs. Just as a person with a splinter in his hand will fixate on that splinter until it is removed, people with negative images will be "self-centered," fixated on themselves, until the negative image is removed. Remove the negative image, and the person's attention will naturally move to the outside world.

The lack of self-consciousness people experience following ImTT allows them to act within the "zone" that is often referred to in sports and creativity. Over days and weeks, new feelings and beliefs will emerge that are flowing in a new direction unimpeded. There is no need for any further treatment on these issues, except, perhaps, to help the person become aware of the changes. The changes will take place in the days, weeks, and months following the release of the negative image.

Two examples of Transformation with ImTT

Jane and Jack's experiences following ImTT show the ImTT effect and underscore how image transformation can first alter one's psychological patterns and then behaviors.

Jane:

Jane began therapy because her memories of a traumatic event were causing problems in her marriage. Jane was sexually assaulted when she was 16 years old. After the sexual assault, she became promiscuous and engaged in other destructive behaviors. Eventually, she married and had a child. After Jane released the image of the sexual assault, she felt sadness about her past behavior after the sexual assault. In addition, her reactions and interactions with her husband changed. Jane reported in a later session that, when her husband made disparaging remarks, she no longer became hurt or sad. Instead, she became angry. This was a new Jane. Not only did she have to get used to her new angry feelings, but

she had to develop new behavior related to the anger. Jane liked the strength of her new sense of self, though the change in her reactions was disorienting for a while.

Jack:

Jack's experience with food is another example of how image transformation can alter, first, psychological patterns and then behaviors. Jack had an image linked with food. He liked to eat sweets. Jack had what he called his "ritual." He would go to different bakeries to get his favorite foods for different days of the week. Once Jack released the image underlying this dynamic, he still had his expectations of what he would do during the day. At first, he continued to buy some of the same sweets he previously enjoyed, only to realize when he started to eat them, that he was not as interested. He went to the bakery for several more days, buying less and less each time until, finally, he realized that he simply was not interested anymore. Jack then began choosing different foods that fit his new emerging self.

ImTT Press, publisher

Working with Fragile People

Some people are fragile and likely to decompensate when thinking even a moment about a terrifying or painful event or image. Therapy should be approached in a gradual manner. The person may have lived with the pain for a long time and is now accustomed to that feeling and the feelings and behaviors related to the pain or terror. If the P/T is released too suddenly, the person will have an anxiety reaction because it feels unfamiliar and the unfamiliar may be frightening.

In this situation, the clinician can elect to release the P/TRP gradually, over the course of several sessions. For example, the client might release the P/T from their legs in one session and their spine in another session. While the ultimate goal is to release the image, the approach should allow a person to become comfortable with the process and the possible disorienting side effects that can occur. A slow approach will allow the person to become familiar and comfortable with the types of changes that occur.

For some people, a traumatic memory may be too overwhelming for the person to focus on. Only do the P/TRP until enough of the P/T has been released so that the person is not overwhelmed by their feelings. If the person is unable to tolerate focusing on the image, the P/TRP should be performed until enough of the P/T has been released so that the person is not overwhelmed with feelings.

While the goal is to ultimately release the image, the approach should allow the person to become comfortable with the process and its disorienting side effects.

A slow approach which emphasizes skill building and confidence building will allow the person to become familiar and comfortable with the types of changes that occur.

ImTT Press, publisher

Chapter 4

THE SURVIVAL MODEL

of

PSYCHOLOGICAL DYNAMICS

The following graphics illustrate the Survival Model of Psychological Dynamics and the results of eliminating the pain and terror energizing the feelings and negative cognitions.

The graphics are presented at the beginning of the chapter to make the discussion easier to follow.

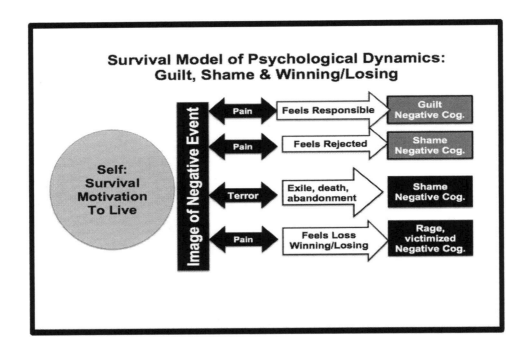

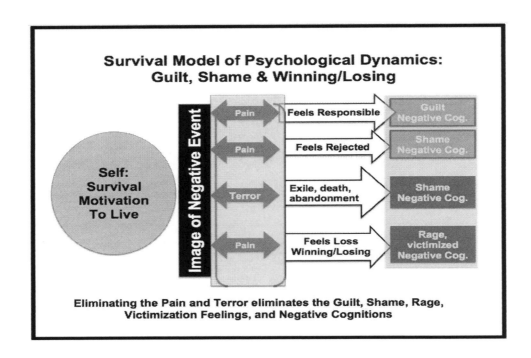

The Survival Model

This section describes the Survival Model of Psychological Dynamics, a concept developed to explain the clinical experiences that result from using ImTT to process psychological issues.

The Survival Model of Psychological Dynamics

The Survival Model of Psychological Dynamics was developed to explain the psychological dynamics that occur when using the P/TRP and IDP protocols. For example, when the pain underlying the feeling of guilt is eliminated, the guilt is eliminated; when the terror underlying shame is released, the feeling of shame is eliminated. Consequently, these and many other clinical experiences required a new model of psychological dynamics in order to understand why eliminating pain and terror releases feelings as well as to provide a new model for developing targets for treatment.

The foundation of the Survival Model is the recognition that the most basic motivation for any organism is to survive, to live. This fundamental motivation to live energizes behavior and the psychological processes that create that behavior. The Survival Model of Psychological Dynamics describes the psychological dynamics that have evolved to optimize the chances of physical survival. These physical requirements for survival include:

1. Protection from immediate death
2. Food, clothing, and shelter
3. Mate selection to optimize the chances of having children that will survive
4. Providing for the species to survive through time

Physical Requirements for Survival

1. **Protection from immediate death**

2. **Food, clothing, and shelter**

3. **Mate selection to optimize the chances of having children that will survive**

4. **Providing for the species to survive through time**

                                       ImTT Press, publisher

In order to meet the physical requirements for survival, the psychological dynamics that have evolved to optimize survival can be separated into three categories:

1. The Primary Psychological Reactions (PPR)
2. Emotions
3. Assured Survival Feelings (ASF)

Survival Psychological Dynamcs

1. The Primary Psychological Reactions (PPR)

2. Emotions

3. Assured Survival Feelings (ASFs)

Category 1: The Primary Psychological Reactions to negative events

The Primary Psychological Reactions are responses that promote immediate physical survival as a response to being endangered. These responses are pain avoidance, terror, shock, freeze, horror, and disgust.

1. Pain Avoidance: Just as with our bodies' avoidance reaction of physical pain (i.e., pulling your hand off a hot stove), we also avoid psychological pain.

2. Terror: When in danger, we experience terror that activates the body's fight/flight response.

3. Freeze: Freeze is the most primitive of survival reactions. By "holding still" or freezing, the person avoids the notice of the predator.

4. Shock: Shock numbs the feelings so that the person is able to extricate himself from danger when experiencing intense emotions which would interfere with the necessary behaviors needed for survival.

5. Horror: Horror is a form of terror—the terror of annihilation of the self.

6. Disgust: In response to physical events, disgust occurs in response to the sight or smell of things we want to avoid such as bad food or road kill. Psychologically, disgust occurs as a response to people or experiences that do not represent immediate danger but that we want to avoid.

Category 2: Emotions

While the PPRs are a response to immediate danger, emotions evolved to meet the long-term-survival physical needs such as food, clothing, and shelter. Humans have a much greater chance of survival if they work together such as in a tribe. The emotions promote the tribe's survival by helping maintain and repair relationships and maintaining the group values that the tribe has determined are necessary for survival.

As a result of clinical experience, it was discovered that pain and terror underlie and generate the emotions guilt, shame, sadness, and anger. This means that pain or terror in combination with the person's beliefs create the emotion. For example, a person who feels responsible for another person's pain will feel guilty. Using ImTT, it was discovered that when the pain underlying that guilt is released with the P/TRP, the person's feeling of guilt will also be eliminated. In other words, the pain is the driving force behind the person's experience of feeling guilty. In short, no pain, no guilt. The same kind of dynamic is present for all emotions that occur when a person perceives that a relationship has been damaged .

The specific survival dynamics of emotions are as follows:

1 Guilt: When a person feels that he is responsible for someone who has become hurt, thereby damaging their relationship, he experiences guilt. The feeling of guilt motivates the person to do something to repair the relationship (i.e. apologize, buy flowers, et cetera.

Repairing the damage to the relationship strengthens the relationship bonds and enhances the possibility that the person will help them in the future.

Pain **Feels Responsible** ⟶ Guilt ⟶ Guilt/Image

ImTT Treatment for Guilt

Feelings of guilt arise when a person feels responsible for causing either physical or emotional pain in the other person. If someone slips and falls because you didn't wipe up the water you spilled, you will likely feel guilt. You did something wrong and someone got hurt. Witnessing the pain you caused causes pain in you. The pain you experience, connected with the feeling of responsibility, activates the feeling of guilt. Then you wipe up the water and help the person who fell.

The ImTT solution for releasing the feeling of "guilt" is to release the pain that activates the guilty feeling. Once the pain is eliminated, there is nothing to activate the "guilt" feeling. In other words, the feeling of guilt is released, not by experiencing the feeling or any type of cognitive reframing, but by releasing the pain that activates the feeling of guilt.

After the pain underlying the feeling of guilt is released (which releases the feeling of guilt), the image linked with the feeling is then released.

ImTT Releases Guilt by:

1. **Releasing the pain (which releases the guilt) and**

2. **Deconstructing the image**.

Evan's Guilt

Evan forgot his wife's birthday. Even though he apologized to his wife and bought her the gift she wanted, he still could not shake off the guilty feeling. The pain that he had caused his wife by his behavior was still activating that guilt.

Evan's guilt was released by releasing the pain that was activating his feeling of guilt. Releasing the pain of that event and the image energized by pain eliminated Evan's feeling of guilt. Eliminating his guilt allowed Evan to stop obsessing about his past actions and focus on his current life.

Releasing the pain of injuring his relationship with his wife caused by not remembering her birthday. → **Eliminated Evan's Guilt**

Irrational Guilt

Irrational guilt is guilt that a person experiences even though he did not do anything wrong. For example, Susan's sister died in a car accident while Susan was driving. Her car was hit from the side by a car that went through a red light. The accident was clearly not Susan's fault. However, Susan felt responsible for her sister because Susan was driving the car and experienced emotional pain because of her sister's death.

As a result, Susan felt guilty about her sister's death, even though there was nothing about the accident that was Susan's fault.

Irrational guilt is created when a person toward whom he generally feels responsible suffers some form of injury. The feeling of pain plus the perception of being responsible activates the feeling of guilt. Statements like, "I should have known" or "I should have seen it coming" evidence this type of guilt.

Questions about irrational guilt are:

:   **"Why** does the feeling persist even after the person knows that *he is not responsible* for what happened to the other person?"

"Why does the person not process the pain that energizes the guilt feelings?"

The answer is the "shock" reaction. As will be described in the section on shock, shock numbs the feelings and prevents processing. The shock of a car accident or even learning of a person's death can prevent the processing of the pain the person experiences as a natural reaction to learning about a person's injury or death. The pain, in turn, activates the feeling of guilt toward whom the person generally feels responsible for. In the above example, Susan felt generally responsible for her sister so that she experienced her sister's death as her fault. The shock of the accident prevented the pain and the guilt from naturally processing over time.

The ImTT solution for irrational guilt is to release the shock of the event. Releasing the shock will allow the person to process the pain, which de-activates the feeling of guilt. If any feelings of guilt persist after the "shock" is released, release the pain that continues to activate the guilt feelings.

There is a complete explanation of "shock" in the section describing the processing of trauma. The script for releasing "shock" is in the Scripts book.

The ImTT solution to guilt, rational or irrational, is to release the pain underlying the feeling of guilt. Once the pain is removed, the feeling of guilt will disappear. Even the "deserved" pain will be released. The person will know what they have done wrong and the pain they have caused. Knowledge of the pain they have caused will be a factor in future behavior.

A person free of painful and terrifying images does not seek to inflict pain and terror on others. There is no need for the person to continue feeling the guilt. Doing so is just a form of punishment that does not help either the person's own survival or the survival of the group.

ImTT Press, publisher

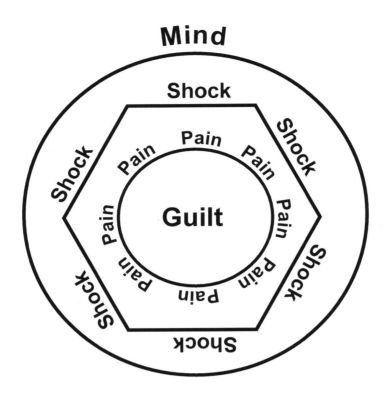

Shock blocks the mind from naturally processing the guilt.

Shame

The feeling of shame is the result of two separate dynamics.

Terror-Shame

Terror-Shame is experienced when the person feels, not just that he has done something wrong, but that he is "bad." A person who is "bad" is a person who is outside the group norms that the group has determined are necessary for survival. Therefore, a person who is threatening the survival of the tribe—a bad person—does not belong in the tribe. A person who is bad must be prevented from threatening the survival of the tribe.

There are two ways that the person can be prevented from threatening the survival of the tribe. The person can be exiled or killed thereby eliminating any danger the person may have posed to the tribe. The other method for eliminating the danger to the tribe is to lower the person's status in the tribe. A person of low status, a person who is always last in line or stigmatized, will not threaten the survival of the tribe by influencing the rules the tribe has determined are necessary for survival.

When the person feels shame, he is signaling to the group that he knows that he is bad but also wants to stay with the group. By signaling the feeling of shame to the tribe, the person is signaling that he will accept a low status within the tribe so that he does not threaten the tribe's survival by challenging the norms the tribe has established as necessary for survival.

From the above discussion, it is clear that the feeling of shame that a person experiences when his survival is threatened by exile or death is generated by the feeling of terror. In other words, terror underlies the feeling of shame. This means that releasing the terror underlying the shame will eliminate the feeling of shame. This model explains the clinical experiences using the P/TRP in which releasing the terror underlying a person's feeling of shame releases the shame.

Richy

An example of the dynamic of shame is Richy. Richy sexually assaulted a woman in concert with other men from his fraternity. As long as this event was only known within his fraternity, Richy only experienced the feelings of power and camaraderie with his fellow fraternity brothers. However, once the event became known in the community, Richy began to feel shame. Richy's feelings changed because, in the context of the larger community, sexual assault was outside the group's values, and this group could exile (imprison) him for his behavior.

Thus underlying Richy's shame was the feeling of terror. As long as Richy feels threatened by society, he will continue to feel shame for what he did.

Cindy

Cindy's experience illustrates a different aspect of the shame dynamic. Cindy was the woman that Richy sexually assaulted. The sexual assault made Cindy feel dirty, and she experienced self-disgust. She felt that the sexual assault meant that she was "spoiled" and that, as a result, no person or group would want to have anything to do with her. Cindy's fear that surviving sexual assault rendered her ineligible for community membership reveals that she experienced the feeling of shame. Underlying her shame was the feeling of terror; she was terrified that the group would abandon her because she was a "spoiled" person. Unlike Richy, Cindy's shame could be completely released because she could be accepted and not threatened by the group.

Pain-Shame

Pain-Shame: Not all ejections from a group threaten a person's survival. If a person is rejected from a group within the tribe but not the whole tribe, the feeling of shame is generated by the feeling of pain.

For example, a 10-year-old girl is snubbed by a group of other girls. The rejection is painful but not life threatening because the girl still has other groups that she belongs to, e.g. school and family. Releasing Pain-Shame, therefore, requires releasing the pain underlying the shame.

Shame

Terror-Shame: Generated when tribe norms are violated.

Pain-Shame: Generated when rejected by group within the tribe but not by the entire tribe.

Summary

Guilt is energized by Pain.

Shame can be energized by either:

Pain or Terror.

When a person feels shame, ask:

"Does it feel painful or fearful?"

ImTT Press, publisher

Relationship and Survival

Guilt and Shame: Emotions with a <u>purpose.</u>

Beyond an immediate physical threat, survival for humans is linked with social relationships.

Relationships are crucial for survival. No person survives on his/her own. As a consequence of the need for relationships for survival, the emotions of guilt and shame have the survival value of repairing relationships with individuals and groups.

Anger

Anger is experienced when the person feels endangered and responds by going into the "fight" mode of the fight/flight reaction to danger. The anger can be generated in response to either pain or terror.

Chris

Chris stated that he became angry at his wife whenever she would ask him to do something but that he hadn't completed something else that she had asked him to do previously. This dynamic was happening two to three times per week. Chris stated if he hadn't completed the first thing before she asked him to do something else, then he was a "bad provider."

The belief that he was a "bad provider' was painful for him. Releasing the pain of being a "bad provider," thereby de-energizing the belief, allowed him to see how unrealistic the belief was.

Chris's belief that he was a "bad provider' was painful because the belief made him feel that he was damaging his relationship with his wife. The result of releasing the pain underlying that belief was that Chris no longer became angry at his wife whenever she asked him to do things.

Sadness

Sadness is experienced when the person experiences a loss of a relationship. The pain of the sadness motivates the person to form other attachments.

Category 3: Assured Survival Feelings

Assured Survival Feelings (ASF) are feelings that provide the person with feedback that their behavior promotes their survival. In contradistinction to the PPRs and the emotions being generated from them, ASFs are positive feelings people seek to feel. For example, the ASF "belonging" gives the person the experience that he is part of the tribe, a tribe that will help with his survival needs.

Other ASFs include feeling powerful, special, important, safe, alive, successful, and high status. ASFs can be divided into four categories:

1. Safety
2. Relational
3. Winning
4. Sensation: Excitement/Alive

ImTT views the basic survival motivations to be the foundation for all feelings, cognitions, and images. These psychological dynamics create feelings of guilt, shame, anger, and sadness that motivate survival behavior. Underlying these feelings is the primary reaction of either pain or terror.

Pleasurable feelings—such as feelings of belonging, bonding, and power—are generated by survival needs. For example, the pleasure of belonging orients a person toward social behavior that ensures both the person's physical survival as well as genetic survival.

The Win/Lose Dynamic

In the Survival Model the motivation for survival extends to the desire to survive through time. The desire to survive through time is often manifested as the intense desire to have children.

Because of the intense desire to have children, there is also an intense desire to find a good mate who will provide both the genes and the support necessary for the children to survive into adulthood so that they, in turn, can have children. Since the number of mates and resources are limited, then there is an intense competition among tribal members for the best mate.

In the Survival Model the competition for genetic survival is the foundation for the Win/Lose Dynamic. In other words, the motivation for genetic survival is the foundation for the intense desire to win. The consequence of not winning is the loss of genetic survival, which is intensely painful.

If we think of a Win/Lose dynamic in tribal terms, a person's choice of mate is determined by the person's status in the tribe. A mate with good genes and who is functional in the world will increase the probability that his/her children will survive to have more children.

In addition to mate selection, the motivation for genetic survival extends to behaviors for providing the physical requirements for the children to survive into adulthood. So the motivation for genetic survival creates competition for food, clothing, shelter, safety for the children, et cetera.

Even beyond mate selection, the person's status within the tribe continues to be important for the survival of his children as his status can affect his capacity for providing for the best possible food, clothing, and shelter for his children. To put it simply, high status increases the children's chance of survival. A high chance of the children's survival means an increased chance of the person's genes surviving into the future.

The Win/Lose Dynamic

1. **Motivated by the desire to survive through time.**

2. **Limited resources (mates, food, clothing, shelter, etc.) means that competition for resources needed for survival is intense.**

3. **Survival through time requires children who need those limited resources to survive.**

4. **Losing the competition is intensely painful.**

47   ImTT Press, publisher

Thus, the Win/Lose Dynamic influences daily behavior. Whether the current need involves money, a mate, or some form of status, the desire for survival motivates the desire to achieve that goal.

The intense motivation to win means that losing is painful, extremely painful. The pain of losing can motivate a person to perform better in the future. As such, the pain of losing has survival value. The problem is that the pain of losing can also undermine survival needs. The pain of losing undermines survival needs when the person keeps trying to overcome the pain of a specific event in which he lost but the current behavior is no longer relevant to his current situation in life.

To avoid the pain or to overcome the pain, people will spend a lifetime trying to "win," to show they're better, smarter, more righteous, of higher status than another person who they feel made the person experience the excruciating pain of losing. Even after decades have passed since the painful event, the person's behavior may be motivated by the desire to win that old, lost battle.

The intensity of the pain of losing can be seen in the adolescent who kills students at a school because he was bullied. A person who is bullied loses status, loses respect, loses a mating prospect because, being labeled a "loser" makes them less attractive—no one wants to be with a loser—and therefore he loses the possibility of survival through time by having children.

The intensity of the pain of losing is seen in the 40-year-old man who is intensely competitive at checkers—he just can't stand to lose at anything. Losing at an insignificant game activates the pain of losing from previous events.

The intensity of the pain of losing is seen in the man who has to keep making more and more money, far beyond what he needs in order to live, so that he can show-up those guys in high school who pulled down his pants.

The intensity of the pain of losing is seen in the woman who has to have just the correct image to overcome being snubbed as an adolescent.

Clearly, the pain of losing has a major influence in people's lives. From the career a person chooses to the person he marries to the friends and enemies he makes, the Win/Lose dynamic manifests as fundamental patterns of behavior. Everybody wants to win. We are hardwired to want to win.

While the pain of losing provides a motivation to succeed, the problem is that the person is attempting to win a battle that he lost a long time ago. The success he is seeking is a success to overcome the pain that his younger self experienced. There are two problems with seeking success determined by pain. First, no amount of current winning will eliminate the pain from previous events. The current "win" may soothe the old pain, but the pain will not disappear. Second, what a person sees as a "win" in high school is usually not the same as what a person sees as a "win" twenty years later.

For example, the pain of being rejected by a girl in high school may motivate a boy to develop a muscular physique. Twenty years later, however, if he is still trying to overcome the pain of not "winning" the girl by having a muscular physique, he is focused on what would be a "win" for his younger self. Without the old pain, the 40-year-old man might think that building a successful business is more important than having a muscular physique.

ImTT Press, publisher

In other words, the old pain of losing may prevent a person from obtaining what he really wants to win in the present. Once the pain is released, the person may find that he has little interest in what he had been motivated to succeed at. The result is that releasing that pain of the loss will allow the person to move on from the past so that he can win what he really wants in the future.

In terms of psychological reactions, the person who loses may experience rage, depression, envy, and feeling victimized because that survival dynamic is threatened. When a person is disrespected, bullied, or victimized, there is a threat to the passing-on-the-genes survival pattern. Even if the person is already married and has children, the template of competition that creates an intense desire to win is still present. Eliminating the pain of losing frees the person from attempting to overcome past losses and allows him to focus on winning.

The most challenging aspect of eliminating the pain of the Win/Lose dynamic is identifying when the current behavior is a consequence of the Win/Lose dynamic.

The Win/Lose dynamic is often not obvious when a person is describing his current situation. Indications that the person's reactions are related to the Win/Lose dynamic are when the person talks about being disrespected, bullied, or victimized. Other indications of the Win/Lose dynamic are feelings of being a loser, worthless, as well as many other cognitions and feelings that are created as a result of the pain of losing. In other words, the pain of losing energizes these feelings and cognitions. Eliminating the pain of losing will de-energize the feelings and cognitions.

The Effect of an Old Loss

The pain of an old loss fixates a person's behavior toward overcoming the pain of an old loss rather than focusing on current needs.

Multiple psychological reactions to events

There can be multiple psychological reactions to experiences. The experience of being bullied may evoke feelings of the pain of shame and the pain of the Win/Lose dynamic. Each of those dynamics will have to be processed separately.

For example, Tom was bullied in the 7th grade. He experienced the pain of both being rejected by the popular boys as well as the pain of the loss of status related to the Win/Lose Dynamic. Both the pain of being rejected and the pain of losing had to be processed.

ImTT Press, publisher

Indicators that the Win/Lose Dynamic is Activated

The person experiences feelings of:

1. Disrespect

2. Victimization

3. Rage

4. Powerlessness

5. Having been bullied

6. Not the favorite child

7. Loss of status

Assumptions Underlying the Survival Model

The Survival Model assumes that both the physical and psychological characteristics that are observed today are the result of a selective pressure that was applied to the human species. In other words, only humans with those characteristics survived. A consequence of this assumption is that each human characteristic and its persistence through time is understood to be the result of the inherent "survival value" of that characteristic.

Summary of the Survival Model of Psychological Dynamics

From the point of view of inherent survival value, the following conclusions can be reasonably postulated:

1. Psychological dynamics, by definition, have survival value, having evolved in the context of humans' physical needs for survival—e.g., obtaining food, clothing, and shelter, and avoiding immediate death.

2. The evolution of Primary Psychological Reactions (PPRs)—pain, terror, shock, freeze, horror, and disgust—has improved humans' chances of avoiding imminent death—i.e., by definition, PPRs have survival value.

3. By and large, humans have a higher chance of surviving (obtaining food, clothing, shelter) by being part of a group; therefore, anything that optimizes humans' ability to live in a group has survival value.

4. Evolution of both positive and negative emotions optimizes the chances for survival of individuals within groups and therefore the groups they belong to.

5. Negative emotions evolved to respond to a variety of challenges within the group. Guilt and shame evolved to repair an individual's relationships with either a member of the group or with the group as a whole. Anger evolved to respond to danger from a particular member of the group. Sadness evolved to allow individuals to break and re-form attachments as necessary.

6. Positive feelings (Assured Survival Feelings)—such as feelings of belonging, connection, aliveness—evolved as identifiers and reinforcers of behavior that would optimize a group's chances of staying together which would enhance survival.

7. The Win/Lose Dynamic (competition) optimizes the genetic composition of children so that the species' chances of having enough members survive any given threat improves.

Chapter 5

IDENTIFYING THE PAIN/TERROR, EMBEDDED FEELING, AND THE IMAGE

Chapter 5 focuses on how to identify the pain or terror and feeling linked with an image, how to develop the image, and how to respond to resistance.

Image Transformation Therapy processes the images that create dysfunctional behaviors. This section will focus on the processing of images that are linked with pain or terror.

Many different feelings and behaviors have an underlying P/T. The P/T may or may not be obvious. Tarry's anger problem is an example of a non-obvious P/T.

Tarry had difficulty arguing with his wife. While he had tried to use the communication skills that he had learned in counseling, their talks usually ended the same way—with Tarry shouting, resulting in hurt feelings for both Tarry and his wife.

The focus on the session was to help Tarry be less reactive when having an argument. When Tarry was asked how he felt underneath the anger when he argued with his wife, he stated that he felt she was saying that he was wrong.

He then said that, when he felt that someone was telling him that he was wrong, that he was really being called "stupid." Asked to remember an event that made him feel stupid, he reported being ridiculed by some boys when he was 10 years old. He felt shamed, which was painful for him. Tarry then identified the pain of shame as blue and released the blue color using the P/TRP. Tarry then deconstructed the image of the event.

When Tarry returned two weeks later, he reported that he was finally able to use the communication skills he had been trying to learn. He was easily able to refrain from overreacting and could understand what his wife was saying without personalizing what she said.

As explained in Chapter 2, ImTT's P/TRP requires the client to identify the P/T underlying an image, state the color of the P/T, and then release it. Sometimes identifying the P/T is easy, such as the pain resulting from the breakup of a relationship. In other situations, the P/T is not so obvious, such as when the client exhibits the behavior of procrastination.

This chapter explains how to identify the P/T.

Categories for ImTT Processing

1. **Pain and terror**
2. **Emotions**
3. **Cognitions**
4. **Behaviors**
5. **Feelings**

Another Worry

"Will it come back?"

After having a splinter removed, would you ask, "Will it come back?"

You would more likely ask, "Did you get it all?"

Removing the P/T and the image is like removing a splinter.

ImTT Press, publisher

Category 1: Pain or Terror

Clients can become flooded with pain or fear when they begin to talk about an event. The clients may be too overwhelmed with feeling to process the event itself. Instead, the P/TRP can be used to release the pain or terror they are experiencing without discussing the event. This approach is extremely useful in crisis management when the person is too overwhelmed to talk about what has caused the crisis.

Since the client is already feeling the pain or fear, there is no need for any further steps. Simply ask the following questions and proceed with the P/TRP.

Once the pain or terror has been reduced, the client will be able to discuss the event more calmly.

A simple script might be:

Therapist: "You look as if you're in a lot of pain." (Or if client appears terrified: "You look as if you're pretty anxious.")

Patient: "Yes."

Therapist: "Why don't we just dump some of that pain (fear). Does that sound okay with you?"

Patient: "Yes."

Therapist: "What's the color of the pain (terror)?"

[Therapist guides the client to release the P/T using the P/TRP. Because no image has been obtained, the IDP is not performed.

After the P/TRP is performed, the therapist proceeds to identify the problem causing the P/T.]

Category 2: Emotions

A second possible target for ImTT is emotions. Emotions such as guilt, shame, anger, and anxiety are "second-order" feelings; they are feelings created by the P/T, in the context of an event.

Guilt and Shame

Guilt, for example, is linked with pain. If a person feels responsible for what happened, the result of the pain will be guilt. On the other hand, shame can have either pain or terror underlying the feeling.

For both guilt and shame, processing these emotions requires the person to:

1. Identify the P/T underlying the guilt or shame.

2. Release the color of the P/T.

3. Deconstruct the image linked with the guilt or shame using the IDP.

> Use the following script to identify the P/T:
>
> **If the feeling is guilt**:
>
> **Question #1**:
> "Can you feel the pain of the guilt?"
>
> **Question #2**:
> "What's the color of the pain?"

> **If the feeling is shame**:
>
> **Question #1**:
> "Does the shame feel painful or fearful?"
>
> **Question #2**:
> "What's the color of the pain (terror)?"

Anger

Inappropriate anger can result from two very different dynamics.

The first dynamic is that anger is linked with a positive feeling such as "powerful," "invincible," or "righteous." In this situation, use the Feeling-State Addiction Protocol or Feeling-State Image Protocol to break the link.

The second dynamic creating anger is the existence of negative cognitions related to experiences such as loss, violation, helplessness, and powerlessness. For example, when a person feels violated by another person, the result of the pain may be anger. When confronted with anger resulting from this second dynamic, the clinician should identify the specific cognition such as "I can't protect myself" and identify the P/T. Then the clinician should ask the person to identify the color of the P/T.

Sam's treatment illustrates the use of ImTT for anger that arises from the second dynamic. Sam had an intense rage towards a man who got a job Sam wanted. Sam did not want to release the rage because releasing the rage would mean accepting that he had lost and that the other man had won.

Sam's feeling of loss was intensely painful; feeling anger kept Sam from feeling the pain of his loss. In a situation such as Sam's, it is important to specifically state something like, "I know it's difficult to hear; but, in this situation, you lost. In life, sometimes you win, sometimes you lose. In this event, you lost. It must be really painful to know that you lost." Once the person acknowledges the loss, the clinician can then ask, "What color is the pain of that loss?"

                                                                           ImTT Press, publisher

Anger (continued)

Question to be asked:
"The fact that you lost must be really painful. What is the color of that pain?"

Anxiety about some specific future event

Just as guilt, shame, and anger are secondary feelings, anxiety is also a secondary feeling.

A person can feel anxious because of anticipated pain or fear.

The clinician should find out what the person is anxious about and then ask what would happen if the worst imaginable outcome were to occur. Then the P/T of the outcome is identified.

> Use the following to identify the P/T:
>
> **Feeling**:
> Anxiety
>
> **Question #1**:
> "What's the worst that could happen?"
>
> **Question #2**:
> "Does that feel painful or fearful?"
>
> **Question #3**:
> "What color is the pain (terror)?"

For example, Ron is anxious because he is about to take his licensing exam. The idea of failure could be either painful or fearful.

Painful idea of failure:

Ron: "I'm having a hard time sleeping because I'm so anxious about the test."

Therapist: "If you fail the test, what does that mean about you?"

Ron: "I'm a failure."

Therapist: "Give me an image of what that looks like."

Ron: "People are laughing at me."

Therapist: "Does that feel painful or fearful?"

Ron: "Painful."

Therapist: "What color is the pain?"

[Therapist guides the release of the color with the P/TRP and the deconstruction of the image with the IDP.]

Fearful idea of failure:

Ron: "I'm no good."

Therapist: "Give me an image of what that looks like."

Ron: "No one will have anything to do with me."

Therapist: "Does that feel painful or fearful?"

Ron: "Fearful."

Therapist: "What color is the terror?"

[Therapist guides the release of the color with the P/TRP and the deconstruction of the image with the IDP.]

Category 3: Feelings

In addition to releasing pain, terror and deconstructing images, the complete processing of an event or belief requires releasing feelings related to the event or belief.

In ImTT the term "feelings" refers to any experience that the person describes with the expression "I feel …". such as "I feel rebellious," "I feel broken," "I have a sinking feeling," "I feel small," and "I feel empty."

The following examples will illustrate the ImTT approach to processing feelings.

Jen

Jen talked about the abuse she had suffered in her family of origin and how she had been unable to get anything done in her life. She stated, "I feel broken." There appeared to be no event that she related to this feeling but the feeling was her overall summation of how she felt about herself.

Jen's ImTT treatment of her "I feel broken" feeling required three steps:

1. Identifying the color of the "I feel broken" feeling

2. Releasing the color of the feeling.

3. Deconstructing the image associated with the "broken" feeling.

The feeling "I am broken" was an "embedded" feeling that needed to be released separately from either the P/T or the image. After releasing the "I am broken" feeling, Jen began to see her life in a totally new way. She stated that she felt as if she were looking through a different pair of lenses.

George

Another illustration of releasing feelings is George's treatment. George reported that whenever he would go home from school, he never knew what kind of mood his mother would be in. When he opened the door to his home, he would experience what he said was "a kind of withdrawal and shutdown." This reaction was often activated in his life whenever he did not know what someone's reaction would be. In other words, this "reaction feeling" was embedded in his psychological system and needed to be released.

In George's treatment, the order of processing was different from Jen's treatment. When George began talking about his returning home from school, he first began identifying his anxiety about what mood his mother would be in.
The feeling that was present "in the room" was anxiety. The order of processing targets for George was:

1. Releasing the terror of what was going to happen when he returned home.

2. The image of his mother when he returned home.

3. The withdrawal/shutdown reaction.

Once George released his "withdrawal/shutdown" feeling, he no longer reacted that way with his partner.

ImTT Press, publisher

Feelings:

ImTT uses the word "feelings" to denote any experience in which the person states "I feel..." such as "I feel worthless," "I feel broken," "I feel angry," "I feel small," "I feel like I'm cringing." Some of these statements are beliefs. ImTT denotes the statements as feelings (even though they have different origins) because the person experiences these statements as feelings. These feelings—no matter what their origins—are embodied in the psychological system and can be released from the psychological system using the ImTT protocols.

This means that a feeling arising from the belief "I'm stupid" and the feeling arising from a physiological reaction to an event such as "cringing" can both be released using the same protocols.

Categories of Feelings

ImTT identifies four different categories of feelings:

1. **Belief/feelings** are feelings that have a cognitive component. For example, the statement "I am broken" is a belief/feeling.

2. **Emotion/feelings** are feelings such as sadness, joy, anger, shame, and guilt.

3. **Physical Response/feelings** are the physical response that occurs during some event. For example, a person who is often abused at home, may have a physical reaction of withdrawing inside or a cringing reaction.

4. **The Primary Psychological Reactions** of pain, terror, shock, freeze, horror, disgust.

All four categories of feelings can be released with the ImTT protocols.

Categories of Feelings

1. **Belief/feelings**

2. **Emotion/feelings**

3. **Physical response/feelings**

4. **The primary psychological reactions of pain, terror, shock, freeze, horror, and disgust**

Embedded Feelings

In ImTT, images and feelings are considered to be embodied throughout the "psychological system." The term "psychological system" is used because the term denotes all the "locations" that the feeling particles and the pixel-particles are released from.

For example, releasing the yellow pain particles from the heart targets an obvious physical location for the particles to be released from, but there is no specific physical location when the yellow pain particles are released from the "depths of the heart." Even though people cannot point to the physical location of the "depths of the heart," they do have a psychological sense of its "location" and can release the particles "located" there. Therefore, the term "psychological system" is used interchangeably with the term "body."

The Difference Between Dynamic versus Embedded Feelings

Definitions:

Dynamic feelings are feelings that are created as a result of either pain or terror. Guilt, shame, anger, sadness, and the different variations of these feelings are dynamic feelings. Releasing the underlying pain or terror released the emotion as previously described.

Embedded feelings are feelings that persist in the psychological system. All the primary psychological reactions—pain, terror, shock, freeze, and horror—are examples of embedded feelings. However, other feelings can also be created as a result of an event.

For example, a person who has been sexually assaulted may feel "dirty" from the assault. Other feelings that may result from events may include "slimy" or "icky," "emptiness," "hollow," and "confusion." These feelings created either during an event or as a result of an event may persist in the psychological system.

A person who has a embedded feeling of "confusion" may have difficulty making decisions because the embedded feeling of confusion makes him feel confused even when he knows what he is doing. A person who has an embedded feeling of "emptiness" may have difficulty with intimacy as the "emptiness" feeling may cause him to either cling to or avoid people.

Dynamic vs. Embedded Feelings

Dynamic Feelings: Feelings that do not persist in the psychological system.

Embedded Feelings: Feelings that persist in the psychological system.

 ImTT Press, publisher

Releasing Embedded Feelings

The treatment for embedded feelings is different from treatment for pain and terror and the emotions with pain or terror underlying them. Instead of identifying the pain or terror underlying the feelings, the embedded feelings are released by identifying the color of the feeling and then releasing the color from the body utilizing the P/TRP pattern.

For example, the feeling of "dirtiness" is released by identifying the color of the feeling of "dirtiness," identifying the location of the color on the body, visualizing the color as being composed of particles, and then breathing into the color particles and releasing the particles from the body. Then following the P/TRP pattern, the particles are released from the rest of the body.

Negative memories or beliefs consist of at least three elements: 1) the image, 2) the feeling, and 3) the pain or terror in regards to the image. Each of these elements should be released so that the negative pattern can be completely eliminated.

Examples of Embedded Feelings

I feel...

unfairly treated, destroyed, crushed, fearful, devastated, broken, like an 8-year-old, small, "I don't want to give it up" (whatever "it" is), dirty, slimed, empty, like I lost a part of myself, confused, chaotic, overwhelmed, hollow, bitter, "people are out to get me," weak, alone, trapped, diminished, hiding.

Category 4: Cognitions

Negative cognitions–such as "I'm stupid," "I'm worthless," "Nothing ever works out for me"–can have a large impact on a person's life. ImTT releases these cognitions by first de-energizing the P/T and the feeling with the P/TRP. After the P/T is released, then the IDP eliminates the image related to the negative cognition. Deconstructing the image will automatically allow the person to re-assess his situation. There is no need to install a positive cognition. The positive cognition will emerge naturally.

The negative beliefs can be beliefs about the self—"I'm stupid," "I'm worthless," et cetera. All of these negative beliefs are the result of the images people hold consciously or unconsciously. These beliefs appear to the person as "facts" about the world. However, once the feelings and images related to the belief have been processed, the person will be able to put those "facts" in a more realistic perspective.

ImTT divides negative cognitions into two categories: 1. Image negative-cognitions and 2. Feeling negative-cognitions. The reason for this division is that these different types of negative cognitions arise from different psychological dynamics. Treatment depends on which type of negative cognition is present.

Image negative-cognition: An image negative-cognition is the result of an event in which the cognition is part of the event. An example of an image cognition is a person believing he is ugly because his father called him ugly.

Image negative-cognitions should be treated as arising from a traumatic event. The ImTT treatment for an image negative-cognition is to use the Shock script (pg. 157) followed by deconstructing the image.

Feeling negative-cognition: A feeling negative-cognition can usually be identified by the person's choice of words. Statements such as "I feel ugly" or "I feel worthless," indicate the presence of a feeling negative-cognition. A feeling negative-cognition is usually the result of how a person "feels" about himself or is "made to feel" about himself in regard to negative event(s).

Feeling negative-cognitions are released by having the person identify the color of the feeling; the color is then released with the P/TRP pattern. This script is on page 131. Images or memories related to the feeling are then released.

Negative cognitions are divided into two categories:

1. Image Negative-Cognitions

2. Feeling Negative-Cognitions.

 ImTT Press, publisher

Examples of Image Negative-Cognition Treatment

Feeling Negative-Cognition Treatment

Ron believed (felt) that <u>nothing he would ever do would work out.</u> This belief was clearly untrue because Ron had accomplished many goals in his life. Nonetheless, this belief often triggered his anxiety whenever he faced new challenges. Ron's feeling that nothing would work out persisted because of the underlying image.

Patient: I believe that nothing I do will ever work out.

Therapist: When you say that, can you feel it in your body or do you just kind of know it to be true?

Patient: I really feel it's true.

Therapist: Where do you feel it in your body?

Patient: My gut.

Therapist: What color is the feeling?

The color (feeling) is released with the P/TRP pattern. Then the image is identified and processed.

Image Negative-Cognition Treatment

June didn't want to return to college because of anxiety about her grades. She had completed the previous year, but the intense level of anxiety that she experienced had become overwhelming. The problem, she stated, was that she believed that she was "stupid." If she stayed in school, eventually everyone would know she was stupid also. She knew she was stupid because her father called her stupid every time she made a mistake. June could vividly see the look on his face whenever he said it.

Therapist: What's the image you have that you're stupid?

Patient: My father yelling at me that I'm stupid.

Therapist: Does that feel painful or fearful?

Patient: Really, really painful.

At this point, the therapist has a choice of two approaches to processing the memory: releasing either the shock of the event or the pain of the event. Which direction is more appropriate depends on the patient. If the patient reacts with intense pain, then releasing the pain is a good direction to begin. The shock is then released after processing the pain.

On the other hand, if the pain is not overly intense, releasing the shock might not only release the shock of the event but also release the pain as well. In either situation, the image is released after the pain and shock have been released. Because June was experiencing intense pain from the memory, the pain was released first, then the shock, and lastly the image.

65   ImTT Press, publisher

In these examples, notice how easy and direct the questioning is. Feelings are not asked about. Eliminating the P/T and image linked with the negative belief releases the belief. No more is necessary to release the image negative-cognition.

An additional area to investigate when releasing an image negative-cognition is whether there is an additional embedded feeling associated with the belief. For example, when June's father called her stupid, she may have felt "small." In this situation, the feeling of being "small" would also need to be released if the feeling is still present after the image is released.

Processing a "Non-Sensory Modality" Image

For many people the word "image" means "visual" image. However, an image can be visual, auditory, olfactory, tactile, or gustatory. In other words, an image is a psychologically energized unit of information that a person translates into one or more sensory modalities.

However, not all images are translated into a sensory form. A person can have a belief without any physical form associated with the belief. For example, a person may have an intense belief "I can't" without any specific memory. Sometimes the non-sensory image can be translated into a sensory form by the use of fantasy or making up a scenario. Other times, the person just has a strong "knowing" or believing that the statement is true.

When the belief cannot be translated into a sensory modality, the image is deconstructed by asking the person to sense or "feel" the belief. The person is then asked to break up the image into tiny "units" in whatever method that makes sense to them. The therapist does not have to understand how the person breaks up the image into units. Most people can find their own method of breaking up the image if they are instructed to do so. Once the image has been divided into small units, the IDP is performed as usual.

Differences between Conventional Cognitive Therapy and ImTT Cognitive Therapy

The Conventional Cognitive Therapy:

1. Identifies the negative cognition
2. Challenges the cognition
3. Focuses treatment on replacing the negative cognition with a positive cognition

ImTT Cognitive Therapy:

Image Negative-Cognitions
1. Identifies the negative cognition
2. Releases the shock & P/T of the NC-image
3. Deconstructs the NC-image
4. Allows a new, more positive cognition to emerge

Feeling Negative-Cognitions
1. Identifies the negative cognition
2. Releases the feeling
3. Deconstructs the image
4. Allows a new, more positive cognition to emerge

Category 5: Behaviors

The fourth possible ImTT target is behaviors. Dysfunctional behaviors linked with an image can be classified as one of two types: (1) avoidance behaviors performed to avoid the feeling of the P/T, and (2) behaviors that result from the P/T. The following scenarios address examples of P/T-energized behaviors.

Avoidance behaviors resulting from P/T

There are different kinds of avoidance behaviors. Overeating, procrastination, and smoking are examples of behaviors that may be the result of avoiding negative feelings and thoughts. Processing the underlying feeling or cognition linked with the image will eliminate the need for the avoidance behavior.

Procrastination

Procrastination may be caused by fear of what will happen if…[client inserts nightmare image.]

Therapist:
"If you do a poor job, what will happen?"

Patient:
"I'll fail."

Therapist:
"What does it mean about you if you fail?"

Patient:
"I'm a failure."

Therapist:
"What does being a failure look like to you?"

Patient:
"I'm sitting outside the room where other people are laughing at me."

Therapist:
"Does that feel painful or fearful?"

Patient: "Painful."

Therapist: "What color is the pain?"

Patient: "Yellow."

[Therapist guides the release of the color with the P/TRP and the deconstruction of the image with the IDP.]

Procastinator? No, I just wait until the last second to do my work.

Because I will be older and therefore wiser.

.....Procrastination

Procrastination results from a P/T-image of what might happen if they do the behavior being put off.

Release the image and the person will immediately stop procrastinating.

Behaviors caused by Feeling Overwhelmed

Feeling overwhelmed is an important cause of hiding behavior such as overeating, playing video games too much, and watching too many hours of television.

People feel overwhelmed, not because of what they have to do, but because of their thoughts about what they have to do.

For example, a person feeling overwhelmed may be unconsciously saying to himself:

1. "I just can't do it," or
2. "It's too much," or
3. "I can't handle it."

The underlying thought is:

"If I can't do it, I'm a failure."

Without a negative underlying thought, a person, given ten things to do, would just write up a list of priorities and proceed to accomplish them as soon as possible. The situation would not be about the person's failure but about getting the job done.

Therapist:
"When you feel overwhelmed, what is the thought you have about yourself? Do you think 'I can't do it' or 'I can't handle it'?"

Patient:
"I can't handle it."

Therapist:
"If you can't handle it, what's going to happen?"

Patient:
"I'm going to fail."

Therapist:
"If you fail, what does that mean about you?"

Patient:
"I'm a failure."

Therapist:
"Give me an image of what that looks like."

Patient:
"I'll be sitting home alone. No one will want to have anything to do with me."

Therapist:
"Does that feel painful or fearful?"

Patient:
"Painful."

Therapist:
"What color is the pain?"

Patient:
"Red."

[Therapist guides the release of the color with the P/TRP and then deconstructs the image with the IDP.]

Dysfunctional Behaviors Resulting from a Negative Image

Dysfunctional behaviors that result from an image have a cognition that intervenes between the P/T and the behavior. For example, a P/T linked with the belief "Nothing I do is good enough" may result in behaviors such as working at a job that is less than expected for the education and talent of the person. A P/T linked with the belief "No one will ever want me" may result in casual sexual relationships in order to feel wanted. Releasing the P/T underlying the belief will release the person from the constraints of the negative belief and allow a more realistic, reality-based attitude to emerge.

Example:

Patient:
"No one will ever want me except for sex."

Therapist:
"Give me an image of what that looks like."

Patient:
"After having sex, the guy gets up, looks at me with disgust, and walks out."

Therapist:
"Does that feel painful or fearful?"

Patient:
"Painful."

Therapist:
"What color is the pain?"

Patient:
"Yellow."

[Therapist guides the release of the color with the P/TRP and then deconstructs the image with the IDP.]

> **When processing an image/memory with multiple feelings, the P/T linked with each feeling must be processed separately.**

Summary of ImTT Model of the

development of dysfunctional behaviors

or

The tail does <u>not</u> wag the dog

The following graphics summarize the ImTT model of the formation of negative behaviors. This graphic illustrates the process through which a negative event can result in negative cognitions and behaviors. Notice that the cognitions and behavior are the last to form.

ImTT eliminates the negative cognitions and behaviors by releasing the pain, terror, and images that result in the negative cognitions and behaviors. Focusing treatment on the cognitions and behaviors is, in the ImTT view, trying to get the tail to wag the dog. Instead, ImTT eliminates the real cause of negative cognitions and behaviors.

Specifically, negative cognitions and behaviors are third- and fourth-order effects resulting from the feelings of guilt or shame, which are energized by pain or terror.

Releasing the pain or terror releases the guilt or shame, which allows the image to be deconstructed and the negative cognition to be released and dysfunctional behaviors to change.

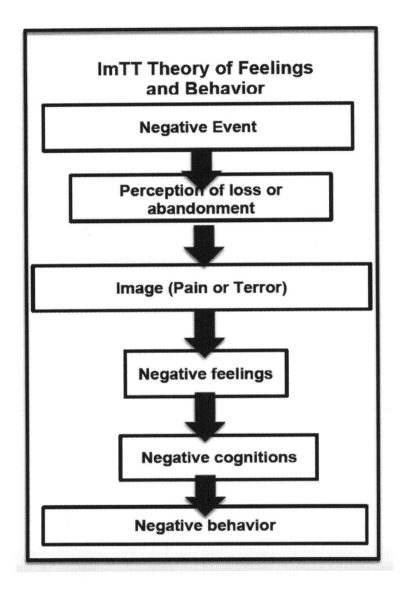

ImTT Theory of Feelings and Behavior

- Negative Event
- Perception of loss or abandonment
- Image (Pain or Terror)
- Negative feelings
- Negative cognitions
- Negative behavior

Pain and Terror energize negative feelings, images, and cognitions.

Releasing the Pain or Terror de-energizes negative feelings and cognitions and allows the negative image to be eliminated.

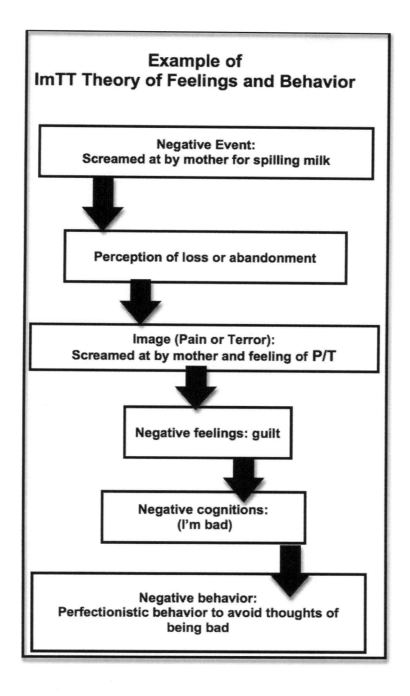

**Example of
ImTT Theory of Feelings and Behavior**

Negative Event:
Screamed at by mother for spilling milk

Perception of loss or abandonment

Image (Pain or Terror):
Screamed at by mother and feeling of P/T

Negative feelings: guilt

Negative cognitions:
(I'm bad)

Negative behavior:
Perfectionistic behavior to avoid thoughts of
being bad

74
ImTT Press, publisher

Chapter 6

ImTT Treatment for Trauma

Psychological treatment for traumatic memories is often very challenging. The feelings are intensely painful, fearful, or both. In therapy, people can easily become flooded with feeling or dissociate from the feeling–neither of which is useful for treatment.

ImTT provides a new approach that releases the pain and terror without the threat of flooding or dissociation during the treatment. The result is that clients can resolve traumatic memories with much less suffering during the process. Less suffering means that the clients will not resist having treatment once they have experienced how easy and gentle the process is.

This chapter discusses the processing of the Primary Psychological Reactions induced by a traumatic event, the order in which feelings and images should be processed, the processing of the trauma memory network of multiple traumatic events, and the ImTT approach to dissociative memories.

ImTT's most important advance in the treatment of trauma is that a person does not have to experience the feeling.

- **They don't have to experience the pain.**
- **They don't have to experience the fear.**
- **They don't have to experience the guilt.**
- **They don't have to experience the shame.**

Primary Psychological Reactions:
Shock, Freeze, Horror

The processing of the Primary Psychological Reactions of pain and terror has been discussed previously. Traumatic events can also cause three other PPRs: shock, freeze, and horror. Identifying and processing these reactions is an important part of releasing traumatic memory.

As with pain and the terror of dying, shock, freeze, and horror create feelings that do not dissipate over time. However, shock, freeze, and horror do not energize negative emotions. Rather, all three inhibit the expression and processing of feelings.

Shock

One of the most overlooked and underestimated reactions to events is the "shock" reaction. The survival purpose of shock appears to be that shock numbs the feelings. If a person is in a car accident, a person becoming emotionally hysterical will not help them get out of the car or do whatever is necessary to survive. The problem is that the "shock" reaction does not go away; rather, the shock reaction becomes less apparent but continues to persist, numbing the person's feelings to both that event as well as interfering with experiencing feelings in other situations.

In addition to the "shock" reaction being present in obvious traumatizing types of events, the "shock" reaction is also present in many types of everyday events. Anytime a person says, "I can't believe that happened," shock is present. For example, "I can't believe I got fired," "I can't believe I got the job," "I can't believe I got married" are indications that a shock reaction is present. Shock, in other words, can be present in both positive and negative events.

Other types of statements indicating shock are:
"Is this really happening?"
"Is he/she really saying ...?"

The key indicator of a shock statement is that the statement indicates a denial of something that happened.

One of the consequences of shock is that shock prevents the person from processing his psychological reactions to the event. The "shock" state is a kind of limbo that makes thinking about and reacting to that event more difficult. Monica came into her session after having been diagnosed with cancer two days earlier. The doctor had discussed with her the different treatment options and had given her specific instructions for what she needed to do immediately. Monica reported that she was having difficulty staying focused on those tasks and making decisions about her treatment. Monica's mental condition was the result of her "shock" reaction to being diagnosed with cancer. The shock was both numbing her from feelings about the diagnosis and also preventing her from thinking clearly.

Statements Indicating Shock

I can't believe...

Is he/she really saying...?

Is this really happening?

                                                                       ImTT Press, publisher

Monica's "shock" reaction was released using the "shock" ImTT script. Once the shock was released, Monica was able to focus on her situation and make decisions about her treatment. The release of the "shock" reaction also allowed Monica to experience how terrified she was that she might die from the cancer or the surgery that she needed. The terror was reduced by using the P/TRP.

In situations where there is an ongoing situation (in Monica's case, cancer treatment required five months of first surgery and then chemotherapy), the P/TRP may need to be performed more than once.

Example of the subtler effects of shock: Shock and a developing relationship

Jill presented with an intense anxiety about her relationship with her boyfriend even though the relationship had been progressing well. Her anxiety was related to fear that if her boyfriend knew how much she wanted to be with him, then he would leave her. Jill thought that, in a previous relationship, she had pushed her then-boyfriend away by wanting him too much. The current relationship had been doing well and there were no signs that her boyfriend was getting "cold feet."

In this situation, it is tempting to focus on her anxiety and directly treat the anxiety, utilizing a future nightmare image. Jill's problem, however, is that she is unable to process her interactions with her boyfriend because of her shock about the current relationship. The shock is a reaction to disbelieving that her boyfriend really wants to be with her. The shock has kept her in a state of disbelief, which had interfered with her being able to realistically evaluate her interactions with her boyfriend.

After processing the shock about the relationship, Jill was able to realistically evaluate her interactions with her boyfriend and emotionally understand that her desire to be with him was not pushing him away.

Treatment for Shock

The ImTT treatment for shock is to:

1. Have the person tune into the "shock" feeling,
2. Visualize the feeling as being composed of tiny particles of feelings of shock,
3. Release the particles with the P/TRP.

For most people, shock does not appear to be associated with a color. However, the shock sensation can be easily visualized as being formed of tiny particles of "shock" that can be released with the P/TRP.

The complete protocol for releasing "Shock" is in the ImTT Scripts manual.

Freeze

The reaction of freeze occurs when the person experiences an overwhelming event in which the person perceives that nothing can be done. When the freeze reaction occurs, as with shock, the freeze reaction may persist in the body long after the event is over. The long-term effect of an unreleased freeze feeling is that the person may "freeze up" when a much less intense event occurs. For example, if the freeze reaction occurred during an incident of assault, the aggressor's anger may trigger the freeze reaction in a victim so that the person victimized is unable to take appropriate action. Just as the shock feeling restricts the person's psychological flexibility, freeze feelings appear to similarly restrict a person's emotional responsiveness.

Treatment: The ImTT treatment for the freeze reaction is to:

1. Have the person tune into the "being frozen" feeling,
2. Visualize the feeling as being composed of tiny particles of feelings of "frozen,"
3. Release the particles of "frozen feeling" with the P/TRP.

For most people, the frozen feeling does not appear to be associated with a color. However, the frozen sensation can often be easily "visualized" as being formed of tiny particles of "frozen" feeling that can be released with the P/TRP.

The complete protocol for releasing "Freeze" is in the ImTT Scripts manual.

Horror

Horror is a different kind of primary reaction. Abandonment issues and even being diagnosed with a fatal disease can create a terror of dying. The feeling of horror is different. Watching someone die by being shot in the heart is very different from watching someone being beheaded or mutilated. Our reaction to seeing someone being beheaded or mutilated is a much more intense reaction–the terror of not just being killed but annihilated. That is horror.

In the treatment of trauma, horror is often overlooked, likely because even therapists have difficulty allowing themselves to be aware of this reaction. However, the feeling of horror is a human reaction that can occur in many different kinds of traumatic events and needs to be processed.

Treatment: As discussed above, the horror primary reaction is a different form of terror—the terror of being annihilated. The terror of annihilation must be specifically identified as the terror underlying the horror reaction. Releasing the terror of abandonment or death does not release the horror reaction. However, once identified, the terror of annihilation is released with the same methods used for the terror of death—the P/TRP. The setup for the release must specify exactly the nature of the terror.

The complete protocol for releasing "Horror" is in the ImTT Scripts manual.

ImTT Press, publisher

Traumatic Memories and the ImTT Treatment

As described previously, the good news about using ImTT for treating traumatic memories is that the person does not have to experience the feelings of pain, terror, guilt, or shame that makes treating the traumatic memories an often excruciating and sometimes overwhelming experience for the client. Instead, these feelings are released quickly without flooding by using the P/TRP to eliminate the feelings.

One of the advantages to ImTT treatment for traumatic memories is that the person's intense feelings that often overwhelm him when he begins to talk about the event can be released before the person even begins to talk about the event. If a person is already crying or terrified before even beginning to talk, the P/TRP can be used immediately to reduce the intensity of the feeling. Once the feeling is reduced, the person will be able to describe the event and an appropriate course of treatment can be determined.

Traumatic events create a number of different possible primary reactions: shock, freeze, horror, pain, and terror. Emotional reactions to trauma include guilt, shame, and anger. Each of these reactions will need to be released separately, most likely over several sessions.

ImTT Press, publisher

The following chart summarizes the primary psychological reactions that are <u>directly</u> released using the P/TRP pattern and the feelings that require the *identification of the underlying pain or terror* in order to be released.

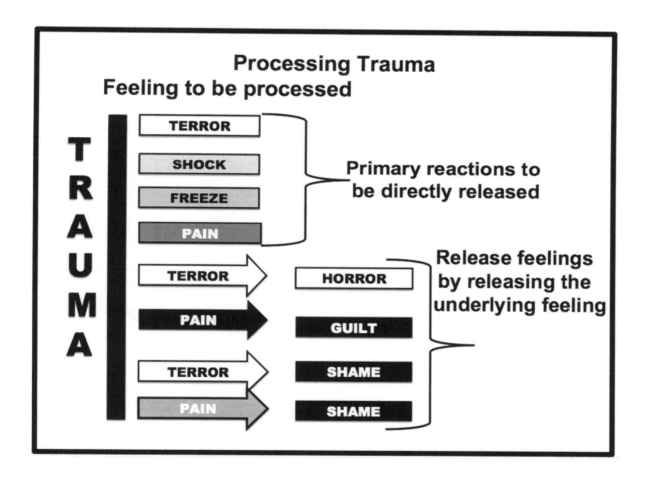

Order of Processing

Since people who have been traumatized have many different feelings related to the trauma, the question becomes what is the order of processing? Because people differ in both their reactions to trauma and in the way they are currently experiencing the memory, there can be no one specific course of treatment. The usual rule of thumb for treatment is to focus on whatever feeling is currently "present in the room." In other words, if the person is in pain, release the pain. If the person is terrified, release the terror. If the person is feeling shame, release the pain or terror underlying the shame. Whatever feeling the person is experiencing when he begins to think about the traumatic event is the feeling to be released first.

The order of processing is to process the feelings "present in the room" during the session. This means processing the pain, terror, guilt, shame, or shock that the person first presents with. The last step is to process the memory or image of the event using the IDP. The reason for this is that the person will be more easily able to "tune into" the feelings, which will allow for a more complete release. This is especially true for the feelings of shock and freeze as these feelings are often more difficult to "tune into."

A problem that may occur is that the image either does not deconstruct or will only partially deconstruct. The reason that an image will not completely deconstruct is that the image is still being energized by a feeling such as guilt or shame. When this occurs, stop doing the IDP and reassess the person for other feelings. After processing those feelings, return to processing the image with the IDP.

ImTT Press, publisher

The ImTT Trauma Protocol

Phase 1: A general history of the client is obtained.

The focus for the general history is to determine which psychological dynamic to process first. For example, if a person is suicidal, releasing the pain, agitation, and anxiety creating the suicidal feelings may be the first areas to process. Also, the level of dissociation may need to be assessed. A person with a high level of dissociation may need multiple sessions to process a trauma so that the person does not react with fear to a feeling of disorientation when the feelings and images related to the traumatic memory are released.

Phase 2: Preparation for trauma processing:

The ImTT protocols are explained. Be especially mindful of explaining that the release of feelings does not require the person to experience the feelings but to view the feelings as if from a distance.

Phase 3: The trauma is processed:

While the steps in Phase 3 are described sequentially, more than one session will be necessary to complete processing. Depending on time constraints and the person's speed of processing, steps 1 – 3 may be processed in one session and steps 4 – 6 may be processed the following session. However, more sessions may be needed depending on the psychological dynamics of the client. In addition, the order of the steps can be altered to fit the needs of the client.

1. The client lightly describes the traumatic event. Instruct the client that he should not allow himself, as much as he can, to experience the trauma. If the person begins to flood or is already flooding when he begins to describe the event, begin the P/TRP immediately on whatever the upsetting feeling is.
2. The pain and/or terror are released using the P/TRP.
3. Release the shock and/or freeze.
4. Release the guilt and shame.
5. Release the image using the Image De-Construction Protocol.
6. Perform the Changing Patterns Protocol.

Phase 4: Evaluate the client's reaction to the traumatic memory.

The person should experience a feeling of freedom, lightness, or just relief from the effects of the memory.

Phase 5: The next session, re-evaluate the traumatic memory.

Re-evaluate the traumatic memory. If the person reports any intensity about the memory, assess for other feelings and earlier memories that may be linked with the memory that was processed. Also, assess the memory for the pain of losing as a result of the Win/Lose dynamic. A person who is traumatized may also feel a loss of status.

ImTT Press, publisher

Deconstructing a Memory Network

People who have experienced abuse over time often have multiple memories that are emotionally linked with each other. The many traumatic memories would be laborious to resolve if each memory had to be processed separately. However, because the memories are linked, the pain and terror of these memories are also linked. The P/T can be thought of as a pool of feeling that energizes the memories (figure 1).

Instead of performing the P/TRP and IDP on each memory, the ImTT approach is to:

1. Drain the "pool" of pain and terror by releasing the P/T from one memory in the network (figure 2).

2. Draining the pool will de-energize all the memories that are associated with the memory network (figure 3).

3. The shock of the traumas is then released (figure 4).

4. Then the person deconstructs all the memories in the network in the image/re-image phase of the IDP (figure 5).

5. Once all the memories are deconstructed, the pixel-particles from all the memories are released from the body at the same time.

6. The images can be deconstructed one at a time or the person may form a collage of the images. Whichever way the person chooses to deconstruct the images, each image must be completely deconstructed. If an image cannot be deconstructed, an additional P/TRP must be performed in order to de-energize the image.

ImTT Press, publisher

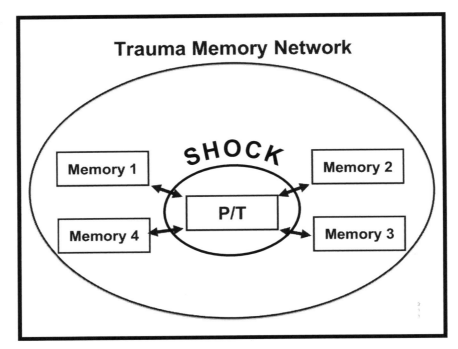

1. A traumatic memory network links similar traumatic memories in a network in which the P/T and shock of one memory adds to the intensity of the other memories.

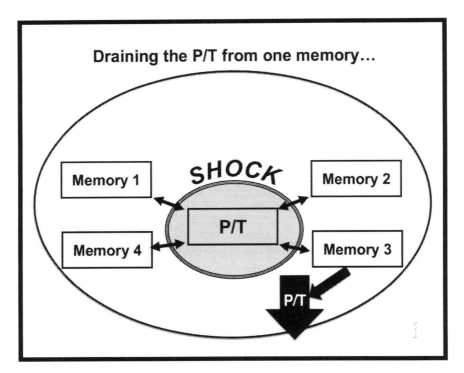

2. The entire network of memories can be drained of pain and terror by releeasing the pain and terror of one memory in the network.

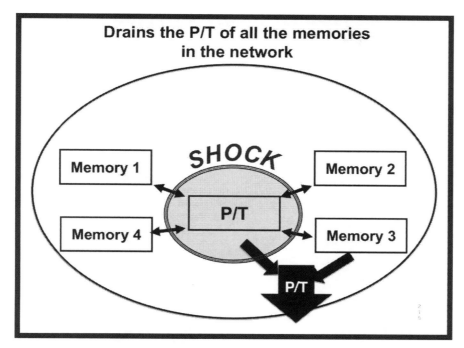

3. All the traumatic memories in the memory network are de-energized of pain and terror.

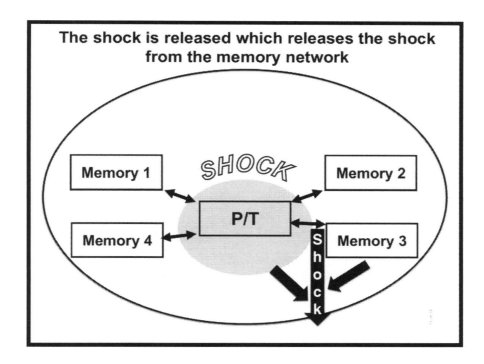

4. After the network has been de-energized of pain and terror, the shock of the traumas is released.

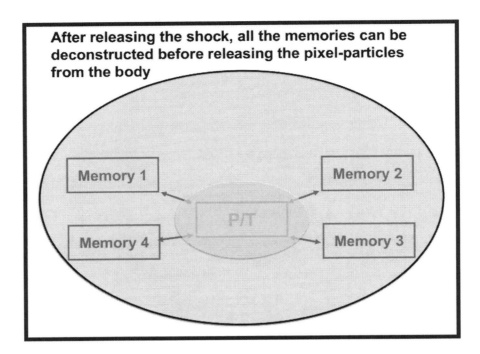

5. *After releasing the shock, all the images/memories associated with the memory network can be deconstructed in the image/re-image phase before releasing the pixel-particles from the body.*

An example of utilizing the processing of primary psychological reactions with a person who has been sexually assaulted

The ImTT treatment of sexual assault was chosen as an example because the treatment illustrates the different stages of treatment when using ImTT on PTSD.

As described above, processing a trauma may require focusing on individual feelings that are linked with the memory.

The following illustrates a possible sequence that might occur when resolving the psychological dynamics of being sexually assaulted.

When a person begins to think about being sexually assaulted, the most available feeling usually on the surface is either pain, terror, or rage. The client may not even be able to describe the event because of becoming flooded with feelings.

Process whatever feeling is present in the room. If the client is obviously terrified, process the terror. The terror or pain can be released without the client focusing on any part of the memory. The point is to release the feeling that is overwhelming the client so that further processing of the event can occur.

At this point, the client may be able to talk about the traumatic event. If the client can now talk about the event, the therapist can then direct the client to begin processing the different feelings and the image of the event linked with the feelings. At any point where the image does not change when doing the IDP, the focus of treatment should change to a different feeling.

Processing a Sexual Assault

Sam was sexually assaulted five years prior to beginning treatment. He had been held down by a much larger man and could not move. He finally sought help because his rage had gotten out of control.

Sam's rage was easily triggered, and had gotten him into some physical fights that could have put him in prison.

He decided that he would rather get help for his rage (which meant admitting to someone the cause of the anger) than go to prison.

In his first session, Sam identified the overall pain of the sexual assault as a gray color located in his stomach. The gray-colored emotional pain was the pain he experienced when he recalled the event afterwards. The emotional pain that Sam experienced from remembering the event

was not the same as the emotional pain that occurred during the event. Since Sam's pain of recalling the event was strongly present in the room, the pain from recalling the event was released first. The P/TRP was utilized without using the IDP. Processing the emotional pain he experienced from remembering the event allowed Sam to focus on processing the traumatic memory.

After using ImTT to release the pain of remembering the event, Sam identified terror as his next feeling–namely, the terror he felt when he was held down and helpless. The terror was processed with the P/TRP and then the IDP of his image. After releasing a black-colored terror from his chest, the image of the weight of the man on top of him and his ineffectual struggle was processed with the IDP.

Success in deconstructing the image was only partial. Sam left the session feeling somewhat better, but there was still a lot of the event to be processed.

In the next session, Sam identified the feeling of shame. He said that he felt shame because, as he put it, "There must be something wrong with me if I was sexually assaulted." Sam said that the shame was green in color and located all over his body.

The shame was released by focusing on the different parts of his body separately. After Sam's releasing the shame, the image was completely released with the IDP. At the end of the session, Sam reported that he still felt angry but no longer experienced the intense rage he had been living with.

In the third session, Sam reported that he felt numb. Sam's "numb" reaction indicated that there was some feeling that he did not want to experience. As Sam talked about the sexual assault, he said that he should have been able to do something. On a rational level, he could recognize that, no matter how good a fighter he was, in that situation he had been helpless. Nevertheless, he felt that he should have been able to do something.

Sam felt shame that he didn't do anything. Sam identified the feeling of terror underlying the shame. The shame was released along with the image of him crying all alone in the darkness.

In the fourth session Sam reported that he was still having nightmares about the attack. The nightmare revolved around the physical pain of the sexual assault, which he had not previously disclosed. He identified the color of the pain as red, which was released with the P/TRP. The image used was the nightmare, and that was deconstructed with the IDP.

In the fifth session, Sam reported that this event no longer bothered him and that he wanted to work on some other areas of his life.

The ImTT Treatment of Dissociation

ImTT views shock as the cause of dissociation. This means that dissociation can be reduced by releasing the shock from the psychological system. However, when processing the dissociation that occurs as the result of an intensely traumatic event, if possible, the pain and terror should be released first. Because the shock reaction numbs feelings, releasing the shock before releasing at least some of the pain and terror could result in the person becoming flooded with the pain and/or terror.

The pain and terror can be released prior to releasing the shock of the event in two ways:

1. If the person remembers the traumatic event, the P/T of the event can be directly released utilizing the P/TRP protocol. Once the P/T has been released, the shock can be released. Releasing the shock feeling may then allow other feelings to surface that had been locked behind the dissociative wall. These feelings will most likely not be overwhelming since the P/T has been previously released.

2. If the person does not remember the traumatic event, current events may be used to access the underlying P/T. Figure1 Illustrates the psychological dynamics of a person who has suffered a severe traumatic event. In this case, the traumatic memory is blocked from memory by the shock reaction, creating dissociation.

Then a current event occurs, figure 2, that activates the P/T caused by the traumatic event. For example, a person's boss mildly criticizes him. The criticism activates the P/T associated with the earlier traumatic event.

Because the current event has activated the P/T of the earlier traumatic event, the P/T of the previous event intensifies the P/T of the current event (figure 3).

Draining the P/T of the current event also drains the P/T of the past event (figure 4) reducing the total P/T (figure 5).

Draining the shock of the current event also drains the shock of the past event (figure 6). The result is that even though the person does not remember the earlier traumatic event, the pain and terror of that event can also be released.

Once the P/T and shock of the traumatic events have been reduced, the person may then be able to remember the previously dissociated event (figure 7).

Then the traumatic memory can be processed using the ImTT protocol for traumatic memories (figure 8).

ImTT Press, publisher

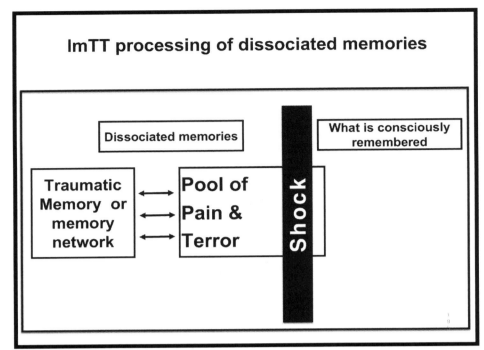

1. *Shock persists in the body long after the event. Dissociated memories are blocked from conscious awarenesss as a result of the shock reaction.*

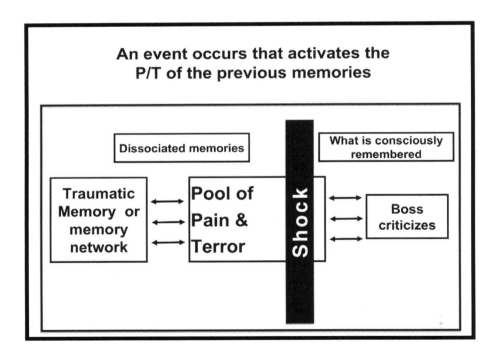

2. *An event may occur in the person's life that activates the feelings and memories of the past traumatic event.*

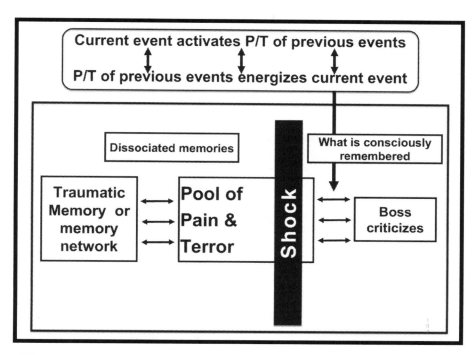

3. The person's reaction to the current event is intensified by the feelings from the past event.

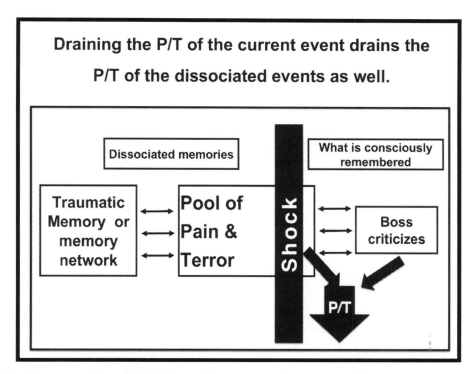

4. Performing the P/TRP on the current event will release some of the pain and terror from the past event.

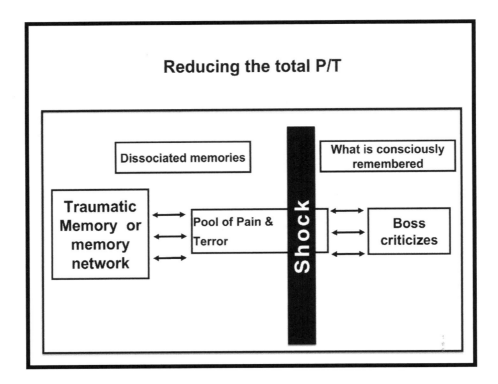

5. The result is that the pain and terror of the past event has also been released. The pool of pain and terror is smaller.

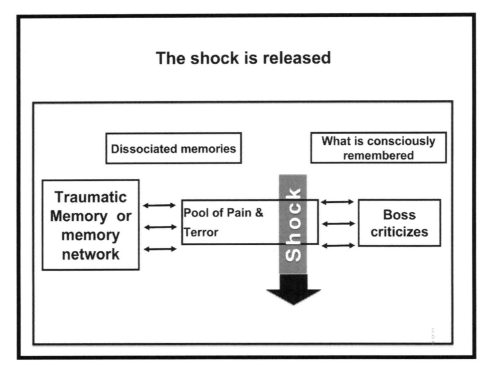

6. Releasing the shock of the current event also releasess some of the shock of the past event lowering the barrier to a conscious awareness of the event.

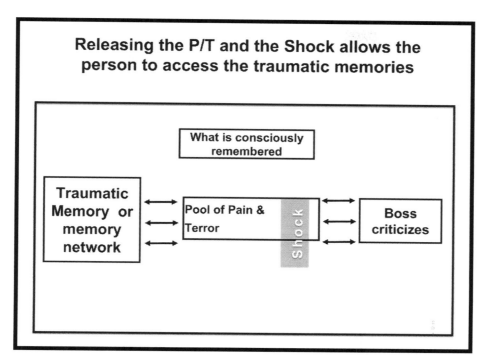

7. The person can now remember events that he had previously been blocked from remembering.

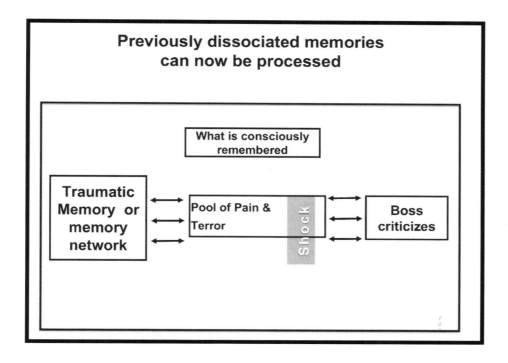

8. Once the person remembers the traumatic event, the event can be directly processed with ImTT.

ImTT Press, publisher

Chapter 7

ImTT TREATMENT FOR SPECIFIC DISORDERS

ImTT is useful in treating a wide range of psychological dynamics. This section will focus on ImTT's treatment of issues that have pain or terror as their immediate energizing force and include depression, anxiety, PTSD, anxiety disorders, anger, eating disorders, paranoia, crisis management, perfectionism, inability to be alone, boundary issues, and blockages.

Depression

Lessening the Load

Depression can be caused by a variety of different painful and traumatic events. When a person is painfully depressed, however, talking about traumatic or painful events may be too difficult. The overall pain may be too intense for the person to process those events. While the image of the events causing the depression will need to be individually processed, the pain of the depression itself can be lightened by processing the depression-caused pain.

Releasing the pain is a useful way of "lessening the load" so that the person can do the psychological work for processing the events. Lessening the load will make the person more emotionally available, allowing them to then work through the difficult memories.

Suicide and Depression

Depression is painful. People commit suicide because the pain of their depression is so intense that they just want it to stop. ImTT can be used in a general way to alleviate the pain of depression.

The response is usually immediately positive, with the person expressing relief and a reduced suicidal ideation.

Example of releasing the pain of depression

> **Therapist: "The feeling of depression is really painful, isn't it?"**
>
> **Patient: "Yes"**
>
> **Therapist: "What color is the pain?"**
>
> **Patient: (Identifies a color)**
>
> **Therapist: (Guides the client to release the color with the P/TRP)**

　　　　　　　　　　　　　　　　ImTT Press, publisher

Depression and

Negative Images of the Self

Negative images of the self such as images of being worthless, unlovable, helpless, et cetera, can create depression. These images appear to be "facts" to the person who holds them.

These so-called "facts" appear to be supported by the evidence of the events that have happened to him/her. Instead of challenging these facts, as in conventional cognitive therapy, ImTT eliminates these "facts" by releasing the P/T and deconstructing the image. Magically, the "facts" disappear.

Once these negative images are deconstructed, the person is able to see that what appeared to be a "fact" was just an image that could be released.

For a more specific explanation for changing negative self-images, see the instructions for changing the self-image.

Will's depression was triggered by his firm's bankruptcy and his subsequent layoff. When asked how he felt about himself, he stated, "I am a total loser. I should have known better." The image that Will had of being a loser was of an old, homeless man pushing a cart and talking to himself. Processing Will's image eliminated Will's feeling that he was a loser. The result was that other, more positive memories surfaced in which Will had performed well.

The Difference between Depression and Anxiety

If Will's image of being a loser was what he anticipated would happen to him, Will would suffer from anxiety–the fear that he would become that homeless man. Instead, Will had accepted the loser image as his current image. He was not afraid of being a loser; he was a loser.

A common psychological dynamic is for the person to swing between depression and anxiety as the person swings from believing in the image and fearing the image.

Depression and Loss

There are two types of pain reactions caused by the loss of a relationship.

The difference lies in the type of attachment.

1. In a relationship with a person who is experienced more as "other" or as a different person, the loss is not experienced as loss of a part of the "self." This loss is experienced as painful, but it doesn't feel as "deep."

2. On the other hand, in a relationship in which the attachment is experienced as part of the "self," the pain is experienced as loss of a part of the self.

Both the loss of "other" and the loss of "self" result in pain. However, it is important to keep in mind the different origins of the pain reaction.

The P/TRP releases the pain that the person is aware of. Pain that is not identified is not released. The importance of this distinction occurs when a person's spouse dies. What the person is usually immediately aware of is the pain caused by the loss of the relationship experienced as "other."

The acknowledgment of the "loss of other" type of pain and its release with the P/TRP is fairly obvious. What is less obvious is that the experience of "losing a part of myself" is a separate reaction creating a pain that requires a separate processing with the P/TRP. Because only pain that is identified can be completely released, it is important to distinguish between the origins of both types of pain from loss.

Only pain that is identified can be released with the P/TRP.

The pain of loss does not necessarily cause depression.

The pain of loss does not necessarily cause depression. The depression is created by the person's images related to the loss. So if a person's image is that he will never get over the pain of the loss or if he feels abandoned, the images related to that loss may create depression.

It is usually best to release the pain of the loss of the relationship before moving on to deconstruct whatever images may be energized by the pain.

Depression and Terror

Loss of a relationship may not only be painful but terrifying. If the person experiences the loss as abandonment, then the primary reaction will be terror, perhaps in addition to the pain of loss. Even the threat of loss can cause an anticipation of abandonment, resulting in terror.

For example, Ruby reported that she had been feeling increasingly depressed over the last few months. She had stopped drinking a few months ago and, since then, her depression had become more intense. She was having difficulty sleeping and had lost weight.

Ruby's depression began seven months prior to the session, when her boyfriend moved to their new home in a different state. Ruby's own timetable meant that she would be joining him in six months but she had to finish a commitment first. They had been talking daily and had seen each other every six weeks since he left. Nevertheless, being away from him physically was emotionally difficult for her.

Ruby was able to identify that she felt abandoned because her boyfriend was not physically present. She then identified and released the feeling of terror of abandonment. The image Ruby identified was that of a little girl holding a doll and crying. Once the image was processed with the IDP, Ruby felt an immediate release of the depressed feeling.

Anxiety

Anxiety disorders—including phobias, Generalized Anxiety Disorder, and Obsessive-Compulsive Disorder—are the result of terrifying images. These terrifying images maybe the result of events that actually occurred or are imaginary, such as a child's image of a monster under the bed. In either case, clearing the image will release the person from both the psychological and behavioral dynamics produced by the anxiety.

While phobias, GAD, and OCD differ in terms of their psychological dynamics, the ImTT approach is the same–identify the image, release its underlying P/T, and then deconstruct the terrifying image.

Lightening the Load of Anxiety

People who have anxiety are usually suffering from a buildup of the feeling of anxiety. As the P/TRP was used to "lighten the load" of depression, this approach can also be used to reduce the intensity of anxiety. The feeling of underlying anxiety may be either painful or fearful. Using the P/TRP in this general way will reduce the overall intensity of a person's anxiety, making it easier to target the underlying source of the anxiety.

After reducing the intensity of the anxiety, the specific events or anticipated events can be targeted.

For example, Betty was getting married in one week. Over the last few weeks, her anxiety level had become so intense that she was having difficulty sleeping and was now having problems keeping up with all the tasks that needed to be done for her large family wedding. Betty's anxiety was so intense she had difficulty talking about what was causing her anxiety.

Instead of focusing treatment on what was creating the anxiety, the sensation of anxiety was the first focus of treatment.

Therapist: "Where do you feel the sensation of anxiety most intensely in your body?"

Betty: "In my stomach."

Therapist: "See the sensation of anxiety as composed of tiny, tiny little particles of the sensation."

Therapist performs the P/TRP pattern on the sensation of anxiety. No color of the sensation is identified. A script for lightening the load of anxiety is in the Scripts book.

After reducing Betty's level of anxiety, the cause of the anxiety was treated. When asked what her nightmare wedding scenario was, she replied that she was terrified she would be jilted at the altar and that everyone would laugh at her. When asked whether this imagined scenario would be painful or fearful, her response was "excruciatingly painful."

After releasing the P/T and the image, Betty's anxiety decreased to the normal level of anxiety that occurs when putting on a big event so that her focus was on the preparations for the wedding, not herself. Betty was now regarding the wedding as a challenge, not a potential disaster. She was able to stay in the zone of action, not reaction. The result was that Betty actually enjoyed her own wedding!

Generalized Anxiety Disorder

Generalized Anxiety Disorder (GAD) is indicated by either the person constantly worrying about many different things or a feeling of being "on edge." The different symptoms require different ImTT treatments.

GAD & worry: The person with GAD who worries expects something bad to happen. So she will worry about first one thing and then another. The content of the worry is constantly changing. The target for treatment is the underlying cause of the worry dynamic, not the current situation. Usually, the expectation that "something bad is going to happen" is based upon something that actually happened. In this situation, the ImTT treatment is to identify the event that the worry is based on. If the person is not able to identify any particular memory, then the Imaginary Scenario Technique is used to create an image that emotionally resonates with the feeling that "something bad is going to happen."

Once either the memory or the image is identified, the terror and then the image or memory are targeted for release.

GAD and feeling on-edge: The on-edge feeling of GAD is usually the result of trauma. The challenge for treatment is to identify the underlying event causing the on-edge feeling. If an event cannot be identified, then the on-edge feeling is used for the initial target for treatment. Releasing the P/T linked with the feeling may then allow the memory related to that feeling to surface. If the memory surfaces, process the memory. If a memory does not process, attempt to create an image that resonates with whatever feeling is present using the Imaginary Scenario Technique. If the client cannot create an image, continue using the P/TRP to release the underlying P/T and thereby reduce the intensity of the feeling.

Generalized Anxiety Disorder

The target for treatment is the underlying dynamic that is causing the worry—not of any particuar worry.

Jill was constantly worrying about anything and everything. She would lie in bed at night worrying about what was going to happen the next day or what she didn't get finished that day.

Jill's worrying began after her parents divorced when she was 13. She didn't see it coming. In her mind, she had to constantly be afraid of what was going to happen that she hadn't planned on.

The target for treatment was the memory when she learned that her parents were divorcing. The memory was enhanced with images of what she feared would happen to her.

Phobias

A phobia is a fear of a specific situation that might happen if.... The person may fear spiders, snakes, taking a test, social situations, or crowds.

Treatment of a phobia involves identifying the terrifying image, releasing the terror, and deconstructing the image.

Phobias are caused by nightmare images of what would happen if...

- **The spider bites.**
- **I'm speaking in front of a group and I forget what I have to say.**
- **I have a car accident.**

ImTT Treatment

Release the P/T and deconstruct the image.

Arachnophobia

Claudia had an intense fear of spiders. She would often clean her house intensely in order to make sure that there were no spiders in her house. The image Claudia had was a photograph she had seen as a child, which depicted a person bitten by a black widow spider. When asked to enhance the image with the nightmare scenario, she pictured herself in the photo. Claudia released the terror with the P/TRP, then released the image using the IDP. The clinician performed CPP by asking Claudia to picture herself in her home, looking in different rooms both during the day and at night.

As a result, Claudia stopped cleaning her house so intensely; ImTT had resolved her fear of spiders.

Social Phobia

The process for treating people with social phobia is virtually the same as the treatment for arachnophobia. The person first creates an image of what he fears might happen when he is in public. If a memory surfaces, then the memory is the target for ImTT treatment. If a memory does not surface, process the image first with the P/TRP and then deconstruct the image with the IDP.

Sandy's social phobia was causing her problems in class. Whenever she had to do a presentation in front of the class, her mind would, as she put it, "go blank." When she was asked to create a nightmare scenario of the worst thing that could happen, she replied, "Everyone will know that I'm stupid and I don't know what I'm talking about." While this image emotionally resonated with her, Sandy could not link the image with any particular memory. Sandy released the P/T associated with the image and then deconstructed the image. The clinician performed the CPP by asking Sandy to imagine that she was speaking in front of her class.

The next session, Sandy reported that she had less anxiety about speaking in front of a group of people. This time she did remember an event in which she was sitting in the audience when the speaker "froze" on stage. The speaker was so embarrassed that she ran off the stage. People in the audience began laughing. From that time on, Sandy was frightened that the same thing could happen to her. This event was processed with the ImTT. Sandy reported the next session that she was no longer afraid of speaking in front of groups.

Panic Attacks

The term "Panic Attack" points to what's causing the disorder–terror. The challenge in treating a panic attack (PA) is to identify what the person is terrified of. People with PAs usually report that the panic appears to happen "out of the blue." Sometimes people report that there appear to be certain "triggers" to the PA but that other times the PA appears to occur randomly for no apparent reason.

The first step in treating PA is to identify the cause of the terror. Sometimes identifying when the PAs first began will be useful. Other times, no particular cause of the terror can be identified. The solution is to begin removing the fear and terror that the person is connected with–the feeling of terror that is occurring at the time of the PA. Even though the cause of the PA is not known, removing the terror that the person feels may allow the person to identify the cause of the terror. ImTT can then be utilized to release the dynamic causing the PA. Even if the cause cannot yet be identified, removing whatever terror the person can release will likely lessen the intensity of future problems.

ImTT Press, publisher

Paranoia

Paranoia is a result of one of at least three different experiences:

1. Being assaulted
2. Family dynamics resulting in perfectionism
3. Psychological boundary violations

While all three of these types of experiences result in paranoid ideation, the difference in how the paranoia was created means that the treatment must target the appropriate underlying dynamics.

Paranoia resulting from being assaulted is a psychological displacement from the real-life event. When the assault event occurs in childhood, the child may suppress the feeling of being threatened, especially if a parent is the perpetrator. Even though the feeling of being threatened is suppressed, the feeling of being threatened is still present in the child's mind.

Later in life, the feeling of being threatened is then projected out into the world or displaced onto people or events. The person will actually look for events in the world that will justify the feeling. Resolving this paranoid dynamic requires identifying and processing the original event that made the person feel threatened.

The second type of experiences that can lead to paranoia are experiences that result in perfectionism. Treating paranoia resulting from perfectionism requires treating the perfectionism first. For treatment recommendations, read the section on treating perfectionism-caused paranoia.

The third dynamic creating paranoia involves boundary violations. When a child is not allowed his own psychological space, a feeling of helplessness and an image of an inability to protect himself may be created. For treatment recommendation of paranoia resulting from boundary violations, go to the section on boundary violations.

The graphics on the next page illustrate the ImTT approach to the paranoid dynamic.

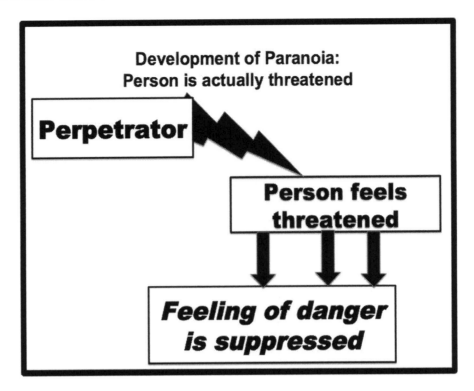

The person feels threatened. Feelings of terror are suppressed.

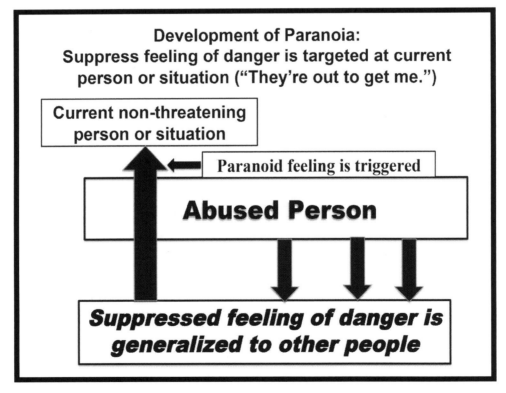

The suppressed terror is generalized toward other, less threatening people.

108   ImTT Press, publisher

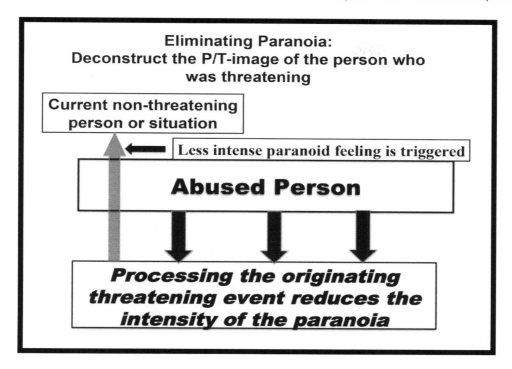

Processing the originating event eliminates the suppressed feeling of being endangered. The current paranoid image must also be deconstructed.

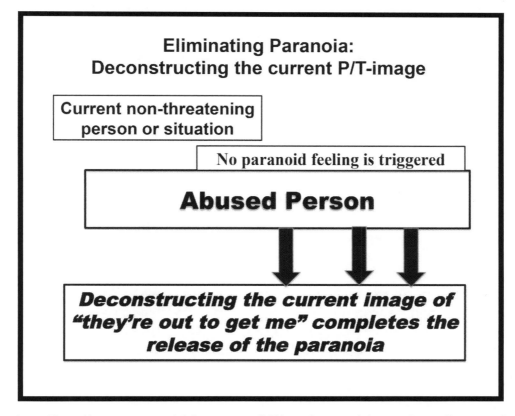

Deconstructing the paranoid image of "they're out to get me" completes the release.

Paranoia Case Studies

The following case studies illustrate ImTT treatment for paranoia resulting from assault. Paranoia resulting from perfectionism is discussed on page 126 and paranoia resulting from boundary violation is discussed on page 132.

Scott's Paranoia

Scott illustrates the first paranoid dynamic. Scott was a 35-year-old man, with a long-standing history of paranoia, who presented for therapy after being hospitalized for expressing his intent to kill two men who had bullied him.

As a child, Scott suffered neglect and endured extreme abuse. Both of his parents used drugs while he was growing up, and his father would often severely beat him.

The first session treated the physical abuse Scott received from his father. Scott was able to tune into the terror he experienced during the beating and release it. He also released some of the pain of the neglect. At the end of the session, he felt lighter and said those events no longer bothered him.

In the second session, Scott reported that the memories processed in the previous session still had no emotional charge. The next topic for processing was the "murderous rage" he had toward the two men. He had been hospitalized to prevent him from acting on his feelings. Scott stated that he did not want to let go of his rage. When asked why he did not want to release the rage, he said that, if he released the rage, he would "lose" to the two men he wanted to murder. Scott then identified the color of the pain of losing located in his heart and released it.

After processing the pain of losing, Scott's rage disappeared. Essentially, the idea of losing had triggered Scott's feelings of helplessness, which, in turn, generated his murderous rage. Releasing the pain resolved his rage.

The next focus of treatment was Scott's distrust of people, which intensified his paranoid feelings. Scott described his paranoia as "not being able to trust anybody." The paranoia was related to an event in his childhood–namely, the time he saved up enough money to buy a car and gave it to his mother for safekeeping. At the end of the summer, when he wanted the money to buy the car, she told him that she had spent it. From that point on, he felt that he could not trust anyone. Scott identified the pain of betrayal and released it.

After releasing the pain of betrayal, the next focus of treatment was Scott's paranoia. He stated that, while that event no longer bothered him, he still felt distrustful of the world. This time he stated the distrust differently: "People are out to get me." He traced this feeling to the beatings he suffered from his father. Scott processed this paranoia by releasing the terror and image of his father physically beating him. Once he released this terror, he stated that the thoughts were still there but that they seemed "empty." In a few days, even the thoughts had disappeared.

The beatings that Scott suffered for years from his father made him feel that his father was out to get him. The suppression of the terror created during these beatings resulted in a generalization of this feeling. So Scott's feeling that, "Daddy wants to hurt me," generalized to the feeling that "People are out to get me." Releasing the terror of his father immediately released the energy behind Scott's feeling that "People are out to get me."

Hypervigilance

Hypervigilance is another form of anxiety-caused behavior. The person is terrified that something bad is going to happen and that he has to always be alert. Hypervigilance is caused by either a traumatic event or the fear of a traumatic event.

When working with combat veterans, they would often state that they were just waiting for something bad to happen. There was always an event that was clear in their minds that marked the point in time when the reality of combat became real for them. That was the moment when their hypervigilance began.

For some veterans, this event occurred when they heard the first bullets fired at them when they were "in-country." For others, the reality-changing event occurred when the red light was turned on in the plane before landing in-country. Whatever the precipitating event, the person now had an intense image that danger could strike at any moment. The feeling of being in danger created the feeling of terror and the hypervigilant behavior.

When combat veterans are asked about what they fear might happen, they often talk about the need to protect their families. Sometimes they feel that someone from their combat zone will come over to the United States and attack their families. Sometimes the danger cited feels directed at them personally.

Whatever the reality is, the mind finds a reason for its feeling of terror—the feeling of terror they almost certainly experienced in combat but had to suppress. Returning home doesn't make the terror disappear; now the mind has to justify the feeling of terror by finding something in their current life to feel endangered by.

ImTT treatment for hypervigilance begins by asking the patient to imagine a scene that evokes the terror. The terror and the image are then processed with the P/TRP and IDP. Sometimes when the created image is processed, another image will surface related to a specific event. The specific-event-related image is also processed.

Anger Issues

Anger issues are caused by two psychological dynamics. One dynamic is that the anger is linked with a positive feeling. Examples of positive feelings include feelings of power, superiority, righteousness, and dominance. Eliminating the dynamic of anger linked with positive feelings requires breaking apart or de-linking the anger from the positive feeling. This dynamic and its treatment will be explained in the book on the Feeling-State Image Protocol (FSIP).

The second dynamic underlying anger is the anger that is a reaction to pain or terror. The P/T differs according to the survival dynamic involved.

1. A person who is emotionally hurt in a relationship may experience the broken attachment as painful. The anger arises because the person is angry at the person who hurt him.

2. If the breakup of the relationship feels like abandonment, the anger may result from terror.

3. If the person feels that he is losing–i.e., losing in status, respect, et cetera– it may trigger the pain of loss in terms of survival through winning or losing the competition for passing on his genetic legacy. From clinical experience, it seems that the rage resulting from loss of status, respect, et cetera, is often the most intense.

ImTT Press, publisher

The Treatment for Roger's Anger

Roger's wife cheated on him with his best friend. His rage was so intense that he would hit a wall with his fist; he had broken a knuckle twice. They had a son whom they co-parented. Seeing his wife triggered his rage again. Anger management classes had not helped.

In the first session, Roger's pain about his wife's cheating and his best friend's betrayal was released using first the P/TRP and then the IDP. He left feeling much better.

At the beginning of the second session, Roger reported that he was no longer angry when he was in his wife's presence. However, when he was not in her presence, he would ruminate about what had happened and become intensely angry, often for several hours at a time.

Because Roger was no longer angry when he was in his wife's presence, it appeared that the previous session had released his anger towards her. The question became with whom was he angry. Roger stated that he was angry with himself for not picking up on the situation with his wife. For Roger, not noticing what was happening triggered his memory of certain events in his childhood that created the painful image of him being stupid. The pain was energizing his anger.

The ImTT treatment focused on utilizing the P/TRP to release the pain of Roger's belief that he was stupid. After the pain was released, Roger's image of a childhood event in which he felt stupid was deconstructed with the IDP. He left the session in a much better mood.

Roger's anger issues were the result of two different pains: the first pain was the pain of his wife and his best friend cheating on him. The second pain was the pain of feeling stupid for not noticing his wife's cheating.

Anger is caused by two different dynamics

1. **Positive feelings linked with the behavior of anger.**

2. **A reaction to pain or terror:**

   a. **An underlying terror if the reaction is to abandonment**

   b. **An underlying pain if the reaction is to a win/lose loss**

   c. **An underlying pain if the reaction is to the experience of rejection**

Eating Disorders

Eating disorders can be the result of a variety of psychological dynamics. As with anger, food can be linked with positive feelings creating different types of food compulsions. The vomiting in bulimia, binge eating, or an intense feeling to eat a certain food are behaviors that may result from a fixated positive feeling. Those dynamics should be processed with the FSIP as discussed previously.

Other problems with food may be the result of a P/T. Overeating, and overeating while watching TV, especially, may be avoidance behaviors. Other eating issues may be the result of feeling overwhelmed or avoiding feelings of anger or anxiety. Food is also used to avoid traumatic memories. Because of the variety of psychological dynamics that can result in problems with food, there cannot be just one protocol for resolving the problem. Rather, as the clinician investigates the timeline of current and past events, the targets will reveal themselves.

One easy and productive place to begin resolving food issues is with altering the client's self-image. There are often feelings of self-disgust, shame, and guilt related to the inability to control food intake. In addition, there are often negative cognitions associated with how the person looks. Negative cognitions such as "I'm ugly," "I'm lazy," and "No one loves me" are beliefs that the person can usually easily identify. The beliefs and associated images create a continuing inner fight between the desired image and the P/T-energized images.

This is an exhausting fight that usually ends in the person losing their battle with food. Using ImTT to change the self-image can be useful for releasing the power of the negative self-images that create this intense inner conflict.

Simultaneously with this inner psychic battle, the person is also fighting off the feelings that created the eating behavior in the first place—feelings such as being a failure, being unloved, being abandoned, et cetera. Targeting these feelings and associated images can help resolve the person's issues with food.

The P/Ts of failure after previous attempts to lose weight should also be processed. Often the memory of these failures is very painful and can contribute significantly to a negative self-image.

In addition to a person's negative self-image and pain from previous attempts to lose weight, the many images a person has of food can also contribute to eating issues. For example, when hungry, a person might say to themselves, "I'm starving."

These words might evoke the image of a starving person eating ravenously and thus trigger an intense urge to eat.

Another image of food can be identified by asking the person to visualize being hungry and then fantasize about what is happening. The fantasy that results is the image that is evoked whenever the person is hungry. This image can be released by using the Image De-Construction Protocol.

Because food issues may involve multiple negative images and compulsions, persistence is paramount. Food problems may not resolve in one golden moment, in which ImTT turns a key that releases the person from their previous behavior. Significant change in eating is more likely to arise following the release of many different images and as a result of the overall work, rather than any one transformation.

ImTT Press, publisher

Chapter 8

OBSESSIVE-COMPULSIVE DISORDER

Obsessive-Compulsive Disorder (OCD) results from suppressed or dissociated feelings and images. People who suffer from OCD report three types of dynamics: Staying-Safe behavior, Avoidant behavior, and Intrusive Thoughts. It is important to note that a person can suffer from all three dynamics.

Psychological Dynamics of OCD

1. **Staying-Safe:** Preventing the "bad thing" from happening.

2. **Avoidant:** Behavior to avoid thoughts, feelings, and memories.

3. **Intrusive Thoughts:** Intense self-negative or violent thoughts that intrude into awareness.

Overview of the Psychological Dynamics of OCD

Staying-Safe OCD Behavior

In the Staying-Safe behavior, the person has a feeling that something bad is going to happen if they don't do some specific behavior. They will often repeat that behavior until they feel that the behavior has either been performed the correct number of times or that the behavior has been performed correctly to ward off the impending doom. The feeling is "If I do this, I'll be safe."

Avoidant OCD Behavior

The purpose of avoidant behavior is to avoid negative feelings. While the behavior, such as counting, may seem similar to the Staying-Safe behavior, the purpose is different. In Staying-Safe behavior the purpose is that the person does not experience that "something bad is going to happen" feeling.

Rather, the purpose of the OCD behavior is to avoid feelings of pain, terror, shame, et cetera. The OCD sufferer keeps doing the behavior such as counting to distract his mind from the unwanted feelings.

Intrusive-Thoughts OCD Behavior

The third dynamic is the Intrusive Thoughts type of OCD. Intrusive-Thoughts OCD is described as the person having intrusive, intense thoughts that appear to have no current rational reason for being present. The person may think thoughts such as "I'm stupid" or have the thought of killing someone they have just met and are not even angry with. The result is that the person spends a great deal of time and mental energy so that he will not act on these thoughts.

Many people with OCD behavior will present with multiple behaviors that are the result of multiple dynamics. A washing-hands behavior for one person may be related to the Staying-Safe dynamic, while his checking/rechecking behavior may be the result of an avoidant dynamic.

For another person, the dynamics underlying the behaviors may be just the reverse. A careful analysis of the underlying dynamic of each behavior is necessary to discern the psychological motivation and the appropriate treatment.

Staying-Safe OCD Behavior

The Staying-Safe dynamic is a form of magical thinking. "If I keep the radio volume dial on even numbers, then nothing will happen to me (or someone else)." The person has the feeling that something dreadful is going to happen. There is usually nothing specific, just a feeling of dread that something bad is going to happen. Common magical warding-off behaviors are counting, washing hands, or setting a dial to a specific type of number (e.g., even, odd, multiples of 3 or 5). What distinguishes the Staying Safe behavior is that the magical thinking contains no rational relationship between the behavior and the feared outcome.

ImTT clears Staying-Safe OCD behavior by releasing the underlying, dread-inducing image. Once that image is deconstructed, the person ceases to perform the behavior. Having eliminated the dread of the pain or terror, the individual no longer needs to perform the magical safety-making behavior. The result is that the person no longer does the behavior. Without the P/T motivating the behavior, there is just no reason to do it.

The key to the ImTT treatment for OCD is to identify the correct image to process. Just targeting the anxiety itself is not sufficient. The targeted image can often be identified by using the Imaginary Scenario Technique. The person creates a fantasy of the disaster that will happen if they do not perform the ritual behaviors. The P/T of the image is identified and processed with the P/TRP. The image is processed with the IDP.

Julian's OCD Treatment

An example of this process is performed in the treatment of Julian.

Julian's OCD began about the age of five. At the time of the therapy, Julian's OCD required that he set the radio dial to an even number and keep his hat and clothes a certain way. Otherwise, Julian would experience intense levels of anxiety.

When asked to imagine that the volume control was on three, he stated that the level of his anxiety was 7 or 8 on a 10-point scale.

Julian recalled that, starting at about the same time as the OCD, he began having a recurrent nightmare. In his nightmare, the sun melted everything on the earth, except him. Julian identified the P/T as terror and

released it. He then stated that the intensity level of having the volume dial on an odd number was 2 or 3.

In the second session, Julian said that, after the first session, he had driven all the way home without looking at the volume control on his radio. He reported that he had never been able to do that previously.

The next target for release was "the devil." Julian experienced severe physical and emotional abuse as a child. He never knew from one moment to the next whether his mother would be calm or whether he would get slapped because of a change in his mother's mood. He felt terrorized by this behavior.

Using the Imaginary Scenario Technique, the clinician asked Julian to create a fantasy representation of all the terrorizing events. Julian imagined that the devil was going to get him. He released the terror and deconstructed the image of the devil. Afterwards, when asked to imagine putting the radio dial on three, he reported the intensity level of his anxiety had dropped to zero.

At the next session, Julian reported that he no longer paid any attention to the volume dial and that the effect of the treatment was also evident in other areas of his life as well, such as the way he wore his clothes.

An interesting aspect of Julian's therapy is that the targets (the nightmare and fantasy), the treatment of which had brought about the most change in intensity and behavior, were mental events—events that only occurred within Julian's mind.

While Julian could remember some of the terrifying events, his mind's ability to "sum up" or represent the totality of the terror in symbolic form provided the key to finding an appropriate target for treatment.

People suffering from Staying-Safe OCD behavior are terrified of images. The focus for treatment is not the behavior but the deconstructing of the images. "The monster is under the bed," "The shadow will eat me," or "I'll be abandoned" are frightening images that must be avoided. Through magical thinking, the person develops behaviors to keep him/herself safe. Releasing the terror and the terrifying image will free the person from the life-and-death urgency to perform magical behaviors in order to survive.

The key focus for treatment of the Staying-Safe OCD behavior is to identify the terrifying or painful image. The clinician leads the person through a series of cognitive steps to discover the P/T image, performs the P/TRP on the P/T, and then the IDP on the image. The feeling that "something bad is going to happen" is also released.

These graphics illustrate the ImTT treatment for the OCD Staying-Safe behaviors

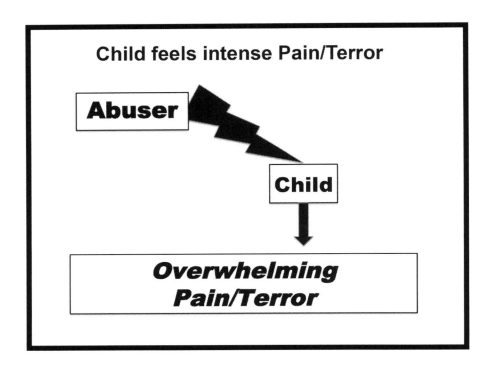

1. Pain and Terror are created during a traumatic event.

2. The person uses magical thinking to develop a "safe place." The person feels that bad things won't happen if he/she thinks or behaves in a specific way.

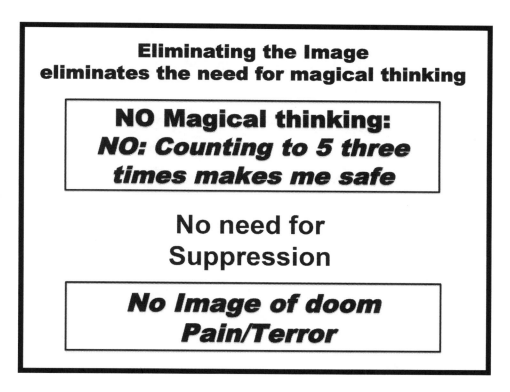

3. Asking the question, "What will happen if you don't do the behavior?" will help identify either the nightmare image which may be totally imaginary or refer to a specific event. Process the image with the P/TRP and the IDP.

ImTT Press, publisher

Hoarding

Hoarding is just another form of OCD Staying-Safe behavior. The person who hoards is preventing something bad from happening by not throwing anything away.

The image that is driving the behavior may be mostly imaginary, or the image may reflect an event that actually occurred. In either situation, the solution is the same: use the P/TRP to release the P/T and then deconstruct the image using the IDP.

Below is an example of identifying an image causing hoarding

Sample Hoarding Script

Th: What will happen if you throw that away?

P: I'll need it for something.

Th: If you need it and don't have it, what's going to happen?

P: I'll lose my job.

Th: If you lose your job, what's going to happen?

P: I'll be homeless.

Th: If you're homeless, what's going to happen?

P: I'll be ragged, smelly, and live under a bridge.

Th: Is that painful or terrifying?

(Process with ImTT whichever feeling the client picks.)

Avoidant Behavior Treatment

The purpose of Avoidant OCD Behavior is to avoid unwanted feelings. This is different from Staying-Safe OCD Behavior because, in Avoidant OCD behavior, there is not a feeling that something bad is going to happen. In Avoidant OCD Behavior the person does not want to experience an unwanted feeling. By performing the avoidant behavior, the behavior distracts the person from the feeling.

The ImTT treatment for Avoidant OCD Behavior is fairly obvious: Have the person lightly experience the feeling and then process the feeling and associated memory or image with the P/TRP and IDP.

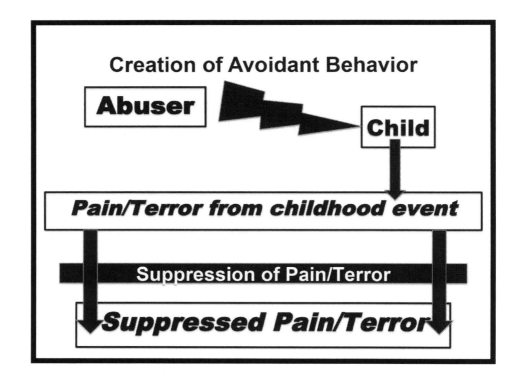

1. An event too painful or terrifying for the person to process occurs. The pain and/or terror is suppressed.

ImTT Press, publisher

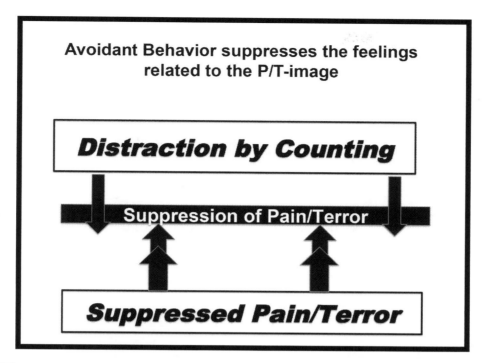

2. The painful or terrifying event is suppressed through distracting behavior such as counting or walking in circles.

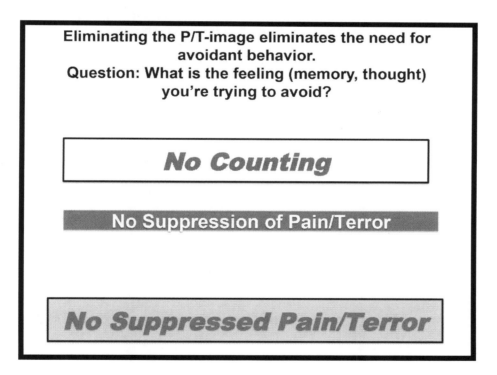

3. The memory, thought, or feeling must be identified and then processed with ImTT, after which, since the person is only doing the behavior to avoid the feeling, the person stops doing the behavior.

Intrusive Thought Treatment

Intrusive Thought OCD behavior usually consists of two types of thoughts: negative self-thoughts (I'm stupid) and angry, hostile thoughts (I'll strangle him). Both types of thoughts are the result of psychological displacement. Psychological displacement occurs when the person cannot let himself experience the thought at the time the event occurred. The person may have been too terrified to feel angry at a person or too shamed to feel the negative self-thought such as "I'm stupid."

Therefore, because of the terror or shame, these thoughts have gone "underground" in the person's mind. In Intrusive Thought OCD, these thoughts are now currently intruding into the person's mind but without the original context in which the thoughts were created.

The challenge for treating intrusive thoughts is that the person has dissociated him/herself from the original memory for a good reason: survival. Whether the thoughts are shameful or guilty, the person has suppressed the feelings (if not the memory) of the event. The challenge is to treat these emotional dynamics even when the person cannot connect with the memory.

Intrusive Negative Self-Thoughts

The ImTT treatment for negative self-thoughts is to release the P/T linked with the thought and then deconstruct the image. For example, Rick's intrusive thought was "I'm stupid." The image he identified that emotionally resonated with the thoughts was of a person pointing at him with contempt on his face. Rick identified the P/T as pain. The image was then partially deconstructed. Upon investigating the

feeling that was causing the resistance to the complete image release, Rick identified the feeling of intense shame. That feeling was processed, and then Rick was able to completely deconstruct the image. Rick was able to completely resolve this issue without identifying any originating event.

1. An event occurs that makes the person feel that he is a bad person.

Because of the intensity of the feeling, the thought is suppressed.

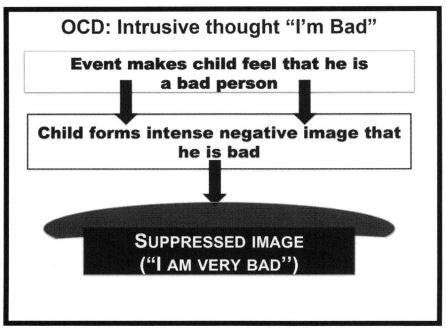

2. As an adult, the person identifies content that matches the "I'm bad" feeling. This content can change as the person's beliefs about what is bad changes. The negative thought intrudes into the person's mind whenever the feeling is triggered by current events.

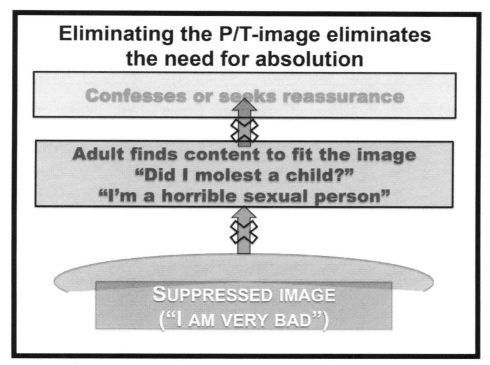

3. Processing the suppressed image and negative cognition eliminates the negative intrusive thoughts.

ImTT Press, publisher

The ImTT treatment for violent or hostile thoughts is different from negative self-thoughts. Negative self-thoughts can be treated without having to identify the foundation for those thoughts. The P/T of the negative self-thoughts is directly linked with the P/T of the originating event.

In contrast with negative self-thoughts, Violent Intrusive Thoughts OCD requires a different approach because the hostile thoughts and images are not directly linked with the originating P/T.

People feel angry and want to hurt anyone who has hurt them. This reaction is a natural response. Anger, however, cannot be processed directly because there is no P/T directly associated with anger. Rather, the feeling of anger can cover up other emotions, such as guilt, shame, or the feeling of loss that do have a P/T linked with them. Releasing anger requires that the feeling and image underlying the anger be identified and processed.

For Violent Intrusive Thought OCD behavior, the client's anger toward the current person is not the result of an underlying feeling related to that current person. The anger, in other words, is completely dissociated from its origins. The consequence for treatment is that the underlying emotion with its P/T cannot be identified. Deconstructing the current image of a recent event will not release that originating P/T and memory.

For Violent Intrusive Thought OCD, it is necessary to identify the originating event or person who the person really wants to hurt. Once this is identified, the event is processed with the regular ImTT protocols. A possible useful approach is to have the person deconstruct the images resulting from current behavior. Then ask the person "Who do you really want to hurt?" The regular ImTT treatment continues from that point.

The most important principle to keep in mind, when treating OCD behaviors, is that these behaviors are the result of prior trauma. There really is nothing mysterious about this dynamic once you understand that normal psychological dynamics are involved.

The person just cannot link the behavior with any particular event, which makes it seem as if it could be a biological problem, for example.

Instead, OCD behavior is just the result of a trauma, the feelings of which have been suppressed. Releasing the P/T images frees the person from the behavior.

1. Person experiences abuse and fear.

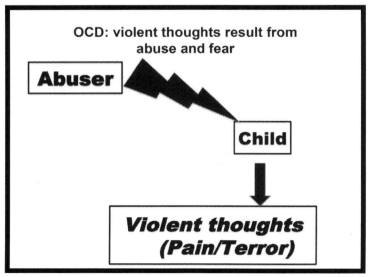

128   ImTT Press, publisher

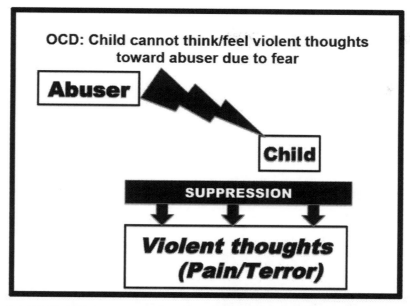

2. Violent thoughts are suppressed due to intense fear.

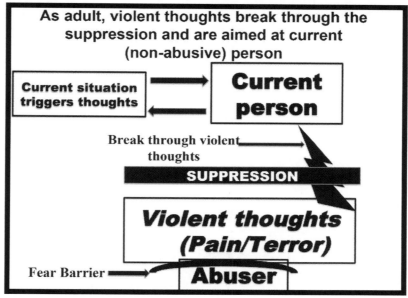

3. Instrusive violent thoughts intrude into the person's daily life when a current situation triggers the underlying feeling.

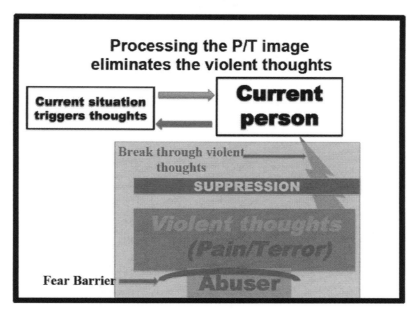

4. Processing the original trauma eliminates the intrusive violent thoughts.

Chapter 9

ADDITIONAL ISSUES FOR
ImTT TREATMENT

Perfectionism

Perfectionism can often be at the root of anxiety and depression. Paranoia and conspiracy theories can also result from the perfectionism dynamic.

Underlying perfectionism are beliefs/feelings such as "I'll never be good enough" or "I'm stupid." These beliefs/feelings can be instilled in childhood as a result of an abusive parent; a controlling parent, a parent with high expectations who withholds love when expectations are not met; or, more subtly, the guilt-inducing parent who makes the child feel the parent's pain when the parent is disappointed. Whatever the cause, the child feels intense P/T when not living up to the parent's expectations. This intense P/T is then internalized so that the child – and later, the adult – demands perfection of himself.

Release Images of Self-Judgment: ImTT treats this dynamic directly at the source. The first step is to identify the negative feeling that the person has about himself when/if he makes a mistake. The person might respond with the statement, "I feel stupid," "I feel like a failure," "I feel no one will ever love me," or "I feel worthless." The feeling is then released with utilizing the P/TRP pattern (page 60).

After the feeling is released, the next step is to identify and to use the IDP to deconstruct the image related to the feeling. If a specific memory surfaces during this process, process the memory. If there is resistance, the resistance should be explored and eliminated by finding and clearing the feelings and image underlying the resistance.

Release Images of Judgment by Other People: Once the initial negative image of self-judgment has been cleared, it is often useful to clear the image linked with the feeling of being judged by other people. The person might have one real person in mind that triggers the feeling of being judged, such as a parent. In this case, focus on the parent.

There may or may not be a specific event that evokes that "being judged" feeling. If there is, clear the image of that event.

Some parents, however, are more subtle, making the identification of a specific event more difficult. In this situation, use the Imaginary Scenario Technique. Have the person imagine a scenario in which he feels intensely judged. If there is more than one person in the scene, ask which person radiates the most feeling of judgment. Then ask "Where do you experience the feeling of being judged in your body?"

Then release the feeling with the P/TRP pattern and then deconstruct the image— real or imagined.

Perfectionism and Paranoia: Paranoia can also result from a perfectionist personality dynamic. Since one of the psychological dynamics of perfectionism is an intense feeling of being judged, the perfectionist may project onto others that, since he is not good enough, they want to get him fired from his job or in some way get rid of him.

    ImTT Press, publisher

For example, a co-worker casually walking by and looking at his office door, for example, may be seen as evidence that the co-worker is trying to find reasons to get him fired from his job. The paranoid's projection that they want to get rid of him can be further developed into a conspiracy theory of a group of people wanting to get rid of him.

Resolving paranoia from perfectionism requires first resolving the perfectionism dynamic and then the image of people trying to get rid of him. In the boxes below are two targets for processing that can often be focused in the beginning of treatment.

Perfectionism Treatment (1)

- **Target: The nightmare image of what will happen if the person makes a mistake**

- **Ask: "What is the nightmare image of what will happen if you make a mistake?"**

- **Ask: "What do you feel about yourself when you make a mistake?"**

- **Release the feeling with the P/TRP pattern.**

- **Deconstruct the image with the IDP.**

Perfectionism Treatment (2)

- **Target: The image of being judged by others**

- **Ask: "What is the image you have of being judged by others?"**

- **Ask: "What would make this image even more intense?"**

- **Ask: "Who do you feel most judged by?"**

- **Ask: "Where do you experience that feeling of being judged in your body?"**

- **Process the feeling and the image with ImTT.**

---

133   ImTT Press, publisher

Jason's Perfectionism Caused Paranoia

Jason's experience with ImTT illustrates treatment for the second dynamic of paranoia–perfectionism.

Jason presented for therapy due to depression. He had been hospitalized several times for depression. Jason also suffered from severe paranoia. Medication moderated the paranoia, but he continued to feel that his co-workers were trying to get him fired.

Jason's depression was the result of his perfectionism. Whenever events did not work out well, he would go into a depression, sometimes so severe that he required hospitalization. Whenever he would make a mistake, Jason's response was to think about how "stupid" he was and about how no one would ever want anything to do with him. Since Jason thought that no one would want to have anything to do with him, in his mind it was logical that they would want to get rid of him. Making any kind of perceived mistake intensified his feeling that "they" wanted to get rid of him. So Jason felt that he had to do everything "just right" to keep his job.

Therapy proceeded by first addressing Jason's perfectionism by releasing his image of being "stupid." The image of "stupid" was the image of being abandoned by his mother. This created a feeling of terror. The feeling of terror was released with the P/TRP, and then the image of his mother abandoning him was released with the IDP.

The next session targeted Jason's paranoid feelings. The image of people conspiring against him was released with the IDP. During the processing of that image, a memory surfaced of his parents intensely arguing.

This argument made him feel that something bad was going to happen. This memory was processed with the P/TRP and IDP.

ImTT Press, publisher

Crisis Management

Crises in the form of suicidal ideation, rage, and overwhelming anxiety are often easily handled with ImTT. A person can be moved from wanting to kill himself or another by releasing the image that underlies their current feeling. Though the crisis arises in the present, it is often the effect of some previously formed image. The current situation can be used to release the previously formed image.

The first type of crisis, suicidal ideation, is usually a result of intense emotional pain. After the patient identifies the pain, the therapist might say, "That sounds really painful. What color is the pain?" If the person has never done ImTT before, telling them that you know that they are in a great deal of pain and that you will help them "get rid of it" will usually get their attention. After getting the person's attention, the clinician can explain the process, and ask the question that leads to the P/TRP.

ImTT is also effective in managing crises in the form of extreme rage. When a person is enraged, the underlying feeling can be either pain or terror. Sometimes it is the pain of betrayal; sometimes it is the pain of losing. The terror could be the terror of abandonment or of being killed (e.g., combat). Whatever the P/T is, naming the cause is important (betrayal, losing, getting killed, et cetera). Thereafter, the clinician should make a blunt statement such as, "It must be really painful to know that you lost." The statement of the fact of the pain or terror needs to be direct and to the point. This bald statement of fact helps the person link with the P/T so that they can release it.

The third type of crisis that the ImTT treats is overwhelming anxiety. The feeling of anxiety may have become an embedded feeling. An embedded feeling of anxiety can be directly released by asking the person where he experiences the feeling in his body and then directly releasing the feeling.

Not Able to Be Alone

After the breakup of a relationship, some people find it difficult to be alone. Going home to an empty house can be very hard. In order to avoid this feeling, they immediately begin seeking another relationship, overwork themselves, drink, or use drugs.

Jill presented for therapy because of her behavior after a recent breakup with her boyfriend of two years. Since the breakup, Jill had begun having casual sexual encounters that she found unfulfilling and that resulted in her feeling bad about herself afterwards. After work, she would go home but then feel an intense urge to go out to bars and find someone to be with.

Jill's problem was that, since her breakup, she could not stand to be alone. Being alone was intensely painful for her. The unfelt, unacknowledged pain of loneliness drove her to have sexual encounters that she did not really want. The image Jill had of being alone was standing in the middle of the desert with no one to hear her voice. Once this image was processed by releasing the feeling with the P/TRP and deconstructing the image, Jill no longer had a problem with staying home in the evenings by herself.

> Not able to be alone treatment
> 1. Release the P/T of being alone
> 2. Deconstruct the image

Psychological Territories (Boundaries)

Boundary Violations

There are 3 types of boundary violations:

1. **Yes/No: Not allowed to say no.**

2. **Psychological intrusion: Blocking or contradicting a person's thoughts or feelings.**

3. **Physical instrusion: Physical contact without permission.**

The Yes/No Boundary Problem

The Yes/No Boundary problem originates in childhood when a child is punished for establishing boundaries. When a child is not allowed to say "no" and is denied permission to set a boundary, the consequence is that the grown-up child will continue having difficulty saying "no." Whenever asked to do something, s/he will agree even when it is not in his/her best interests. The result is either not being able to accomplish the agreed-to task or the constant sacrifice of what is important to him/her to accomplish what is important to others. A person who wants to accomplish certain goals in life must have the energy to accomplish those goals. The ability to say "no" reserves that energy for the person's own personal goals.

ImTT resolves this dilemma by targeting the image of what the person imagines will happen if she says "No." This image may be something that exists only in the person's imagination or may be related to a memory. Whatever the situation, the P/TRP is performed on the image and then the image is deconstructed with the IDP.

ImTT Press, publisher

Psychological Intrusion

The establishment of psychological territory is an inherent drive in every human being.

From the "terrible two's" on, a person begins developing a psychological territory that he controls. Saying "No" is just the beginning of such development. The ability to feel and express what one wants and dislikes is important to the cultivation of this territory.

Psychological intrusions occur when a person is not allowed to express what she thinks or feels. A child who is not allowed to express his anger or sadness is experiencing psychological intrusion.

Another type of intrusion occurs when the person's thoughts or feelings are contradicted.

Example of Psychological Intrusion

Child:
"I don't like Auntie."

Adult:
"Yes, you do; you love Auntie."

The following are examples of other types of intrusions: a mother who has to know everything that her child is feeling, a mother who is overly involved in her child's life or a father who is very controlling. All of these behaviors violate a person's psychological territory. These types of violations prevent the person from establishing the psychological territory necessary for developing an understanding of who she is and what she wants.

Psychological intrusions are subtler than the yes/no boundary problem. Asking a person what his image is of what will happen if he says "No" is a very direct pathway to the dysfunctional image. In contrast with the yes/no violation, there are many different types of psychological intrusions. The central dilemma created by psychological intrusions is that they prevent the person from even understanding that an intrusion has occurred. The person has become accustomed to being treated in that way and is often not aware of his lack of knowing what he likes and dislikes—and knowing what he wants to do and what he doesn't want to do. This psychological dynamic persists into adulthood because of the images created as a result of the childhood psychological intrusion.

For example, a child whose parent contradicted his feelings may have developed an image of not knowing what he wants. His behavior, acting from that image, might be that he seeks out the opinion of another person because he cannot decide on his own. A child who was not allowed to be angry may have an image that disallows him from being angry. In adulthood, the anger might be somatized into headaches or other physical problems. Various forms of behavioral and substance addictions may be an exhibiting of the ramifications of psychological intrusions.

The most difficult challenge in resolving psychological intrusion dynamics is identifying the interpersonal dynamic that created it. The interpersonal dynamic of intrusion has usually been occurring for many years while the child has been growing up. So the grown-up child thinks that the intrusion behavior is normal and has developed no understanding of the negative consequences of this "normal" behavior. The challenge for the therapist is to help the person identify the intrusive behavior.

Once the person becomes aware of this behavior, then the processing is straightforward. For example, Jack's father was very controlling so that Jack had difficulty making decisions. He would usually seek out the opinions of other people for his life's decisions. Jack would usually choose the opinion of the person who was most sure of himself. Jack's image was of his father telling him that he (Jack) didn't know what he was doing. That image would stop Jack from attempting to make any decision.

The invasion of psychological territory can create at least four possible dynamics, all of which can operate within the same person at different times in different situations:

1. The person becomes a "doormat" for other people because they have lost the capacity to defend their territory. This dynamic can manifest as promiscuity after a sexual assault or the inability to say no to other people's requests.

2. Inside, the person shuts down emotionally. This dynamic can produce behavior such as depressive symptoms and addiction.

3. The person develops an intense rage, which presents as a general rage toward the world.

4. The rage may further develop into a paranoid state, directed either at an individual or a more global view of perceiving conspiracies. There is a feeling that people are "out to get them." The lack of defensible territory leaves them feeling vulnerable and easily attacked. Looking through the lens of fear, the abused person will easily see external events as threatening.

Behaviors Resulting from Psychological Intrusions

1. **Doormat Behavior: Doing what other people want even when the person doesn't want to.**

2. **Emotionally shutting down.**

3. **Intense rage from not being able to protect one's own personal space.**

4. **Paranoia: terrified that someone will "invade."**

5. **All four previous behaviors, depending on circumstances.**

Physical Boundary Violations

Abuse violates a person's feeling of safety within their own territory and the trust that other people will not invade their territory. Normally, other people are allowed within one's territory only with permission. If a person is standing too close to someone, they will step back because the discomfort is "painful." No lasting damage occurs because the event is not intense enough to create a P/T event. An abuser, on the other hand, violates these boundaries and enters the territory without permission, which may create images that block the person from protecting himself in the future.

Physical and sexual abuses create additional boundary problems resulting from images derived from the abuse. When a person is physically abused, the person feels that he cannot protect his own body.

The violation of physical as well as psychological territory creates an image of helplessness: "I can't control my space" (territory). If we think of the boundary as a fence, the abuse breaks the fence.

The image of helplessness energized by the P/T prevents the mind from repairing the fence. This image of helplessness (i.e., the broken fence) overrides the mind's natural inclination to repair the "fence" and establish appropriate boundaries. Even when the person becomes aware of the broken fence, the image will stop them from developing boundaries. Releasing the image will de-energize the pattern and allow the person to establish his own psychological territory.

The target for processing is therefore both the image or memory of the event and also the image of how he sees the world in regards to himself. For example, a person who was physically abused as a child may have the image that he cannot protect himself in a world full of people who will hurt him. Eliminating the negative image allows the person to create his natural boundary protections.

Physical boundary violations including physical and sexual abuse have additional dynamics:

1. The abuse creates an image of not being able to control the person's own personal space.

2. Terror is created when the person is unable to protect his/her own personal space. There is no feeling of safety or security when the person does not know what will happen within his/her space.

3. Treatment: Process the image of the person not being able to control his/her own personal space.

Against the Self: Self-Hatred and Self-Punishment

A person hating himself or deliberately hurting himself seems to contradict the Survival Model of Psychological Dynamics. In the Survival Model's understanding of behavior, no one can directly act to hurt himself because hurting oneself is contrary to the primal motivation to survive. Yet people cut and hurt themselves in a variety of ways. So if people are hurting themselves, the primary motivation to survive by avoiding pain and danger and seeking pleasure appears to be either not operating or overridden in some way.

The answer to this apparent contradiction is that the person who hurts himself has a positive feeling linked with the painful behavior. For example, a person who cuts may have the pain of cutting linked with a positive feeling such as an adrenaline rush or a feeling of belonging with others who cut. This positive feeling linked with self-harming behavior is the reason that these behaviors have been so difficult to change—as the positive feeling linked with the behavior has not been recognized as the cause of the behavior. For a more complete explanation of this phenomenon, see Feeling-State Theory (Miller, 2010, 2012).

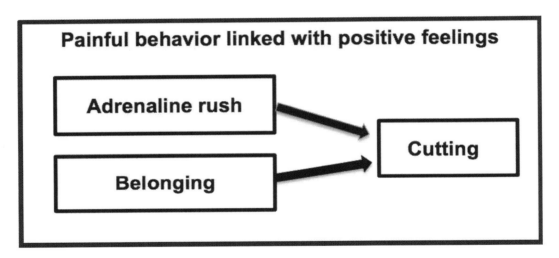

1. *Deliberate painful behavior is linked with a positive feeling.*

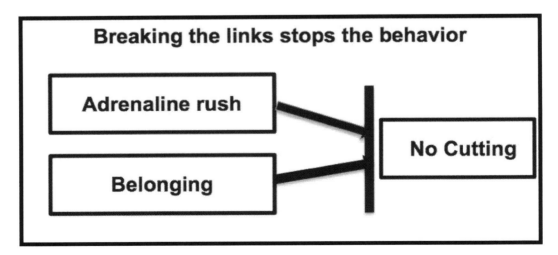

2. *Breaking the links between the positive feelings and the behavior stops the behavior.*

                                                 ImTT Press, publisher

Self-Punishment

Clinical experience suggests that feelings of guilt or shame can lead to self-punishment behavior which seems to contradict the Survival Model's stated motivation for behavior. However, ImTT views self-punishment as similar to cutting in that there is a positive feeling linked with the self-punishing behavior. For example, after a person has done something "bad," self-punishment is a way of saying, "I know I've done something bad. But because I'm punishing myself, I'm not really that bad." Self-punishment allows the person to feel the positive feelings of being moral, righteous, or linked with the people he feels are judging him. In other words, it is the positive feelings that drive the self-punishing behavior. The Feeling-State Image Protocol can be used to break the link between the positive feeling and the self-punishing behavior.

Even though there must be a positive feeling linked with the self-punishing behavior, that does not mean that the feeling is fixated. The feeling may be more associated with the behavior than intensely linked. In this situation, Feeling-State processing may not be necessary. The best approach to treating self-punishment is to eliminate the negative self-image that makes the person feel bad about him/herself. In generating the image, ImTT relies on the Imaginary Scenario Technique.

Specifically, the clinician should ask the person to make up a fantasy nightmare image of himself which represents how awful he is. He might see himself as some kind of monster or devil. Whatever the image is, it should not contain any positive elements. The point is to create an image of his darkest, worst side. After creating the image, treatment proceeds with the Image De-Construction Protocol.

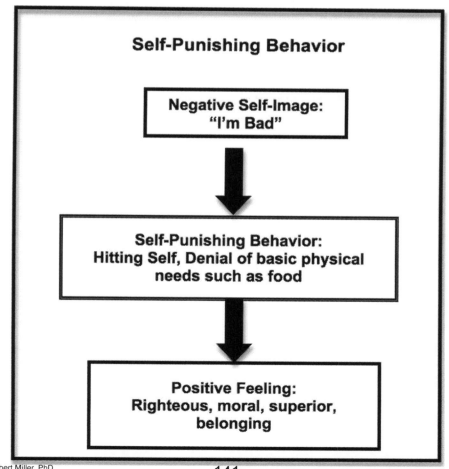

Upon eliminating the negative image, the person will no longer feel the need to be moral or righteous in order to overcome the negative self-image and will no longer feel the need to punish himself. One of the additional benefits from this kind of formative change is an alteration of the person's relationships. People with intense negative self-images have difficulty connecting and maintaining relationships because they either withdraw from relationships or overcompensate for their "monstrousness." Consequently, removing the negative self-image also removes barriers to interpersonal connections.

Self-Hatred

Self-hatred is another form of self-punishment. The self-punishment is the forming of the image of hating oneself. As in all self-punishment, there is a positive feeling linked with the image. The challenge is to identify that positive feeling. Instead of approaching this challenge directly, the positive feeling may be identified by asking the person what is the positive feeling he has when he hates someone else.

That positive feeling may be the positive feeling that is linked with his hatred of himself.

ImTT treatment for self-hatred is the same as for self-punishment: deconstruct the image of hating the self.

> ## Self-Hatred Treatment: Deconstruct the Image

Self-Love

This discussion brings us to the idea of "loving oneself." The need for "self-love" only exists as an antidote for self-hatred. Once the self-hatred goes away, there is no need for what is thought of as "self-love." The drive toward life, toward feeling alive, provides all the motivation necessary for a person to take care of himself and to act in ways that will ensure adequate self-care.

This understanding of "self-love" is consistent with the concept that no positive cognition should be installed to replace a negative cognition. Positive thoughts and cognitions will naturally surface as the contrary negative cognitions are eliminated.

ImTT Press, publisher

Attachment Issues

Difficulties with attachment are often the result of images from childhood. For example, children have an intense desire for a relationship with their parents. A person whose dysfunctional family relationships prevent appropriate attachment patterns from forming may have difficulty connecting or attaching in his/her adult relationships because of the images created in childhood.

The ImTT treatment for attachment difficulties is to process the images that are blocking the person's desire for a relationship. Because people have an intense desire for having relationships, once the image-block is removed, the person will begin seeking out and forming connections with others. Unless the person has grown up with the "wire monkey" mother, the capacity for relationships is intact. The difficulty is that their dysfunctional images prevent them from developing the appropriate psychological patterns.

The effect of the attachment difficulties can be seen in long-term relationships. At the beginning of the relationship, the desire for a relationship overrides any attachment problems. However, as time moves on and the relationship settles down to a calmer tone, the image-generated feelings have more effect.

Once the dysfunctional relationship images are activated, the person may use avoidance tactics such as overeating, smoking, drinking, or breaking off the relationship to avoid the feelings generated by the image.

In ImTT, the approach to attachment difficulties is to identify the current image that is causing the problem. Understanding how the image was formed is not necessary. Exploring childhood dynamics might sometimes be fruitful in developing the image, but the focus should be on identifying the current image, not on the history of what caused the image to be created.

An image can often be identified using the Imaginary Scenario Technique. The clinician should ask the person to make up an image of what a relationship looks like or an image of what will happen if he allows himself to connect with another person. For example, does it feel safe or dangerous? Does she feel that the person will betray or leave her? This image should contain as many of the negative elements that have emotional resonance as possible—the nightmare-scenario relationship. Then the clinician should perform ImTT utilizing this image.

Once the images that have blocked the formation of healthy attachments are deconstructed, the person will automatically begin to develop the psychological patterns and behaviors for a healthy relationship.

ImTT Press, publisher

Attachment Dynamics

1. People have a strong desire for attachment that is based on survival needs.

2. When a person is resistant to changing relationship behaviors, there is a P/T image.

3. P/T images block the development of the skills needed for relationships.

4. Eliminating the P/T images blocking attachment will result in the person automatically seeking relationships and developing relationship skills.

Chronic Physical Pain

A person with a long-standing physical injury or other physical problems causing pain can often obtain temporary pain relief using a modified version of the P/TRP. Chronic pain is a sensation that appears to build up in the body over time. The P/TRP can reduce the sensation of pain. The reduction in pain makes it easier for a person to utilize less pain medication.

There are two major modifications of the P/TRP for managing chronic physical pain. The first modification is to focus on the origin of the physical pain. For example, if the pain is located in the shoulder, the shoulder is focused on almost exclusively until the pain diminishes. After the reduction in the area where the pain is located, the "pain-particles" in the other areas of the body are then released.

The other modification of the P/TRP is the sequence of the areas the colored pain-particles are released from. For example, if a person has pain in his shoulder, first the color of the pain is identified.

However, instead of beginning the release of the color from the shoulder, the color is first released from the hand and wrist. The focus of release then moves up to the elbow flowing down to the hand and out the palms. Then the color of the pain in the shoulder is visualized as flowing down the arm and out the palm.

The reason for the change in the sequence is that the colored pain-particles seem to be both harder to move and become "stuck." This description is how people have described problems in visualizing this release. By following this release sequence from the distal part of the limb to the area of the pain, people report that the colored pain-particles are more easily released. It is as if the channels downstream from the area where the pain is located have to be cleared first of any "blockages." Clearing the path makes releasing the colored pain-particles easier.

The full ImTT Chronic Pain Protocol is in the Appendix.

The Chronic Pain Protocol has also been successfully used after surgery, reducing the need for pain medication.

In addition to the Chronic Pain Protocol, the Shock Protocol may also be useful, especially when the pain has been caused by surgery or an accident. Shock appears to intensify the feelings of pain.

ImTT Press, publisher

Chronic Physical Pain

Chronic physical pain builds up over time.

Chronic Physical Pain

The P/TRP can release the built-up pain. When a person experiences pain for a long time, the sensatsion of pain builds up in the body.

Releasing the built-up pain will reduce the sensation of pain.

Chapter 10

ImTT FOR CHILDREN

By Dana Tennison, MA, LMFT

ImTT for Children follows the same principles and basic format as the adult theory, but modified to compensate for age-related challenges.

While certain variables are present with clients of any age, such as motivation or level of insight, ImTT for Children was developed to accommodate the following dynamics unique to children:

- Children have shorter attention spans than adults.
- Children have limited awareness of their bodies and body sensations.
- Children have limited knowledge, language and awareness of their own emotions.
- Children have limited awareness of self-talk or negative cognitions.
- Children think and process in more concrete terms vs. abstract.

This chapter will explain ImTT for Children by walking through the ImTT protocols, P/TRP, IDP, and CPP. Case examples will illustrate how each protocol has been modified for young clients. In addition, the following child-friendly supplies have been added as part of the modification process. Use of these supplies will be discussed in greater detail throughout this chapter and in each case study.

- White board and dry-erase markers
- Pom-poms
- Drawing supplies, such as paper and markers
- A stuffed animal "helper" and a container (this therapist uses a stuffed owl and his "owl pot")

ImTT Press, publisher

Illustrating ImTT for Children with a Case Study

While most adults can identify their P/T and target image through verbal processing, children do best with a more concrete identification process. Some children struggle simply to know what they are feeling, much less why they have such feelings. Especially with younger children (ages 4-8 years), it is important to use their language for how they feel; many children understand "icky" feelings more than they understand "emotionally painful." Additionally, children often describe multiple fears and worries, making it difficult to know where to begin. In these situations, it is important to ask the child, "Which is the biggest worry?" and target that first. A benefit of ImTT is that other fears will subside, even though they haven't been addressed, because the child's overall fear level will drop with this intervention.

The following case study illustrates the use and effectiveness of ImTT for Children.

Identifying the Pain/Terror and the Image

A natural way for children to express themselves is through drawing, and this is a necessary tool to use when identifying the P/T and target image. Significant information can be collected when children are willing to draw their feelings, a situation that bothers them, or how their bodies actually feel when the "icky" feelings are around. In one case, an 8-year-old girl named Holly reported she was afraid of going to the dentist.

Holly's parents described numerous failed attempts to have her teeth cleaned; in fact, they had tried (without success) four times over many months, with two different dentists. While Holly said going to the dentist was "scary," it was critical to identify the worse part of the dentist, the part she feared the most. After making a list of all the scary things about the dentist, she said the worst was her fear of getting a shot, even though she knew she would not have to get one for her upcoming visit. Holly drew her worst fear, the shot.

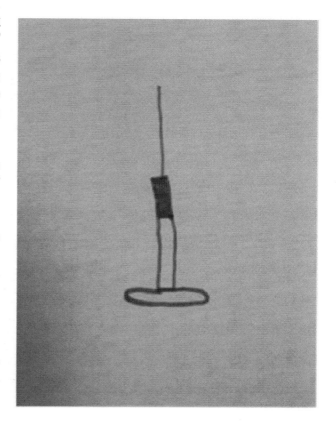

Processing the Pain/Terror with the P/TRP

After identifying the P/T and target image, it is helpful if children can understand the concept of the P/T residing in their bodies. To make this concrete, it is best to use an external representation of the child's body, such as drawing a gingerbread man outline on a white board. To make the location of the emotions more concrete, children can use dry-erase markers or pom-poms to place their emotions in the gingerbread body outline. In Holly's case, she selected pom-pom colors that represented her scared feelings (red = scared; blue = crying) and placed them in her body outline drawn on the board.

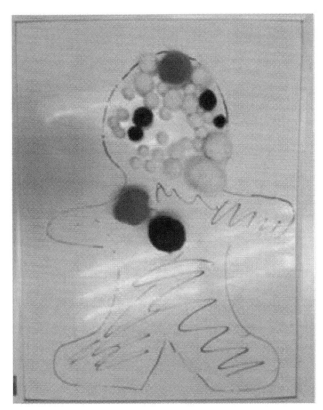

Using one's breath to release the P/T remains the most abstract part of the P/TRP. However, most children grasp the concept with minimal coaching. I explain that breathing out icky feelings is like washing their hands or brushing their teeth. Children easily understand that it is just as important to clean their insides as it is to clean their outsides.

It is best to do a practice release first, guiding children to clear one hand, using their breath. Most children eagerly follow the clinician's lead in breathing in, sending their breath down the arm, through the hand and out the fingertips. During a release itself, younger children tend to use full body breaths instead of clearing different parts of the body one at a time. Most children clear their bodies more quickly than adults, usually in 2-5 breaths. It can be helpful to ask them, "Where do you want the feelings to leave your body?" This extra guidance provides helpful imagery for them to notice and feel the colors being released, such as through their fingertips, toes, or ears.

Providing a container (such as the "owl pot") for this step is another way to make the release process as concrete as possible. Once their bodies feel clear, encourage children to transfer whatever pom-poms they have released (from the white board body outline) into the container. If they have used dry-erase markers alone, most children will erase the markings and place the "pretend" erased matter into the container. The same container can be used for the IDP, as described below.

Processing the Image with the IDP

As with adults, once the P/T has been completely released, children are guided to deconstruct the image. Again, because this is so abstract, a more concrete approach is to have them tear up the image they drew. A sense of agency often emerges at this point as children eagerly rip up their image, delighting in tearing it up into tiny pieces. As explained in the P/TRP section above, the container (at this point filled with released pom-poms) is a concrete way to collect the pieces of the image.

This therapist uses a stuffed owl and pot (ceramic container with lid) as a concrete way to collect the released emotions and deconstructed image pieces.

                                                           ImTT Press, publisher

Children are told that the owl is magical as is his pot. The owl's job is to help anyone who wants to get rid of unwanted feelings; you can put them in his pot and he will take the contents away. This therapist explains that owls do their work at night, which means the owl flies to wherever he is told and empties the pot. Children get to tell the owl exactly where they want him to bring their unwanted feelings. Common destinations include outer space, the center of the earth, and heaven. One clever 9-year-old told the owl, "Bring ¼ of the pieces to Africa, ¼ to Australia, ¼ to the Atlantic Ocean and ¼ to China. That way they will never meet up again." To clear the body of any particles left over from deconstructing the image, this therapist uses the Magic Water Technique as explained in the protocol section of this book.

Using The Changing Patterns Protocol

Depending on the child's age, attention span and energy level, the CPP may take a few seconds or a few minutes. Most children are fatigued by this point and have little energy left to complete the CPP. If time and energy permit, ask children brief questions to help them picture themselves in the domains of family, school and friends. Sample questions include, "Can you remember your teacher from last year?" "Can you remember summer camp last year?" "Can you picture yourself going home tonight?" "What are you going to do this weekend?"

In Holly's fear of going to the dentist, she did a second release on the same fear of getting a shot. Afterward, she declared she was no longer scared about going to the dentist and turned down subsequent opportunities to release any other fear associated with the upcoming dental appointment. A few weeks later, Holly happily shared with this therapist that she tolerated the entire dentist appointment with no fears or hesitation. However, she was told she had two cavities that needed to be filled; that appointment was set for two months out.

During the intervening months, Holly declined multiple invitations by this therapist to release any fear associated with the upcoming cavity appointment. She repeatedly responded that she did not have any fear about going the dentist to release. True to her word, Holly successfully tolerated getting two cavities filled. She said she "cried a little" and was able to be brave and scared at the same time. Her parents corroborated Holly's report, describing the appointment as "starting out rough," but stabilizing and ending with an unexpected decision by Holly. The dentist had planned to work on the cavities in two appointments. To everyone's surprise, Holly decided she wanted the dentist to work on both cavities in the one visit. She explained, "I figured he should just do them both because it wasn't that bad, and then I wouldn't have to go back another day." Four months later, her parents told this therapist that Holly had gone back to the dentist for a routine cleaning without issue.

THE ImTT TRANSFORMATION EFFECT IN CHILDREN

Similar to the transformation effect described in Chapter 3, after using ImTT, children also develop a new lens through which they view their whole world. Holly's parents had originally brought her in for therapy because of impairing anxiety during their morning routine. Holly's anxiety symptoms had included crying, difficulty concentrating and making decisions, and school avoidance. During school drop-offs, she often cried and refused to get out of the car so that an adult had to walk a tearful Holly to her classroom. After using ImTT twice about going to the dentist, Holly's parents reported that school drop-offs were going "much better" and that Holly was able to walk herself into the school building without crying. This is often the case for both adults and children: using ImTT to address P/T around one part of life often has the same effect on other parts of life, even if they were never directly targeted during ImTT.

Another example of the transformation effect of ImTT with children is Sophie, an 11-year-old who came to therapy with features of OCD. She would repeatedly rub her hands in a specific way that resulted in red, cracked, chapped skin. In the first session, Sophie showed her hands to this therapist and we all commented on how painful they looked. After two sessions using ImTT, Sophie's parents reported that their daughter's hand-rubbing behavior had significantly decreased. They also noted how healthy her skin looked. Thus, at the next session, this therapist asked Sophie how the rubbing behavior was. She replied, "About the same," contrary to her parents' observations. (It is quite common for clients, including children, to be unaware of changes in their behavior at first, even when the people who live with them notice the changes). This therapist then asked Sophie, "Well, how are your hands?" To which she answered, "I don't know." At this therapist's suggestion, Sophie looked down at her hands. Shocked at how healed they looked, she exclaimed, "Wow, look at that!"

Sophie's reaction reinforces the observation that clients can experience changes in behavior without being conscious of the changes.

Peeling the Onion Layers

As in Jane's case, described in Chapter 3, children also benefit from ImTT's ability to peel back layers of P/T, revealing more P/T and associated images underneath.

One such case involved a 6-year-old girl, Sarah, who came to therapy because she had anxiety around her bowel movements (BMs). Anemic as an infant, Sarah had been prescribed iron supplements from age six months to two years. This caused chronic constipation, difficult BMs, and one event of excessive bleeding due to anal fissures. Twice she was given enemas, once as a toddler in the emergency room and a second time at her doctor's office around age 5.

Sarah developed a persistent fear of BMs. She had a history of withholding BMs and avoiding related behavior such as wiping herself or even talking about BMs. She eventually explained that she was afraid her BMs would be "too big or too fast." In addition, Sarah would often lose control of her bowels, but she refused to use public restrooms. This behavior made it difficult for the family to leave home because they never knew when Sarah would need to use the bathroom.

During the first session, Sarah seemed motivated and eager to work on this issue. She was articulate, compliant, and engaged in the release process. Sarah stated that, "I have scary feelings that tell me not to poop." Sarah came for three sessions, releasing her fear of BMs each time. After the first two sessions, her parents reported little change in Sarah's BM avoidance. However, they said she was able to discuss BMs more freely than before and was more productive when she did attempt a BM. Two days after her third session, Sarah's parents reported that she spontaneously used the bathroom at her grandparents' house for a BM. Sarah grabbed her mom's hand, brought her to the bathroom, sat on the toilet and exclaimed, "Look what I can do!" and proceeded to have a BM with ease and confidence.

Approximately two months later, Sarah came in for a follow-up session due to a regression in her BM behavior. Two acute stressors had occurred; her father had been unexpectedly hospitalized and a new school year had just started. Sarah's anxiety became heightened and her old behaviors took over. She willingly participated in the session, released more fear, and resumed fairly normal BMs the next morning. Another session was scheduled for the following week to maintain progress and help Sarah manage this time of transition. At that session Sarah seemed uncharacteristically silly, non-compliant and slightly antagonistic toward her mother.

She softly kicked her mother, seemed antsy, and often needed re-direction. She agreed to release more fear, but did not seem wholly engaged in the process.

Near the end of the session and seemingly out of the blue, Sarah told the therapist about a visit to the doctor's office (for an enema) she had experienced seven months before starting therapy. After she described the procedure and how scary it was, she looked at her mom and asked, "How could you let them do that to me?" What followed was a touching example of a parent remaining engaged, present, and loving while her child asked some tough, emotional questions. Mom and therapist helped Sarah understand that her angry feelings were okay and couldn't scare mom away; that mom's love for Sarah was bigger than Sarah's angry feelings. This provided a natural transition into working on the P/T surrounding Sarah's scary doctor visit. Her previous work to release fear enabled Sarah to feel safe enough to start talking about the enema procedure.

CLIENTS WITH SPECIAL NEEDS

While most of the case studies in this book are about neuro-typical people, it is important to note that ImTT is not limited to this population. Clinicians have found the child version of ImTT effective with adults who are developmentally delayed or with any clients who seem emotionally immature. Clients with autism may find the ImTT approach particularly helpful because of the therapy's visual approach to working with emotions and thoughts.

A variation of ImTT for Children was used with a 21-year-old female client, Paula, diagnosed with Generalized Anxiety Disorder and autism spectrum disorder. She lived with her parents and was about to start a new job. Prior to the first session, Paula's mother described her as high-functioning and also high-needs.

In many ways Paula was a typical 21-year-old (wanting to fit in with peers and have a boyfriend), yet was about 10 years old in her emotional maturity and body awareness. Paula's mother also cautioned the therapist that Paula was extremely sensitive to being treated like a child. For these reasons, this therapist decided to use a modified version of ImTT for Children.

At the first session, it was clear that Paula was extremely verbal, easy to talk with, and highly motivated to work on her anxiety as well as perseverating behavior. She reflected on the pain of never feeling like she belonged to a peer group as well as her fear of being bullied. Paula said these feelings and beliefs started in first grade and persist today. She described the pain as "a big sore or hole in my heart," directly connected to the negative belief, "No one wants me because I'm not perfect." She also connected this pain with hypervigilance and the walls she put up to protect herself from being bullied. Paula was motivated to try ImTT, noting her anxiety was particularly intense due to starting her new job. She was afraid her anxiety would fuel more perseverating behavior and ultimately interfere with or jeopardize her new position.

With ImTT, Paula used her own starting images or stock photos provided by the therapist. The white board was used to help her identify and locate the P/T in her body and assign it a color using dry-erase markers. The owl and owl pot provided a concrete way to end the processing and emphasize what she released. Often at the end of a release, Paula would open her eyes and comment about how the world looked different. After one session, observing the familiar office surroundings she said, "I feel like I am looking at the world through different eyes."

After the second session, her mom reported Paula's mood was much better and she seemed more relaxed. About three weeks into her new job, Paula reported that her perseverating behavior was "not an issue at all." She noticed subtle urges but said, "I don't act on them." When asked about her anxiety level, Paula described it as "peachy." She reported the ImTT sessions had helped her feel more confident overall and able to believe, "I am perfectly whole as I am."

Successive ImTT sessions continued to focus on Paula's layers of pain and terror around her social life. Her target images were about feeling judged because of her disability. Eventually Paula was able to articulate that she was scared to get rid of her protective wall of fear. She had a growing insight that anxiety caused impairment, yet it also felt protective. In session she wondered, "Who is the real Paula? My whole life I've been Paula plus fear." Just like neuro-typical clients, the more pain Paula released, the more clarity she gained about herself and existing limiting beliefs.

Whether the client is an adult or a child or has special needs, ImTT can help to peel back the layers of emotion and explore deeper issues that contribute to maladaptive behavior. Taking care to modify ImTT for children or anyone with special needs allows clinicians broad use of this intervention. ImTT for Children is a gentle, adaptable, age-appropriate intervention with substantial benefits.

ImTT Press, publisher

Chapter 11

TRANSCRIPTS OF THERAPY SESSIONS

The transcripts in this chapter illustrate how ImTT can be used to resolve a variety of psychological dynamics. Difficulties with pain, guilt, shame, trauma, OCD, and other issues are addressed in these sessions. The only editing that has been done is to make the sessions more understandable and to delete the parts of the transcripts where the client is being guided to release the particles of the P/T or the image from the body to avoid unnecessary repetition. This is indicated in the transcript

Ann: Shawn's Death—Pain/Terror Release Protocol

Ann's brother Shawn died in a flood when he was 7 years old. Ann was 18 years old at the time. Currently she is 25 years old. The memory of Shawn's death has continued to be extremely painful. In the first session, Ann is taught to do the P/TRP and processes the obvious pain of his death.

Dr. Miller: What I want to do is teach you to do the P/TRP, the Pain/Terror Release Protocol, on something simple to work on. That's your brother. That may seem kind of odd.

Ann: I would love that. [Laughs]

Dr. Miller: When you think of your brother, how old was he when he died?

Ann: Seven.

Dr. Miller: Let me give you, first, some instructions.

I do not want you getting into the pain. Do not do that. I'm going to be asking you very clearly, what color is the pain and where it is in your body?
This time, we're not going to have to work hard to get to the pain. That's going to be simple. Other times, we're actually going to have to work harder to get to the pain because sometimes it's not so obvious. Like under anxiety, there's pain under there or terror, whatever it is.

What I want you to do, though, is, once we identify the color and where it is in your body, don't think about Shawn. Do not think about the pain. I don't want you to feel it. I want you to just pay attention to the color itself. What we are going to do is do something on the color itself. That's all we are going to do. Then at the end of what we are doing, we are going to re-check our work and see what's left.

When you think of the death of your brother—what's his name?

Ann: Shawn.

Dr. Miller: Shawn.

What color is the pain?

Ann: Like a deep, deep, deep blue, like midnight blue.

Dr. Miller: Like what?

Ann: Like a midnight blue, almost black but not navy.

Dr. Miller: Where is it located in your body?

Ann: Right here.

                                       ImTT Press, publisher

Dr. Miller: What I am going to ask you to do is to take a breath and visualize the breath going in to where the blue is. Then I want you to see the midnight blue going directly out of your body as you breathe out—not out with your breath, but see the blue releasing directly away from your body. That's all we are going to focus on now is the midnight blue. Can you concentrate better with your eyes closed? Or just two thirds of the way down?

Ann: Yeah.

Dr. Miller: Then visualize your breath going into where the midnight blue is, and see it going directly out of your chest, that part of your chest. [Silence]

Very good. Again. [Silence]

How does the blue look to you now?

Ann: I don't really see a color, but it just feels so light, like airy.

Dr. Miller: I want this to go to the rest of your body, though. Visualize the breath going into the middle of your brain and see whatever blue or color you can, going right out the forehead, middle of your forehead.

Ann: It's any color? Or we are still focusing on the...

Dr. Miller: Midnight blue.

Ann: Okay. [Silence]

Dr. Miller: Do that three times. [Silence]

Now breathe into the middle of your brain, and breathe out the color out your eyes. [Silence]

Now, breathe into your chest and breathe the color down your arms and out the palms of your hands. [Silence]

Ann continues to release the color particles using the P/TRP

Dr. Miller: Now, scan your body and see if there is any of that midnight blue left in your body. Did it change colors? What color is it now?

Ann: It's clear. It's like clear water.

Dr. Miller: It's clear water?

Ann: Yes.

Dr. Miller: Does it feel like it's painful or just nothing there?

Ann: Nothing. Air.

Dr. Miller: So now, let's check what's happened. I want you to think of Shawn right now and tell me how charged that is for you.

Ann: It's not that charged. Even the name "Shawn" didn't...

Dr. Miller: What was it like before when we began?

Ann: I was planning on sitting down and saying his name and bawling my eyes out.

Dr. Miller: That's your usual?

Ann: Well, when I know...

Dr. Miller: When it happens, that's what happens.

Ann: Yes.

Dr. Miller: So now with Shawn now, this is not a problem.

Ann: No, that was okay.

Dr. Miller: How does that feel now?

Ann: Almost it's giving me a little bit of anxiety just because I feel like I am letting him go a little more.

Dr. Miller: Okay. You still have the good memories of him.

Ann: That's so true.

Dr. Miller: You need to be connected with him through the good memories, not the pain.

Ann: Sure. Yes, I agree.

Dr. Miller: So now when you think of Shawn, how does it feel?

Ann: Like I am just thinking about my little brother.
That's weird. It's not like a heavy "little brother." I guess that's how I would put that.

Dr. Miller: This is our stopping point now.

Ann: Shawn's Death — Second Session, Guilt & Shame

While the pain of her brother's death has been released, Ann has other issues related to her brother Shawn's death. This session focuses on releasing the pain or terror that energizes the negative feelings underlying Ann's guilt and shame.

Dr. Miller: Let's re-evaluate what we did last week about your brother. When you think of your brother, how does that feel now?

Ann: It's not painful. Over the last week, I chatted about it with my father or, excuse me, my step-dad. I guess I've been getting sick to my stomach when I think about it. But it's not like the hard pain, like "Okay, let's not go there. Let's not even indulge." I sat and talked about it. It was nothing, but just getting a little queasy.

Dr. Miller: You're getting a little queasy. What's the feeling there?

Ann: I guess. I didn't explore anything besides feeling sick to my stomach. Then my Dad's like, "All right. We don't have to talk about it anymore." Then after I noticed it then, I noticed it throughout the week a little bit.

Dr. Miller: We're not finished with that event.

Ann: You think? All right.

Dr. Miller: If you're still feeling somewhat queasy, it's a lot easier to talk about it. It's not so obviously painful, but something is still there. Why don't you let yourself fully picture him? What comes up for you? What does he look like? What is he doing?

Ann: When you tell me to picture him, I picture a photo of him that I have. It's just his face and his big ol' blue eyes, and his bright blond hair and his little dorky smile.

Dr. Miller: When you were talking to your father about him, I know you didn't feel anything directly there. But when you're thinking about it now, what is your reaction?

Ann: Right now, I don't have anything.

Dr. Miller: Oh, there's no queasiness? There's nothing?

Ann: No, it's not bad. But now that we're starting to talk about it, I think my body might get a little queasy just because it will respond to what my brain is thinking a little bit, if I'm thinking about getting queasy.

Dr. Miller: Just thinking about being queasy? [Chuckles]

Ann: It might start a little bit of queasy, I guess. [Chuckles] But no, I feel okay now that I'm talking about it.

Dr. Miller: Tell me a little bit about him.

Ann: He was just a very special little boy—super happy, always joyous. He was like my little son. Whenever I was there, he always had to be right next to me, up on my arm and in my lap. I had to carry him everywhere. We just were super tight.

I didn't get to see him as much as I would have liked, but I suppose that comes with the father issue. He was just happy. He always wanted to be doing stuff. He was a mischievous little boy. He'd hide my stuff when I came so I couldn't leave. He would hide it around the house.

I don't know...he was driving tractors since he was like four. He was in front all the time, and he just ran the family, I guess. He was a boy, I guess. I don't know...the "golden child" would be a good term, I suppose. We all just loved him.

In the accident, we all didn't think it was true because he was the only one that died. We couldn't find his body; so the whole family, was just, I guess, awkwardly joking that we just expected him to come running through the woods—"Hey, guys. I'm hungry. Where's my dinner?" —making a big, ol' joke or something. But that didn't happen. I don't know... he was just a "bright child" would be how I would describe him.

Dr. Miller: Now that you've talked about him, how does it feel?

Ann: Honestly, I feel a little empty. It's not pain, or I don't feel queasy. I just feel...or like light is another term.

Dr. Miller: You feel "light," you said?

Ann: Yeah.

Dr. Miller: Floaty light?

Ann: Mm-hm. I don't have a feeling. I wouldn't say "high," but I don't feel pain—which is weird. Before last week, I would not have said any of that about him. I didn't talk about him.

Dr. Miller: You know what, you haven't been able to talk about him, the positive memories, right?

Ann: I just don't know if I have that many memories of him. I wouldn't say that I have very many negative memories, but they're all just kind of neutral. All I remember is picking him up, standing in line with him, or little stuff like that.

159   ImTT Press, publisher

Dr. Miller: He would cling to you, be with you, and a lot of stuff. When he's doing that, how does that feel? When you think back, do you feel warm and connected with him? You don't have that anymore.

Ann: I guess not. No.

Dr. Miller: Do you miss it?

Ann: Yeah. I guess I just don't let myself go there. There's a little bit more to the story. My stepmother took him and my little, I guess technically, step-sister and disappeared to Minnesota for a few months. We had to work to get a detective to find him. I think that was my freshman year, and I vowed that I was going to adopt him and take him away from my family.

When I turned 18, I applied to the U of A, and they offered a free lawyer to potential students. I went and sat with him. We talked about adopting Shawn. The lawyer said it wouldn't work out. I wouldn't win the case because I'm 18 and I'm doing nothing. He suggested that I go to college and re-evaluate everything afterwards.

Then, my freshman year, Shawn died. I guess maybe there was a lot of guilt underneath it all, more towards me.

Dr. Miller: What color is the pain of guilt?

Ann: I want to say black. It's the first thought that came to mind.

Dr. Miller: Where do you see it in your body? Close your eyes. Breathe into the black. Forget about everything else except the black. Now, breathe out the black from that part of your body.

Ann releases color particles with the P/TRP.

Dr. Miller: Think of Shawn again. Do you feel guilty towards him?

Ann: No. I feel clean.

Dr. Miller: Is any queasiness left?

Ann: I'm feeling slightly queasy, but I think that's because I'm getting all anxious.

Dr. Miller: What are you anxious about?

Ann: I'm a little anxious about maybe this all being aired for a bunch of people to see, maybe not want me to see their kids in the future, I suppose. Is that random? I want to work with kids. I don't want this weird thing with my brother to affect that part.

Dr. Miller: You just got through explaining how much you loved your brother, how you wanted to take care of him.

Ann: You're right. I don't know.

Dr. Miller: He died, and it wasn't your fault.

Ann: [sigh] I know that.

Dr. Miller: The fact that you came up with that idea, that anxiety, means there's a part of you that feels like it's your fault, doesn't it? No. You feel ashamed, don't you?

Ann: That's it.

Dr. Miller: Underneath that shame, it sounds like fear.

Ann: Fear of...

Dr. Miller: Not being welcomed, being excluded.

Ann: Yes.

Dr. Miller: There's something wrong with you and they're not going to want anything to do with you, right? Tune into the terror. What color is it?

Ann: Red.

Dr. Miller: Where is it located in your body?

Ann: My chest.

Dr. Miller: See the red as composed of tiny, tiny particles of red.

Ann: I can do that.

Dr. Miller: Breathe into the red, and let it out.

Ann releases the red particles with the P/TRP.

Dr. Miller: Is it all gone?

Ann: I'm not anxious anymore.

Dr. Miller: How does the shame feel?

Ann: No shame.

Dr. Miller: Are you worried now about somebody seeing this?

Ann: No. [Laughs] That was an easy fix.

Dr. Miller: Okay.

Ann: That's awesome.

Dr. Miller: How do you feel?

Ann: I feel relaxed. I could hang out all day. [Laughter]

Dr. Miller: Good. Think of Shawn now, think about him.

Ann: It's nothing. Even when I think about what used to make me feel guilty like having to leave or wanting to be on my phone or something silly like that. It's nothing, nothing.

Ann: Overwhelm and Phobia

This session illustrates the full use of the ImTT protocols. In this session, Ann works on her feelings of being overwhelmed. After processing the feelings of being overwhelmed, Ann is taken through the Changing Patterns Protocol. During that process, Ann's phobia of driving surfaces. This fear is then processed with the ImTT.

In the beginning of the session, Ann talked about attending her evening class at the end of her workday. When someone asked her about her day, she broke into tears. The transcript begins after she talked about this event.

Ann: I lost it, and now I'm embarrassed about it.

Dr. Miller: Okay. It's hard when you're working this hard, isn't it?

Ann: Yes.

Dr. Miller: I think what's going on, on an emotional level, isn't tiredness. The tiredness is there, but you're clearly feeling overwhelmed.

Ann: Yeah.

Dr. Miller: What's happening is that, as you go about your day, you're doing this, doing this, doing that. The next thing you know is that in the background you're telling yourself something like, "I can't handle this. It's too much." Does this make sense?

Ann: Yeah, it sounds probably about right.

Dr. Miller: Okay. If you "can't," what would you think is going on in your head? What phrase would fit?

Ann: I can't handle this.

Dr. Miller: "I can't handle this." If you can't handle this, what's going to happen?

Ann: I'm going to lose the practicum. Then what am I going to do? I'm not going to get my hours. I'm not going to graduate. I'm going to ruin these kiddos' lives. There's a thousand and one things that could happen.

Dr. Miller: You'll never be a psychologist, right? This is what's happening in your head. You're stressing yourself out by what you're unconsciously thinking. If you can't do all that, then you're a failure. Right? You are probably putting about ten times more stress on yourself because of your thought pattern. What we're going to do is clear it up.

Ann: All right. I have a negative thought pattern of myself.

Dr. Miller: There's never a reason to feel overwhelmed, ever. Feeling overwhelmed is not about how much you have to do. If I give you a thousand things to do, there's no reason to feel overwhelmed. You may not be able to do them. [Laughs] Right? You may look at it and go, "Okay, this is how I'm going to have to divide it up.

This is how long it's going to take me. That's it. You gave me a thousand things to do. This is what it's going to require including my breaks [Laughs]. Right? Feeling overwhelmed isn't about what you have to do; feeling overwhelmed is about your reaction—what you tell yourself about what you have to do.

Ann: That makes sense.

Dr. Miller: There's never a reason to feel overwhelmed.

Ann: That makes me feel better. [Laughs]

Dr. Miller: It's all about your reaction. Your reaction is, "I can't handle this." When you think that in your mind, it's "I'm going to fear all these things are not going to get done." You're going to fail school. You're never going to become a Dr. Miller. This is what has kept going on in your head. No wonder you feel stressed out. Right?

Ann: So much on the line.

Dr. Miller: If you had a lot of things to do and you went from one thing to another, to another, you will eventually exhaust yourself if you overwork. That's still doesn't mean you'd feel overwhelmed. Feeling overwhelmed is totally separate from working too much, from finally wearing out your body. What we're going to do is change that image of yourself.

Ann: Okay.

Dr. Miller: When you think "I can't handle this," what's the image of what's going to happen if you can't handle this?

Ann: I'm going to be sitting at Tyco Park on the wrong seats, not the graduating class. I'm going to be watching everyone else graduate.

Dr. Miller: Is that painful or fearful?

Ann: Fearful.

Dr. Miller: What color is the terror?

Ann: Black.

Dr. Miller: Black. And where is it located?

Ann: In my gut.

Dr. Miller: All right. See the black as being composed of tiny little particles. Breathe into the black particles and breathe them directly away from your body.

Ann releases the black particles of terror with the P/TRP.

Dr. Miller: Okay, how do you feel?

Ann: I feel amazing. I'm light as a feather. My tummy is still in knots a little.

Dr. Miller: You're saying it's feeling a little queasy there?

Ann: Yeah.

Dr. Miller: Okay.

Ann: That helped connect me to my whole body.

Dr. Miller: Okay. What do you think is the feeling?

Ann: I don't know. As we're going through the process, my stomach got tighter and tighter.

Dr. Miller: Did it relax, or is it still in a knot now?

Ann: It's not in much of a big knot, but maybe I'm still a little anxious.

Dr. Miller: Let's finish off the image, and then we'll see where we are from there.

Ann: Okay.

Dr. Miller: Okay. Remember what the image was or is?

Ann: Yeah.

Dr. Miller: Okay. See it composed of tiny little particles. Drop them to the floor. See the particles soak into the earth.

Ann drops the image particles to the floor.

Dr. Miller: Re-image it again. Tell me what you've got.

Ann: I pictured me in the stands at Tyco Park, sitting around a bunch of people that were happy and cheering. I was sitting there moping. When I re-imaged it, I was smiling.

Dr. Miller: You were what?

Ann: Smiling.

Dr. Miller: Okay. Re-image it again. See it composed of tiny little particles. Drop them to the floor. See the particles soak into the earth.

Ann drops the image particles to the floor.

Dr. Miller: Re-image it again. Tell me what you've got.

Ann: I'm cheering.

Dr. Miller: Okay. Re-image it again. See it composed of tiny little particles. Drop them to the ground.

Ann drops the image particles to the floor.

Dr. Miller: Okay. Re-image it again, Tell me what you've got.

Ann: Is it weird if the picture switched?

Dr. Miller: No. What did it switch to?

Ann: It's me standing in the mirror with my cap and gown.

Dr. Miller: Okay. Does that feel good? Good. Now we're going to release the particles of the original image from your body.

Ann: Okay.

Dr. Miller: Breathe into the center of your brain and see the tiny particles going out your forehead.

Ann releases the particles of the image from her body.

Dr. Miller: Okay. How do you feel now?

Ann: [sighing] That was overwhelming. I feel great.

Dr. Miller: How is your stomach?

Ann: It's fine.

Dr. Miller: No knots?

Ann: Not anymore.

Changing Patterns Protocol

Dr. Miller: Let's think of your day on Monday. Just think about it. Just focus on it.

Ann: Okay.

Dr. Miller: Then your day on Tuesday. You go to school on Tuesday, right? And Wednesday going to work. Thursday going to work and school. Friday going to work. How does that feel now?

Ann: It's funny. It's like how my week is. When you asked me to think about my Monday and Tuesday, I instantly got anxious, but by the time I was thinking about Wednesday, Thursday, and Friday, I was fine. I don't know why I instantly go to anxious feelings thinking about it. I don't know.

Dr. Miller: So go back and think of Monday again. Does it make you anxious?

Ann: Slightly, but not as much as the first time you asked me to think about it.

Dr. Miller: So focus on Monday again, and then Tuesday, then Wednesday, Thursday, Friday. So think of Monday again. How does it feel now?

Ann: I don't know. I am really anxious. But I think that's because I'm thinking about how anxious I am.

Dr. Miller: You're thinking of what?

Ann: How anxious I am. And now I just really feel anxious. Throughout the whole week, thinking about each day, I felt anxious. I feel that's maybe because I am focusing and sitting here and trying to notice where my anxiety is.

Dr. Miller: Okay.

Ann: My thought pattern now is, "Not a big deal, I'll go see that kiddo". That's what I am thinking, but what I am feeling is like the butterflies in my chest.

Dr. Miller: Okay. So let's talk about what's causing you to have butterflies in your chest.

Ann: I don't know. I mean...

Dr. Miller: What are you scared of? What's an image? Give me an image. What are you scared of?

Ann: I don't know, I really like what I do. So I don't know...

Dr. Miller: Anxiety is not about disliking what you do.

Ann: I don't know what I am afraid of. I guess the generic feeling that I'll mess up. I don't know.

Dr. Miller: Well...

Ann: Because I feel pretty confident in my job, but...

Dr. Miller: We are triggering something where you don't. So let's focus on Monday. When you focus on Monday, go through the day in your mind and see where the anxiety starts or is most intense.

Ann: I don't know. I feel calm now.

Dr. Miller: [Laughter] Okay.

Ann: I don't know, I don't know.

Dr. Miller: Right.

Ann: I tried—every session, I have it every Monday, every Wednesday. I feel confident. I feel comfortable in the home. I have a plan. I know what my role is. I'm trying to think of everything. I don't know.

Dr. Miller: Okay. No more butterflies?

Ann: There is still a little bit of butterflies but not as intense as when you asked me to think about...I feel like "Monday"—this word is a trigger or something.

Dr. Miller: Okay. Well, focus on Monday. What do you get?

Ann: Like crawling out of my bed, the day after my day off, like "Monday blues," I guess, if that's what you call it.

Dr. Miller: "Blues" are not anxiousness. Anxiety is a whole different thing.

Ann: I don't know what it is.

Dr. Miller: Is there anxiety now, when you think about Monday?

Ann: I am anxious about getting to work, the drive. I guess that's triggering for me and then—in between kiddos, I have to drive and I hate driving. So I've been anxious while driving.

Dr. Miller: So driving is making you anxious? So what do you think is going to happen when you drive?

Ann: Car accident.

Dr. Miller: A car accident.

Ann: I am going to hit something.

Dr. Miller: You were recently in a car wreck, right?

Ann: Yes. Yeah. My brother died in a car accident. My mother ruined her life in a car accident. My grandma killed her mother in a car accident. I don't like cars.

Dr. Miller: There is a lot of stuff here about cars. You've got a job where you drive from place to place. Okay. So give me an image of driving, a terrifying image. You are going to be in a car wreck. Make it more specific. What's going to happen?

Ann: What I hate is there are a lot of people crossing the street, a lot of close streets with parking, and everyone's parked on the street—like downtown. It's terrifying. "Okay, I am going to turn. I am turning."

Dr. Miller: Okay.

Ann: I don't know how to parallel park; so parking is a nightmare for me. I'll drive around for half an hour to find a spot. I'll plan out where to park at a parking lot where there's no other car. So if I need to back out weird—I am getting anxious thinking about it.

Dr. Miller: So you are pretty terrified about this whole thing about it, aren't you?

Ann: I hate it.

Dr. Miller: Okay. What color is the terror?

Ann: [Whispering] It's black.

   ImTT Press, publisher

Dr. Miller: Black.

Ann: [Laughing]

Dr. Miller: Okay. What else could it be?

Ann: There is nothing else. [Laughing]

Dr. Miller: Where is it located?

Ann: It's in my chest.

Dr. Miller: Okay. See it composed of tiny little particles, and breathe into the particles, and breathe the black particles out.

P/TRP releasing the black particles of terror.

Dr. Miller: When you think of that image now, how does that feel to you now?

Ann: Very good. I'll be okay.

Dr. Miller: Okay. Now let's deconstruct the image. See that image? See it composed of tiny little particles? Drop it to the ground.

Ann deconstructs the image.

Dr. Miller: Re-image it again. Tell me what you've got?

Ann: My initial image was like the image that I saw when I hit the car in front of me, in my last car accident. The swoosh—like my hands are here. When I re-imaged it, it was like before I hit the car; I stopped.

Dr. Miller: Okay.

Ann: There was no hit.

Dr. Miller: Now see the image composed of tiny, little particles. Then drop it to the ground.

Ann deconstructs the image.

Dr. Miller: Re-image it again. Tell me what you've got.

Ann: There is no one in front of me, and I am just driving.

Dr. Miller: You are just driving?

Ann: Just driving.

Dr. Miller: How do you feel just driving?

Ann: Fine.

Dr. Miller: Okay. Let's clear out the old particles of that image. Breathe into the center of your brain and see the particles of the image go out your forehead.

(It is important to note that the Ann is asked to release the particles of the <u>original</u> image that she deconstructed.)

Ann releases the particles of the image from her body.

Dr. Miller: When you think of that image, what comes up for you now? What's your reaction?

Ann: Nothing. Just driving.

Dr. Miller: Okay. Now go through the week again including driving from place to place and tell me what's happening.

Ann: Nothing.

Dr. Miller: Nothing?

Ann: Nothing.

Dr. Miller: Go through the whole week, focus on every day of the week.

Ann: So all my triggers are school related.

Dr. Miller: Excuse me?

Ann: All my anxious moments are school related because there is a lot of stuff due next week.

Dr. Miller: Okay. That'll be for another day.

Ann: Okay. Good.

Joan Session #1:

Drinking Problems and Avoidant Behavior

Joan has become concerned that she has begun drinking too much in the last few months. The first challenge is to discern whether Joan's drinking is the result of a positive feeling—a feeling-state—or is the result of an avoidance behavior. The difference is extremely important, as the different psychological dynamics require different approaches.

Joan: The thing that I would be very interested to try this with is drinking alcohol.
I don't drink masses, but I drink more than I think is a good idea. I notice that there are two things. One is that I really love the initial hit of drinking a glass of wine or Vermouth. But I don't really want to give that bit up. The initial bit is absolutely fine.

The thing that is not so brilliant is that I seem to have a second thing that I really like or have a bit of more of a weird liking for, which is getting to the point of feeling a bit—well, "sloshed" is an English way of putting it.

Dr. Miller: How much are you drinking?

Joan: I'd say about two large glasses of wine in an evening—not every evening, but most evenings. And some evenings, instead of two large glasses of wine, I'd have a glass of wine, and then I'd have a glass of Vermouth Martini, or sometimes, instead of the wine altogether, I might fancy something like Baileys. You know, that Irish Cream liqueur? I don't know if you get that in the States.

Recently, I think it's crept up a bit; so it's these two large glasses of wine. The second one, I definitely don't need. That's the bit that I would quite like not to be doing because, at that point, I'm looking at being slightly inebriated—not inebriated—slightly...

Dr. Miller: "Sloshed"?

ImTT Press, publisher

Joan: Yeah. And slightly zoned out—something like that feeling.

Dr. Miller: How long have you been doing this for?

Joan: This amount of two large glasses of wine a night is more of quite a recent thing over the last couple of months—maybe two, three months. But I've always really enjoyed drinking wine.

My parents were absolute piss artists. I mean they drank ridiculous—well, my mom is still alive, and they drink crazy amounts but in a very controlled, Protestant-work-ethic-y sort of—there's a big thing in the family about—it's seen as quite funny to have this enormous sobriety thing going on in the background—some idea of hard work and all the rest of it—and then every night they drink—my mother—she'll easily drink half a bottle, two thirds of a bottle of wine herself. I've got three sisters, and they all do the same thing.

I think it's quite unusual actually amongst people I know. Most people are not that uptight followed by that plastered. Most people are more relaxed in the first place, and then it's a sort of natural extension; whereas, this is a bit more weird, I think.

Dr. Miller: When did you first start drinking?

Joan: You see, my parents were quite—I'd say certainly not liberated in any sense of the word—but with drinking, I think they quite enjoyed introducing us to a small glass of something from mid teens onwards probably—about 16, 17. But that would be only very occasional. I didn't like alcohol at that age. If I were going out with my friends, I'd have a Babycham, which is a sort of sweetened fizzy thing that me and my friends drank, but we didn't drink much of it, and we just pretended to be drunk really at that age.

Dr. Miller: You say that your drinking increased just a few months ago.

Joan: Yeah.

Dr Miller: What happened a few months ago?

Joan: Well, it's difficult to say, really. I think not much, actually, except that—I can't think of anything particular, except now I'm thinking about it, I think there's a sort of—I've noticed being slightly more—what's the word?—slightly more easily fed up recently. And I think it's a hormone—I'm 55, and although I absolutely sailed through—well, relatively speaking—sailed through menopause at 50-odd—and that didn't seem to create any particular mood change or anything; whereas, recently, I've been aware of being more flat—which is probably a bit relevant, I suppose, actually—for the odd day at a time, maybe more than that. It probably is linked, actually.

Dr. Miller: When you say "flat," what do you mean?

Joan: Well, just a bit fed up. I'm normally quite an enthusiastic sort of person, and I've always really enjoyed my job, generally speaking, and love seeing friends and all that. And I still love doing all that. But the work's got more stressful, I think, in the last few years in terms of how I find it. It's just straightforward adult out-patient clinical psychology in private practice. But I'm noticing it's more tiring as I get a bit older, actually—or draining.

Dr. Miller: How many hours a week do you work?

Joan: I do three days of seeing five people a day: Monday, Wednesday, Friday. But I've only just changed that. I was doing Monday, Tuesday, Wednesday for a long time; and that was—by Wednesday evening, I was absolutely like a zombie. It was just too much together. So now I do those three days a week, and then I also do weight loss work on a Tuesday in a separate clinic. That's in Bristol, which is separate.

                                       ImTT Press, publisher

Dr. Miller: When did you change your work schedule?

Joan: About a month ago. It has been really a good move.

Dr. Miller: It sounds like you were starting to get to be very exhausted, zombie like. And somewhere in there, you started drinking before you actually changed your—

Joan: That's right. That's definitely right.

Dr. Miller: How's your marriage?

Joan: Brilliant. There've been periods of stress. We've been married 20 years this year, and there have been periods of stress, but I'd say it's extremely strong.

Dr. Miller: Has there been any change in your sex life in the last year?

Joan: Only—right, this is another interesting thing—only that I've noticed recently that the menopausal changes have led to it being really quite uncomfortable. I've started taking something to make that easier, but we do have quite a very regular sex life, and that has been more uncomfortable recently.

Dr. Miller: How recently?

Joan: Well, funnily enough, I think probably the last couple of months, maybe three months, I think. But it's very recent.

Dr. Miller: And so is the increase in your alcohol.

Joan: Well, yes. Now you mention it. [Laughter] It's quite an interesting—but I hadn't made that connection at all; so I'm just paranoid about the— [Laughter]

Dr. Miller: Recently you're more zombie like?

Joan: Yeah.

Dr. Miller: You have become more fed up?

Joan: Yeah.

Dr. Miller: And your sex life changed?

Joan: Yes, yes, yes.

Dr Miller: This is probably less about feeling-states than it is about avoidance. What is the feeling that you're avoiding?

Joan: Right. Well, that's interesting. What's the feeling I'm avoiding? I suppose what it achieves—that second glass of wine—is—it achieves that whole—I mean, the problem is the zombie state, but by drinking that extra glass of wine, I induce a—more of a zombie state. It's more—yeah—disconnected.

Dr. Miller: Precisely. There might be a feeling-state—as a matter of fact, I'm pretty sure there's a feeling-state with the first glass of wine.

Joan: Yes, there is. There's definitely one there.

Dr. Miller: But the one that is bothering you the most is the second one, and you are definitely doing an avoidance behavior there.

Joan: Right. Can you just tell me—so for my professional purposes now of learning—how that became clear to you. What it is—how do you—

Dr. Miller: The first glass of wine—you like the feeling. And my guess is that the feeling-state probably has something to do with your family and belonging and joining—something like that.

Joan: Right. That's a bit excruciating. Go on. We'll have to move on to that then.

Dr. Miller: But with the second glass of wine, the question is what changed? And it's unlikely that a new feeling-state formed.

Joan: Because?

Dr. Miller: Number one, most feeling-states are going to form in your younger years. Usually, by the time you're in your 20s, that's it for most—not always, but—

Joan: Yeah, that makes sense.

Dr. Miller: It could always happen, but—and partly that's because the psychological—the needs—number one, your body can be intense, and your psychological needs are really there—whatever the deficits are, if you remember me talking about that.

So you're going after those feelings—whether it's in a relationship or a substance or a job, whatever it is—you're more likely to go for it then and have a positive experience that creates a feeling-state. Later on in life—partly because our psychological needs are less in terms of belonging, in terms of joining, in terms of feeling special—more likely, whatever you haven't gotten by then just goes into depression. By that time, you're not going to have the positive experience. You're more likely to have the negative experiences.

So you're 55 years old. And you say the last few months—so now it's time to start asking what happened? What changed? So it's pretty clear that, when we really start analyzing it, we realize a lot of things were happening. One of the things you know. The zombie-like state that you were having before you changed—when you're doing that, it doesn't just affect—you say you worked Monday, Tuesday, Wednesday, right? It probably wrecked the rest of your week too.

Joan: Well, it certainly—yes, it took me a while to recover.

Dr. Miller: I've been there. And it takes the joy out of life. Part of it is that before, when you were younger, it was probably really cool. You'd have four days off. You'd work three days and have four days off. You probably had more energy to do it; and therefore, it didn't put you in a zombie state. But my guess is that zombie state has been creeping up on you for a long time.

Joan: I think that's very true.

Dr. Miller: What's happened is that it started taking the joy out of all of your life because you're overworking. Then there's—probably some of the stuff, you've worked through; and some of the stuff, you haven't—like with the menopause, in terms of the psychological changes, what that means—you're getting older; you're now moving into a different state, you're looking mortality in the face, how many more years do you have left?—that kind of stuff. So this whole thing—it's pretty clear it's avoidance.

So now we get back to the question. What are you avoiding?

Joan: I don't know the answer to that immediately. What am I avoiding in that second glass of wine? I think what I am doing is essentially—it feels like just disengaging from everything. It's sort of not—you know, like the opposite of connecting.

Dr. Miller: Are you feeling overwhelmed?

Joan: With that three-day thing—pattern of working, yes, definitely.

Dr Miller: You know, what may have happened is that you did get to the point where you were feeling overwhelmed. Do you remember my talk about the overwhelm?

Joan: Yeah.

Dr. Miller: In your mind, there's a part of you going, "I can't handle this. I can't do this. It's too much." That's going on in your mind. And what may have happened is that, even though you switched the number of days, that feeling is still there. You're still saying that to yourself. You walk into your office in the morning, you know. It's like there's another part of you that, in the back of your mind, is going, "Oh, my God. Here we are again." Even though it's not the same, your mind is making—it's like—when you think back, how many years have you been moving toward that zombie state?

Joan: I think I've gone into it a few years ago—probably about six years ago, I was in it when I got as far as working four days a week. And that was too much, definitely. So then I came—did less, and then down to two days a week after a while. And then it crept up again to three. And what I kept trying to do—my thinking on this was, if I did Monday, Tuesday, Wednesday, then it was over by Wednesday evening and I had the rest of the week free. My husband said to me a couple of times, "Why don't you separate out the days so you don't have this accumulation by Wednesday evening because," he said, "you look as though you've been beaten up by the time you get home on a Wednesday because, you know, it's just too much." I didn't really take much notice of my husband's saying it. I just thought, "Oh yeah, that's fair enough," but I didn't take much notice. But when one of the secretaries at work then said the same thing, I thought, "Well, maybe I should give it a go, even though it means giving up that idea of having a long weekend." And, actually, I've only done about a month of it, but it's miles better—miles better.

Dr. Miller: Right. So you have now an image of working with people that is of when you were overwhelmed. And that image is still there. So I think the first thing we need to do is to clear that image. What is the image? There's an image that creates dread. What is it?

Joan: The real dread, to do with the overwhelm, is looking at the list of people and seeing one or two of the people who are really worrying or really intensely draining to work with, amongst a list of five or six.

Dr. Miller: That's the first part of it. Now make that a nightmare image. What's going to happen? They're going to be really draining. So what's the image of what's going to happen to you?

Joan: What's going to happen is I'm going to feel more and more and more depleted. They're not going to really benefit from the whole thing anyway; so there's a sort of pointlessness to it. Well, I suppose, if we make a real nightmare scenario out of it, I then get—in my incompetence, I then make a serious mistake—this isn't quite how I think, but this—taking it further, this is definitely there in the background somewhere—that I then make some sort of error and get struck off so I can't work anymore.

Dr Miller: And if you get struck off and can't work anymore, what's going to happen?

Joan: I'd hate that.

Dr Miller: No, I know that, but what would happen to you?

Joan: What would happen?

ImTT Press, publisher

Dr. Miller: What is the nightmare scenario?

Joan: The nightmare scenario then is the humiliation of being seen to be somebody who was that bad at her job, that stupid, as to miss something big.

Dr. Miller: Is that painful or fearful?

Joan: Painful, more. Well, is it? Perhaps both. But my instinct was to say "painful" there.

Dr. Miller: Okay. You ready to clear it?

Joan: Yeah.

Dr. Miller: So what color is the pain?

Joan: I don't know. Yellow—I don't know—is the word that comes to mind; so we'll go with that.

Dr. Miller: And where is the pain located?

Joan: In my chest somewhere.

Dr. Miller: I want you to see the yellow in your chest as composed of tiny, tiny little yellow particles. Tell me when you've got it.

Joan: Yeah.

Dr. Miller: Breathe into the yellow particles; breathe them directly away from your body.

Joan releases the yellow pain particles with the P/TRP.

Dr. Miller: Okay. How do you feel?

Joan: Extremely relaxed, I must say.

Dr. Miller: When you think of that nightmare scenario, does it seem as charged as it was?

Joan: No. It's interesting doing that. To begin with, I found it hard to actually concentrate on the color and everything. And I was thinking, "Oh dear, I'm thinking too much about this stuff," but interestingly, after we went through it, I had a couple of thoughts, one of which was very simply to have the first glass of wine later in the evening. Just practically. And the other thought I had was just about the idea of being struck. I know the idea of being struck off is a bit wacky. I know I am extremely competent, thanks to being extremely well trained and supervised. I've been qualified for 25 years; the first 10 years, I was given amazingly good clinical psychology training. Then I had amazing first supervisors and so on. I'm quite old. I've been doing it for quite a while; so it's a bit of a preposterous—

Dr. Miller: Now we're going to finish it off. We're not finished. I want you to see the nightmare image. What I want you to do now is see the nightmare scenario, the image you have. Can you tell me when you've got it.

Joan: It's a bit vague, but I've got an image.

Dr. Miller: Now I want you to pixelate it like pixels on a TV screen; tell me when you get it.

Joan: Yeah.

Dr. Miller: Now I want you to deconstruct the image. You can do it by dropping all the particles or the pixels to the floor, you can blow it up, you can take a hammer to the image, whatever you want to do, but deconstruct the image. Just tell me when you're finished.

Joan: Okay.

Dr. Miller: Re-image it again and tell me what you've got. Is it as intense as it was? Is it even more blurred? What's going on? Is it falling apart?

Joan: Instead of a mixture of things, it's now just one particular patient who's very worrying.

Dr. Miller: Pixelate it. [Silence]

Joan: Okay.

Dr. Miller: Deconstruct it.

Joan: Okay.

Dr. Miller: Re-image it again and tell me what you've got.

Joan: I can still picture the same patient, but I think there's a slight drawback, in that my initial image was a bit of a muddle. Then it was the patient and now it's the patient again.

Dr Miller: Is it the same intensity of that patient?

Joan: No, I don't think it is. No.

Dr. Miller: All right. Pixelate it. [Silence]

Joan: Okay.

Dr. Miller: And deconstruct it.

Joan: It's interesting doing that. I immediately have a series of thoughts that come with doing that. Like "If I don't hold onto the image of her, who's going to?"

Dr. Miller: What does holding the image have to do with it?

Joan: I don't know. But there's a sense of it's a bad idea to let it go because letting that image go is quite anxiety provoking. It sort of sums up the problem with this patient, actually, which is I've got too much riding on my support of her.

Dr. Miller: What's riding on your support of her?

Joan: She's rather fragile and sometimes actively suicidal. It's a bit like, if I let the image go, then somehow that means letting go of her, which then means that I would bring about a sort of catastrophic sequence.

Dr. Miller: So what you're doing is you're living with this image that terrifies you that she is going to kill herself. It doesn't work that way, you know, consciously. You can let go of the image and still be supportive of her. You just don't have to live with it 24 hours a day. As a matter of fact, it weakens you in terms of working with her and supporting her.

Joan: Yeah, it does.

Dr. Miller: Now pixelate that image and deconstruct it. [Silence]

Joan: Yeah, okay.

Dr. Miller: Re-image it again. Tell me what you've got. [Silence]

Joan: Well, not much, really.

Dr. Miller: Now we're going to go through the body and remove the particles of the image from your body. Okay? So visualize that you're breathing into the center of your brain and see the particles of the image go out your forehead.

Joan releases the particles of the image from her body.

Dr Miller: How do you feel?

Joan: Relaxed. I think with a sense of that person—and somebody else came to mind who was even more difficult to work with that I worked with a long time ago—and I was just noticing a sense of I don't have to hold these people in my mind in this way.

Dr. Miller: Okay.

Joan: Which is good.

Dr. Miller: Now, when you think of having that second drink at night, how does that feel to you now?

Joan: Well, it's obvious to me that I've been having it to sort of get me to the point of not thinking; and that it will be interesting to notice probably not deciding to do that this evening. Because I think I'll enjoy the first and see what happens.

Dr. Miller: How do you feel about what we just did?

Joan: Well, I think it's extremely interesting. I think you're absolutely right about it being an avoidance thing and that the avoidance has been a sort of—just one thing to sort of shut down, basically, just really abdicate any sort of responsibility basically for anything and a sort of "Just leave me alone" sort of state. It's very interesting. It's very useful to have done it with you, going through that.

And I would like to do the other bit, even though I don't want to give up the first hit of the wine.

Dr. Miller: Nobody's making you give up anything. Remember?

Joan: No, no, no. [Laughter]

Dr. Miller: Okay.

Joan: But I really would like to do that.

Joan Session #2:

Processing a Feeling-State Involving Alcohol

This is the second session for Joan, who presented for therapy to work on her use of alcohol. In the first session, Joan was able to identify that her second glass of alcohol was an avoidance behavior. Joan was avoiding the feeling of being overwhelmed, resulting from an image of being a failure. Joan reports that this behavior has improved.

In the second session, Joan wants to work on her first glass of alcohol. The feeling-state is identified and processed with the Image De-Construction Protocol. While the Feeling-State Image Protocol (FSIP) is not discussed in this book, this session is included to illustrate a different protocol that may be necessary to resolve a compulsive behavior.

Dr. Miller: How have you been doing?

Joan: Fine. I think I definitely have had a bit of a difference this week. It's not the total wiping out of that pattern, but it's definitely—A, I've been more conscious; and, B, I've also thought less about it, which—the second is more relevant to this, in a way, isn't it? It's more of a relevant sign. But, actually, to start with, at the beginning of the week, after I spoke to you last time, the thing that was quite helpful was just being more conscious of the whole thing. And that was good for a week—I mean for a day or two.

Dr. Miller: Tell me about what the behavior is now.

Joan: Well, the other thing, which is this thing that I didn't want to give up, paradoxically, but would like to reduce, is this thing of the—what I don't want to give up is the hit of the first bit of the first glass of wine or Vermouth. But I sort of—well, it's obviously completely conflicted because, otherwise, I wouldn't be talking about it.

I think if I did some of this on it—my main thing is I just want to learn about this stuff, and I think the best way to learn is to have it done to you, basically with anything. I try most things when I learn about them. But it would be useful to—

Dr. Miller: Do you want to work on the hit, then?

Joan: Yes.

Dr. Miller: Describe the hit to me.

Joan: It's a really nice feeling—which comes back to this distinction I made—it's a really nice feeling that includes a sort of physical warmth going through my body, but, even though it's only the first couple of sips, it also involves a sense of very mild intoxication.

Dr. Miller: Can you remember the most intense time that ever happened?

Joan: No, I don't think I can. I don't think I can.

Dr. Miller: Do you remember when you first started?

Joan: Well, the sort of relatively early memory I have, which I think has got something to do with it, is New Year's Eve—which was a regular thing, I don't know how old I was, which particular New Year's Eve—but each New Year's Eve, our family would have a very small—I'm one of four so there was six of us altogether and my parents—and we'd have some friends over, which was a family of two parents and two children and some neighbors. So it was only a small party. But there was about 15 of us altogether.

And there'd be nice food and, crucially, salted peanuts as a thing that was put out—we never had food like that normally—salted peanuts and—which I absolutely love and—I think this is my relatively early memory of it—is having sweet Martini in a Martini Rosso. I really get this feeling from that more than anything. I get it from red wine, which is probably my favorite drink, but I get it even more from red Martini.

Dr. Miller: The red Martini took place at New Year's?

Joan: Yeah, I'd say I was probably in my mid to late teens at this point because I wasn't drinking Martini any younger than that, probably. It was just a family thing, and that was the most social or most likely time for it to happen. We'd occasionally have wine with meals and things. And my parents—I think I mentioned before they really liked drinking alcohol. It was a thing that they encouraged us to do, frankly—not in an excessive way.

Dr. Miller: The New Year's party sounds like that's one of the most intense, pleasurable memories.

Joan: Yeah.

Dr. Miller: What we need to do is identify the feeling. There's certainly a good feeling. The question is does it feel like you're belonging? Does it feel like you're connected or joined with your family? What does it feel like, at that point? the party? Or is it the party?

Joan: No, it's not the party, I don't think. It's difficult to say, but I suspect it's something to do with the connected or belonging feeling. Belonging, probably.

Dr. Miller: Go ahead.

Joan: What was interesting is, actually, it's quite difficult or—very logically, I know that would be quite a big deal for me and my family. It's actually quite hard to access what that—now you're asking about it, and this is obviously relevant to me dealing with people—it's quite hard to tell what that bit of it was. I'm very clear about the physical feeling I get when I have the Martini. It's a bit difficult to—do people normally readily see what they associated—no? Okay. Right. That's all right.

Dr. Miller: This is the hard part. This is always the hard part. I'll present different possibilities. When they don't fit, people will just tell me, but it gives them something to compare with, rather than letting them try and figure it out all by themselves.

Joan: The picture I have, you see—the picture I have of this thing is actually kneeling down, sitting in my obviously party clothes by the—we had this low coffee table with a thing of peanuts on it.

One of the things about these bloody peanuts is that we didn't have free access to any food. The cupboards weren't locked, but there was nothing that you would ever want to eat in that house. Food was a big issue, really, in the sense that it was incredibly boring— off-the-scale boring. There was no onions, no garlic, nothing used in cooking because my father hated them. The food was unbelievably plain, and I really quite like strong tastes and so on.

Anyway, the thing about the peanuts is that I could just have them. I could just literally get a handful of peanuts and eat it.

Dr. Miller: Now, how are you with peanuts now?

Joan: I'm fine with peanuts. I absolutely love them. One of my children has a severe nut allergy, unfortunately; so they're now off limits for another reason.

Dr. Miller: I was wondering if you would eat them with your—

Joan: With my Martini?

Dr. Miller: Yeah.

Joan: Yeah, I actually do that.

Dr. Miller: Now?

Joan: Well, I actually—I suppose what I do is—I hadn't thought of it, but I do tend to have crisps or savory things.

Dr. Miller: By having savory things, that elevates the whole feeling?

Joan: Yeah, it does.

Dr. Miller: It's becoming clear now, isn't it, that that's where this focus is on?

Joan: Yeah.

Dr. Miller: Does it feel more like you can have what you want?

Joan: With the savory stuff, that's definitely there.

Dr. Miller: Even with the drink—what I'm looking at is the whole picture. Is the whole picture like, "I can have what I want"?

Joan: I think it is, actually. Yeah. I think it is.

Dr. Miller: It's really not about belonging at all but "You can have what you want."

Joan: I think it's more that, yeah.

Dr. Miller: What would enhance the picture even more? What would you put into there?

Joan: What? Nowadays?

Dr. Miller: Anything to enhance the picture, whatever would enhance the picture "You could have what you want," or whatever would intensify the picture.

Joan: Now we've hit a bit of a nerve here because I'm not sure whether you mean now or then, right? I'm then thinking, right, "Okay, if we go back then," and then I immediately think, "Well, what would enhance the picture is actually having some connection with my family or a sense of belonging," which I did not have very much of.

Dr. Miller: You know something, then belonging is part of that picture.

Joan: Yeah. I think it is part of it.

Dr. Miller: Because at that one point, you probably did feel connected to your family.

Joan: Yeah.

Dr. Miller: Because at that one point, you probably did feel connected to your family at that one point. See, what happens is that what you wanted was to belong with your family. Of course, everybody wants to feel connected, bonded with their family.

When you finally kind of get it—and probably the peanuts had a lot to do with it—you could have what you wanted, and you were getting what you wanted through your family, by the way. They were the one offering the salted peanuts—your family.

Joan: My mother—that's where the action was, in terms of the aggravation. In fact, this is interesting because it was a very conventional division of labor between the two of them. My dad—in anything like this, he would do the drinks, and my mum would do the food. Neither would cross that boundary really. [Laughs] They would serve the things—interesting, too, actually.

Dr. Miller: So now what we have is you drinking your drink, eating your salted peanuts. In that picture, you're connected with your family. There is that feeling of connection or bonding with the family, right?

Joan: Yeah. Just—it's pretty precarious even then, but yes.

Dr. Miller: This isn't about reality now. This is about what's in your head.

Joan: That's right.

Dr. Miller: When we're talking about the image that's in your head, the fantasy that's in your head. The fantasy that's in your head is that you're drinking the drink, having the salted peanuts, and you're connected with your family. Ready to work on it?

Joan: Okay.

Dr. Miller: What I want you to do is now see that picture, close your eyes, and really get into the picture of it and then the feeling that you have that you're drinking, you're having the salted peanuts, and you're feeling connected with your family. Just feel that whole picture in there at that point and tell me when you've got it really clearly. And, again, it's not the memory; it's the fantasy.

Joan: Got it.

Dr. Miller: See these composed of tiny little pixel-particles, like we did last time, and tell me when you've got it formed with pixels–the visualization.

Joan: Yeah.

Dr. Miller: Deconstruct it. You can let all the particles go to the ground, you can wash them away, you can blow them up, whatever you want to do. Tell me when you're finished.

Joan: Done that.

Dr. Miller: You've already done it?

Joan: Yeah.

Dr. Miller: Re-image it again, and tell me what you've got.

Joan: I notice now the family of neighbors, the children—I was more connected to them than my siblings were; so they're now more in the picture.

Dr. Miller: Pixelate it again.

Joan: Yeah.

Dr. Miller: Deconstruct it.

Joan: Mm-hmm.

Dr. Miller: Re-image it again and tell me what you've got.

Joan: That just moves on to a different bit of the memory now.

Dr. Miller: Pixelate that now.

Joan: Yeah.

Dr. Miller: And deconstruct it.

Joan: Mm-hmm.

Dr. Miller: Re-image it again and tell me what you've got.

Joan: It keeps moving on to different bits of memory now.

Dr. Miller: That's okay.

Joan: It's another bit.

Dr. Miller: Pixelate it.

Joan: Yeah.

Dr. Miller: Deconstruct it.

Joan: Mm-hmm.

Dr. Miller: Re-image it again and tell me what you've got.

Joan: Well, not much now.

Dr. Miller: Is it all gone? You say, "not much."

Joan: It's now just the playing with the neighbors and the children from the other family at Monopoly in a room separate from the adults which were all in the other room.

Dr. Miller: Pixelate that, as well.

Joan: Mm-hmm.

Dr. Miller: Deconstruct it.

Joan: Okay.

Dr. Miller: Re-image it again and tell me what you've got.

Joan: The same thing. Just the same scene.

Dr. Miller: What's your emotional reaction to that scene?

Joan: Now? To that one? Well, it is a pleasant one. Because that part of the whole evening was always fun because we'd all play some sort of board game in this—you know, the children together. There'd be about—I don't know—six of us.

Dr. Miller: I mean you say it's "pleasant." Is it intensely pleasant? Does it feel like unified belonging or just a little bit of fun?

Joan: Well, definitely, I didn't feel excluded from that group. I did feel as though I belonged in that group of all the children. It's not a powerful positive; it's just a nice positive.

Dr. Miller: Let's go back to the original image. How does that scene look to you now?

Joan: I'd say probably still quite appealing but strangely slightly more distant or something.

ImTT Press, publisher

Dr. Miller: When you go back to it now, you can re-image it again; is that right? [Joan affirms] Pixelate that original image again, please. [Joan affirms] Deconstruct it. [Joan affirms]

Re-image it again. Tell me what you've got. [Silence]

Joan: Well, I can see it, but strangely, it's just like the Martini and the peanuts are just there, I think, rather than—I can imagine—maybe if I imagine eating them and drinking them again, I might get more.

Dr. Miller: Okay. Go ahead and try that.

Joan: Well, there isn't the same—that's a bit weird—there isn't the same sort of—

Dr. Miller: So you still see them there. So pixelate whatever is there.

Joan: The glass and the bowl.

Dr. Miller: Deconstruct it. [Silence]

Re-image it again, and tell me what you've got.

Joan: It's hard just to do that now, actually.

Dr. Miller: Okay. Is there anything still left, like little bits of it, pieces, are there?

Joan: Yeah.

Dr. Miller: Okay. Pixelate whatever is left. [Silence] Deconstruct it. [Silence]

Re-image it again and tell me what you've got. [Silence]

Joan: Well, the sense that I—a sort of "Oh, dear, I hope I don't want to have another"—No.

"I hope I don't not want to have another Martini" is one thought. And the other is like a—"photograph" isn't quite the right word. It's just like a picture in a frame or something.

Dr. Miller: Okay. Pixelate it. [Silence] And deconstruct it.

Joan: Okay.

Dr. Miller: Re-image it and tell me what you've got.

Joan: I can picture myself at the coffee table kneeling down, and the glass and the peanuts are there; but it isn't the same connection at all.

Dr. Miller: Pixelate what's left. [Silence]

Deconstruct it. [Silence]

Re-image it again, and tell me what you've got.

Joan: I can still see it. I don't think I would be able not to see it. Maybe it's just me.

Dr. Miller: Is there a table to see in the memory?

Joan: Yes, there is.

Dr. Miller: You're still seeing it, rather than recalling just a memory.

Joan: Sorry?

Dr. Miller: It sounds as if you're still seeing it, rather than recalling just the memory of it.

Joan: The "seeing" is the more removed, dispassionate thing; whereas, before, I was very engaged and involved in it.

Dr. Miller: Let's try it one more time. Pixelate it, please. Pixelate it all the way through, three-dimensionally. [Silence]

Deconstruct it three-dimensionally. [Silence]

Now re-image it again, and tell me what you've got.

Joan: Not much really.

Dr. Miller: It continues to go away?

Joan: Yeah.

Dr. Miller: That means it was still psychologically powered.

Joan: How is that?

Dr. Miller: The difference between an image and a memory, in the way I describe it, is that a memory is just a memory of something like 2+2=4. You have a memory of that. There is no power to it; it's just like there it is. An image is something that is psychologically powered. It can be powered by either pain or terror or powered by some kind of pleasure, like belonging.

That's what gives the image its vivid quality. You're still able to see parts of that, and my guess is, as long as you can do that, you're still powering it with your mind.

That's why I'm pretty relentless about making sure every little piece is gone. That way we know the image has been totally deconstructed and that all the feeling has been released from the image.

Joan: Yeah, brilliant. It's just that—I think it's interesting.

Dr. Miller: What we are getting to is that, that the feelings and those behaviors linked with those feelings will be disconnected.

Joan: Yes, but in terms of the image, as I go back to that pixelated deconstruction, keep going like that, what normally happens? What does this mean? It keeps shifting.

Dr. Miller: Actually, two different things happen. The first time we did it, you kind of went off into other memories about that memory. They weren't really the real thing. I let you do it to see what was going on because I wasn't quite sure.

After you got into a place that was clearly not important, having fun with the other children, you went back to the original memory, and it was still there—just less intense. That distance was normal. The first image we worked on had deconstructed to some degree, but it was still there.

This time we kept working on that same original memory until it blanked out. Now, sometimes good memories do show up, and I let that happen. But I always want to go back to that original memory and make sure there is nothing left of it at all because that's where the real feeling-state is.

Joan: I see. When you said about adding more food to that image, I know that will make it more, that wasn't the thing I said, was it? I was saying something else about family, but that will really enhance it, actually. Is that—this is partly the point? that it's still enhanceable?

Dr. Miller: Right now, when you think about it, if you add food into it, does that enhance it? Does that intensify it?

Joan: Yes. Definitely.

Dr. Miller: We need to work on it some more. Or else you will have to start eating a lot of salted peanuts.

Joan: Yes. [Laughs] I've now got all sort of other snacks on this table.

Dr. Miller: Make all the snacks on the table whatever you want and pixelate it. [Silence]

Joan: Interestingly, I immediately start thinking, "Oh, I don't want this to go."

Do people say this?

Dr. Miller: Yes, of course.

Joan: Great.

Dr. Miller: Now, see the food. There you are; there is the food.

Joan: Loads of it.

Dr. Miller: Loads of it. Pixelate it—you can have what you want—and deconstruct it.

Joan: Yeah.

Dr. Miller: Re-image it again, tell me what you've got. [Silence]

Joan: I can see it again.

Dr. Miller: Pixelate it, all the way through.

Joan: Yeah.

Dr. Miller: Deconstruct it.

Joan: Yeah.

Dr. Miller: Re-image it again, and tell me what you've got.

Joan: It's a pile of dust.

Dr. Miller: [Laughs] Is that it now? Is there nothing left?

Joan: I could get it back. This is my slight confusion here. I know I could, obviously—I could just have that image memory in my head. I could easily get it back.

Dr. Miller: Try it again; get it back again.

Joan: Okay. Yeah.

Dr. Miller: Pixelate it, and deconstruct it. [Silence]

Joan: Okay.

Dr. Miller: Re-image it again, and tell me what you've got. Really try now.

Joan: Really try.

Dr. Miller: Really try.

Joan: Okay. [Silence]

It's not as clear, I have to say.

Dr. Miller: Pixelate it. Really pixelate it now. [Silence]

Joan: Mm-hmm.

Dr. Miller: Deconstruct it. [Silence]

Joan: Mm-hmm.

Dr. Miller: Re-image it again, and tell me what you've got. Really re-image it again. Harder.

Joan: I can't do it as well now.

Dr. Miller: That's the point.

Joan: Yeah.

Dr. Miller: Pixelate it and deconstruct it. [Silence]

Joan: Mm-hmm.

Dr. Miller: Re-image it again, and tell me what you've got.

Joan: Nothing. I would have to really start all over again to get it now.

Dr. Miller: Let's clear the pixel-particles from your body.

Joan: Can I just ask you something? This is really interesting. Is this exactly the same protocol after the pain and terror?

Dr. Miller: Yes.

Joan: Yeah.

Dr. Miller: Not exactly. When you're doing a trauma, there's pain and terror. First you clear the pain or terror, then you do the image deconstruction protocol. When you're dealing with a feeling-state, there's no pain and terror.

Joan: Yeah.

Dr. Miller: There's only the feeling-state. There's only the image; so all you do is the image deconstruction protocol. Now, think about the particles of the image, and you're going to breathe into the center of your brain and see the particles of that old image go out your forehead.

Joan releases the particles of the image from her body. [Silence]

Dr. Miller: How do you feel?

Joan: Very relaxed. I've got extremely relaxed after that last week. I'm more relaxed now, just now.

Dr. Miller: When you think of having your drink tonight, how does that seem to you?

Joan: During that exercise, I kept thinking all sorts of different things like "Should I go and buy some peanuts?" You know what I mean? I'm sort of tempted.

Dr. Miller: How does that feel?

Joan: First up, I don't feel an urgent need to rush out and get them. I don't know what to think, actually.

Dr. Miller: That's the norm, by the way.

Joan: Is it?

ImTT Press, publisher

Dr. Miller: You have all these years of expectations of how you're going to feel. When people feel differently, it's like, Where did it go? What's going on here? It takes a while to understand the changes that have taken place.

Joan: Which is fine. That will be interesting.

Dr. Miller: I was dealing with somebody who had an anger issue, and we processed it through. I asked, "Well, how do you feel?" That person answered, "Well, I don't feel angry." And it took him a couple of weeks before he realized, "Wow, I'm really just not getting angry anymore."

You've got to go out in the world and test it and say, "How do I feel?"

Joan: Absolutely. Well, that will be very interesting. I'll email you to let you know. If I remember.

Dr. Miller: [Laughs]

Joan: If I even think about it.

Sarah's Paranoia

In this session, Sarah works through her issue of feeling that people are out to get her.

Sarah: I was thinking. I've been reflecting about the stuff that's going on in the office—some of the changes there and then thinking about my life in general—and what I noticed is that, when some change happens and I don't get an explanation for the change that makes sense to me and, like all human beings, then I make up my story to fill in the gaps, the stories that I make up are always scary stories. So I end up scaring the living daylights out of myself with the stories that I make up and tell myself. Then I go to anger and fear and all this sort of stuff. Then there's a touch of paranoia in there, where I think, "Man, they're just doing this to get to me," and all that.

But the good news is I'm able to catch that much sooner and realize, "No, no. Nobody has said anything about this. That's me putting this all together."

But if there's some way that we can interrupt this automatic response of going to telling myself the worst-case scenario—whatever it's going to be in that situation—and literally scaring the shit out of myself, that would be helpful.

Dr. Miller: So what's the worst-case scenario?

Sarah: It varies. But it usually ends up with some version of "They're out to get me"—whoever "they" are, and whatever "out to get me" means. Neither one of those is well defined, but "They're out to get me."

Dr. Miller: Okay. What that means is that you have an image of "They're out to get me" that gets put on the different current events.

So they're out to get you. And what's going to happen when they get you? What is the nightmare scenario?

Sarah: They're going to kill me.

Dr. Miller: Ah, well, there you go. How are they going to kill you? Does it matter?

Sarah: The most general one is I'm going to get just shot—somebody has a gun, and they're going to shoot me—or tortured in some way.

That's interesting. Now it explains why when—I love reading murder mysteries, but if there are scenes like this in the murder mystery, I skip them.

Dr. Miller: So the idea that they're going to kill you, is that painful or fearful?

Sarah: That's painful.

Dr. Miller: Painful?

Sarah: It's painful—because it's actually a fear. Well, it's both. It's a fear of a very painful death.

Dr. Miller: Okay. So it's painful. What color is the pain?

Sarah: It's a dark red that's almost black.

ImTT Press, publisher

Dr. Miller: Where is it located?

Sarah: Front of my head.

Dr. Miller: See that dark red as composed of tiny, little, dark red particles.

Sarah: Okay.

Dr. Miller: Breathe into those dark red particles, and breathe them directly away from your head. [Silence]

Sarah releases the dark red particles using the P/TRP.

Sarah: Okay.

Dr. Miller: So now does that feel as charged as it was?

Sarah: No. And my image, I realized, comes from an Edgar Allan Poe story that I read when I was very young called "The Tell-Tale Heart" and it's that heart that's running around free and the body—the person has been killed, but the heart's still beating.

That was a terrifying image to me when I was about fourth or fifth grade.

Dr. Miller: It's coming to get you.

Sarah: It's coming to get me [chuckles].

Dr. Miller: All right. So pixelate it.

Sarah: Okay.

Dr. Miller: Deconstruct it.

Sarah: Okay.

Dr. Miller: Re-image it again; tell me what you've got.

Sarah: A lot less vivid. Not full of blood anymore.

Dr. Miller: Good. Pixelate it again.

Sarah: Okay.

Dr. Miller: Deconstruct it.

Sarah: Okay.

Dr. Miller: Now re-image it again, and tell me what you've got.

Sarah: Now, what I'm seeing is like an open coffin in the ground and the heart is the only thing that's left there intact. Everything else has disintegrated.

Dr. Miller: Okay. Pixelate it again.

Sarah: Okay.

Dr. Miller: And deconstruct it.

Sarah: Okay.

Dr. Miller: Re-image it, and tell me what you've got.

Sarah: It's much fainter. It's not quite as vivid.

Dr. Miller: Pixelate it again.

Sarah: Okay.

Dr. Miller: And deconstruct it.

Sarah: Okay. I have a picture of a cemetery plot with the grass growing over it. It's a bright, sunny day.

Dr. Miller: Pixelate it.

Sarah: Okay.

Dr. Miller: Deconstruct it.

Sarah: It's turned into a picture of a cemetery where I have several family members buried. There are some tall trees that provide shade, and it's a nice, sunny day. It's a place that, when I'm back in my hometown area, I just love to stop and visit, for some reason. I feel closer to those relatives when I'm there, and it's just a very quiet, peaceful place, and I just like that.

Dr. Miller: Pixelate it.

Sarah: Okay.

Dr. Miller: And deconstruct it.

Sarah: It turned into an image of me walking along the shoreline by the ocean someplace.

Dr. Miller: What's your reaction to that?

Sarah: It's just calming. I love the sound of the waves and the water and the cool breeze. It just feels really nice.

Dr. Miller: Now, let's remove the particles of image from your body.

Sarah: Okay.

Dr. Miller: Breathe into the center of your brain and see the particles of the old image go out your forehead.

Sarah: Okay.

Sarah releases the image-particles from her body.

Dr. Miller: How do you feel?

Sarah: I think "free" is the word that comes to me. There's kind of a contentment, but there's also a sense of freedom.

There's also a sense of humor in realizing that that Edgar Allan Poe story has been affecting me for so long and I hadn't even really realized it.

Susan OCD Session #1

Susan's OCD behavior began when she was 7 years old. The behavior that bothered her the most at the beginning of therapy was her need to tap her forehead. In the first session, Susan is introduced to the ImTT concepts and techniques and the potential effects of this treatment.

Dr. Miller: The major side effect, really, of this is that, for a few days after the session, you can feel strange to yourself. Often people feel weird because something that has been with you for a long time is just gone. And you are wondering, "Where did it go?" [Laughs] And you're waiting for it to come back.

Susan: Okay.

Dr. Miller: After a few days, in a week or so, you get used to it. "Okay, life's different." That is actually one of the biggest side effects of this, you might say, or impacts of this. It's not really a side effect. It's actually what we're looking for.

Susan: Yeah.

Dr. Miller: This is something you have lived with for a very long time.

Susan: Correct.

Dr. Miller: Have you done previous therapy with this? The gold standard—what they normally use is exposure with response prevention. Have you done anything like that?

Susan: Yeah, I have.

Dr. Miller: What were the results of that?

Susan: I did a couple sessions down at Mayo Clinic back in 2011 and 2012. I worked with a psychologist up here. He mainly specializes in OCD.

Dr. Miller: Have you noticed, with either one of the therapies, any change in your behavior?

Susan: No. I still do my compulsions.

Dr. Miller: You've gotten some relief from the exposure therapy?

Susan: Yeah.

Dr. Miller: Well, this is not behavioral management therapy.

Susan: Yeah.

Dr. Miller: Okay. There is no exposure involved here. The basic idea is very simple. If you release the underlying terror that involves what would happen if don't do these thoughts or behaviors, you just stop doing the behaviors. I am never going to ask you to stop doing a behavior nor ask you to do exposure where you have to endure something. As a matter of fact, what you'll do is you'll tell me if the behavior has changed or not.

Susan: "Behavior" meaning compulsion.

Dr. Miller: Exactly. Name the behavior that you do that bothers you the most.

Susan: My compulsion—I tap my head and go like that with my eyes and then tap my head again.

Dr. Miller: What we want to do is see that you don't need to do that anymore.

Susan: Correct. That will be great.

Dr. Miller: How many times a day do you do that?

Susan: I can't guess, but I know I will lay in bed at night some nights—I have to do it more some nights than other nights—I can tell you I've probably done it like 15, 20 times, and then I am okay.

Dr. Miller: Let me ask you a general question here. Was your childhood difficult?

Susan: I'd say yes.

Dr. Miller: Okay. Was there physical abuse in your childhood?

Susan: No.

Dr. Miller: Okay.

Susan: But there was sexual abuse.

Dr. Miller: There was sexual abuse? Okay. Starting at what age?

Susan: When I was four years old.

Dr. Miller: Okay. Was it painful or pleasurable?

Susan: Painful.

Dr. Miller: Painful? Okay. I have noticed a pattern for people with OCD. They all seem to have some kind of terrifying experience in their childhood.

Susan: Yes.

Dr. Miller: So far I haven't found an exception to this. The idea is that the behaviors that you do—the forehead tapping, whatever they are, all of them—are what we call the "magical behaviors" of a child. "If I don't step on the cracks, I'm safe."

Susan: Right.

Dr. Miller: It's a child-like kind of thinking. Right?

Susan: Yes.

Dr. Miller: We're just going to work on the underlying terror. Now, we might have to go back to your childhood and process something in regards to that.

Susan: Okay.

Dr. Miller: What happens is that you have this underlying terror that just comes out in different ways.

Susan: Mm-hmm.

Dr. Miller: We would just have to follow that terror, where it goes, and release it.

Susan: Okay. Is it like a real, living experience?

Dr. Miller: No. As matter of fact, that was going to be my next statement. When I ask you to "feel" something, I don't want you to get into it.

Susan: Okay.

Dr. Miller: What I want you to do is go, "Oh, yes, it's there." That's all. "Oh, yes, I see it."

Susan: Yes.

Dr. Miller: Right. If I say, "What's the terror?" I don't want you to feel the terror. I want you to say to yourself, "Oh, yeah, there it is. I see it's here." Then I will ask you "What's the color of the terror?"

Susan: Okay.

Dr. Miller: Once I've asked you what the color is, I don't want you to think of anything else except the color, from that point on.

Susan: Okay.

Dr. Miller: I don't want you to think of the event. I don't want you to feel the terror. I just want you to focus on the color. That's the only thing we're going to be working on.

Susan: Okay.

Dr. Miller: At the end of releasing all the colors, I'm going to ask you to look at the event again and tell me what you feel.

Susan: Okay.

Dr. Miller: But I don't want you to get into the feelings.

Susan: Okay.

Dr. Miller: Really, it makes it more difficult if you get into the feelings. I don't want you to get into the feelings. We're going to release the terror without you ever getting into it.

Susan: Okay.

Dr. Miller: Okay? It's so much easier than anything you have done before. Okay?

Susan: Yeah.

Dr. Miller: How do you feel right now?

Susan: Good. It would be just the first color that comes into your head?

Dr. Miller: Yes.

Susan: Okay. It seems complicated, but the more you're explaining to me, the more natural it seems.

Dr. Miller: Yes. You know something? It's going to be really simple.

Susan: Okay.

Dr. Miller: Let's get started.

Susan: Okay.

Dr. Miller: Do you want to start with that tapping?

Susan: Okay.

Dr. Miller: Is that the one that bothers you the most?

Susan: Yes.

Dr. Miller: When you think about not doing it, the anxiety starts to come up, right?

Susan: Yes.

Dr. Miller: And so there is a dread that something bad might happen, right?

Susan: Yes.

Dr. Miller: Give me an image of what bad thing is going to happen. And it doesn't have to be realistic, by the way. It could be an asteroid is going to hit the earth and wipe everything out. It could be you're going to get clobbered or somebody's going to kill you. Whatever it is, I want an image. What does that image look like if you don't do it.

Susan: That I will die.

Dr. Miller: All right. If we do have an image of you dying, what does that look like?

Susan: Just like lying on the floor.

Dr. Miller: And you are just dying?

Susan: I think it's like me—not dying, but me having a meltdown and crying and stuff.

Dr. Miller: It feels like you're dying. It must be pretty intense, that meltdown, right?

Susan: Right.

Dr. Miller: You're just falling apart, the whole world is falling apart. Is that what it feels like to you?

Susan: Yeah.

Dr. Miller: When you think of that meltdown, is that terrifying to you that something could happen?

Susan: Yes.

Dr. Miller: Okay. What color is it?

Susan: Yellow, I would say.

Dr. Miller: Where do you see the yellow in your body?

Susan: Like my skin color.

Dr. Miller: Let's start with you telling me where is the most intense part of your skin, the most yellowish part of the skin. Where would this be?

Susan: My face.

Dr. Miller: Your face. Okay. What I want you to do is now see the yellow in the skin as being composed of tiny, tiny, little yellow particles. Okay?

Susan: Okay.

Dr. Miller: You can close your eyes and visualize this now, whatever it takes to really focus. I am going to take you through a guided visualization/breathing technique. We are going to release the yellow. See the yellow in the skin composed of tiny, tiny, little yellow particles. Just nod your head when you get it. You got it? Okay. Breathe into those yellow particles, and breathe them directly away from your face.

Susan: Okay.

Dr. Miller: Now, when you think of that image of you dying, lying on the floor, melting, does it seem as charged as it did?

Susan: No.

Dr. Miller: Now, what we are going to do is deconstruct that image. Okay? What I want you to do is close your eyes. I want you to see that image as being composed of tiny, tiny, little particles. When you have that whole image composed of tiny, little particles like pixels on a TV screen, just nod your head.

Susan: Okay.

Dr. Miller: Now let all the pixel-particles fall apart and be absorbed into the earth. They are just falling to the floor, falling deep into the earth, and being absorbed into the earth.

Susan: Okay.

Dr. Miller: Now re-image it again and tell me what you have. Is it as intense as it was? Is it starting to blur? What do you have?

Susan: No. It's more clear.

Dr. Miller: Okay. See it being composed of tiny, little particles.

Susan: Okay.

Dr. Miller: Drop them down into the earth. Let the earth absorb the particles. Okay?

Susan: Yeah.

Dr. Miller: Re-image it again, and tell me what you've got.

Susan: I picture the first thought, when I saw yellow, was like me in one of our bathrooms at home, on the floor crying. But then, when I got the last image, it was like me in my room on my floor crying.

Dr. Miller: Okay.

Susan: It's more clear, like it's going to be okay.

Dr. Miller: Good. See that image as being composed of tiny, little particles again.

Susan: Okay.

Dr. Miller: Drop them. Let them be absorbed into the earth. All the particles of the image fall apart, they drain into the earth, and the earth takes them away, as you let them go.

Susan: Okay.

Dr. Miller: Re-image it again, and tell me what you've got.

Susan: Just me in my room on the floor. That's all.

Dr. Miller: Are you crying now?

Susan: No.

Dr. Miller: Re-image it again. See it being composed of tiny, little particles.

Susan: All right.

Dr. Miller: Drop all the particles to the floor. Let them be absorbed into the earth.

Susan: Okay.

Dr. Miller: Okay. Re-image it again and tell me what you have.

Susan: My floor being really clean.

                          ImTT Press, publisher

Dr. Miller: [Laughs] Okay. What does that mean to you?

Susan: There is no dog hair on the floor.

Dr. Miller: Okay. That's good?

Susan: Yes, it's good.

Dr. Miller: Re-image it again. See it as being composed of tiny, little particles. Drop them all to the ground. Let them be absorbed into the earth.

Susan: Okay.

Dr. Miller: Re-image it again and tell me what you've got.

Susan: Just me up, getting ready.

Dr. Miller: Getting ready for what?

Susan: To go out, like after.

Dr. Miller: Does that feel good?

Susan: Yeah. Like, I'm picking myself up and like getting myself to feel better.

Dr. Miller: Re-image it again and see it as being composed of tiny little particles.

Susan: Okay.

Dr. Miller: Re-image it again and tell me what you've got now.

Susan: Just a picture of my room—nothing really.

Dr. Miller: Does the room have a good feeling to it? a bad feeling to it? a neutral feeling to it?

Susan: Neutral, but more of a good feeling.

Dr. Miller: You're happy there in this image?

Susan: Yeah.

Dr. Miller: Now we're going to go through the body, as we did before, but instead of releasing terror, we're going to release the particles of the image from your body. Okay?

Breathe into the center of your brain and visualize the particles of the image going out through your forehead.

Susan: Okay.

The particles of the image are released from the body.

Dr. Miller: How do you feel?

Susan: Good, pretty good.

Dr. Miller: When you think of that image, what is your reaction to that image now?

Susan: It's gone.

Dr. Miller: That's good.

Susan: Yeah.

Dr. Miller: Now, when you think about not performing your forehead taps, how does that feel to you now?

Susan: Fine. I don't have a desire to do it as of right now, but...

       ImTT Press, publisher

Dr. Miller: If you normally think about it, would you normally have a desire to do it?

Susan: Yes.

Dr. Miller: Maybe something has changed?

Susan: Okay.

Dr. Miller: Now, what you may notice is that you may feel strange to yourself. How is it going to feel not to do this?

Susan: Weird.

Dr. Miller: You are used to doing it when you go to sleep at night, right? Right now, what I want you to do is think about going to sleep tonight. Just let your mind focus on going to bed. You normally do it while you're in bed? Just imagine that you're in bed right now. Just be there as if you're in bed right now. You don't try to resist anything. Just focus on being in bed right now.

The CPP is done on the times Susan usually taps her forehead.

Susan: Okay.

Dr. Miller: How does that feel to you?

Susan: Good.

Dr. Miller: Next week, when we do it, we'll see where we're at. Probably this image that we just did won't be there; it will be gone.

Susan: Yeah.

Dr. Miller: If you're still tapping your forehead, you'll probably be doing it less intensely.

Susan: Okay.

Dr. Miller: Maybe there's less frequency; maybe the urges are just less. Then we'll go to the next image.

Susan: Okay.

Dr. Miller: We just have to work through until all the images related to these behaviors are gone.

Susan: Okay.

Dr. Miller: That wasn't very hard, was it?

Susan: No. It was really easy.

Dr. Miller: That's what we'll be doing pretty much every time.

Susan: Okay.

Dr. Miller: I just don't want to do too much change at any one time.

Susan: That makes sense. Yeah, I agree.

Dr. Miller: You can see this is nothing like anything you've ever done before.

Susan: No.

Dr. Miller: And yet that image is gone, isn't it?

Susan: Okay. It's just like it leaves, like an atomic bomb.

Dr. Miller: What's that?

Susan: Like atomic bombs, like them just like going away.

Dr. Miller: Yeah. Okay. We will go through the images as long as you still have them causing your behaviors.

Susan: Okay.

Dr. Miller: I can't tell you how many of them are there because I don't have a clue. Neither do you. [Laughs]

Susan: No.

Dr. Miller: What we do is we clear out one after another. It depends on how your mind is set up. Sometimes we clear out an image, and five out of nine behaviors just go away. The other four behaviors were related to two other images that we had to process.

But I don't know how you've set this up. You could have this one tapping behavior related to three images or more.

Susan: Four. It could be four; it could be ten.

Dr. Miller: We'll find out how it works, how your mind set it up, as we go along; and we'll just process each one every week until it's all gone.

Susan: All right. That's good, good with me.

Dr. Miller: All right.

Susan: I'm eager to see what happens and how it goes.

Dr. Miller: Okay.

Susan: Especially with the unwanted thoughts.

Dr. Miller: Yeah, we'll do that next week.

ImTT Press, publisher

Susan OCD Session #2

In the first session, Susan processed the image linked with tapping her head. Since that session, she reported that the intensity of her tapping had decreased. In addition, Susan stated that the underlying dynamic of why she had to tap her head had become clearer to her.

The second session focused on releasing the feeling of shame that triggered the shameful thoughts that triggered her tapping behavior. The treatment concept is that the feelings of shame from childhood create thoughts that justify the feelings. Then Susan performs the OCD behavior of tapping her forehead to make the thoughts go away. By releasing the shame, Susan will no longer feel the need to perform the tapping behavior.

While Susan is aware of her feelings of shame in regards to her current thoughts, she is unaware of where those feelings may have originated. The discussion about shame and her childhood was necessary in order make the process understandable to her. When a person understands the process, the changes that occur are less frightening.

Even though Susan wants to change her tapping behavior, she has lived with it so long that it's a familiar difficulty. If this behavior is suddenly changed, she needs to understand why it has changed and that the change is something that she is causing rather than something that is just happening to her.

Dr. Miller: Do you remember what we did last week?

Susan: Mm-hmm.

Dr. Miller: What was the image we worked on exactly?

Susan: It was the compulsion, like when I tap my head.

Dr. Miller: And if you didn't do it, you would lie down and die. Something like that, right?

Susan: Right.

Dr. Miller: How was that behavior this week?

Susan: It's good.

Dr. Miller: What does that mean?

Susan: I am doing it less, but I am still doing it. But over this week of time, I've realized why I do the actual compulsion.

Dr. Miller: Why is that?

Susan: If I think of an unwanted thought, I feel like I have to do the compulsion because, if I don't do the compulsion, I am going to think that. So if I get a thought like an unwanted thought in my head, I feel like, if I don't do my compulsion, I think that. Therefore, I have to do my compulsion and make it pure and cleanse it.

Dr. Miller: Good. Do you notice that you are doing it less, or is it less intense or less frequent or—what is it?

Susan: Less intense.

Dr. Miller: Same frequency?

Susan: Yeah. Well, I would say the frequency has gone down a little bit.

Dr. Miller: But the urgency is less?

Susan: Yeah.

Dr. Miller: All right. Good. What that means is that what we did last week helped.

Susan: Yeah.

Dr. Miller: Let's focus on those unwanted thoughts today. Okay?

Susan: Okay.

Dr. Miller: Give me an example of a thought you don't want to think.

Susan: Like if I molested a child.

Dr. Miller: So your thought is, "I molested a child," right?

Susan: Yes.

Dr. Miller: Or is it fear that you are going to molest a child? What exactly is the thought?

Susan: The thought is that "I've molested" so-and-so—like somebody in the nursery at church or somebody that was in my childhood—and that convinces me that I did that—or something.

Dr. Miller: Is the tapping behavior a form of confession, or is it, "This will stop me from thinking the thought"?

Susan: "This will stop me from thinking the thought."

Dr. Miller: Okay. Does it work?

Susan: It makes the thought go away for a short period of time.

Dr. Miller: Got it. When you think that thought, are you afraid that you did it?

Susan: Yes.

Dr. Miller: These intrusive thoughts are all about something horrible that you did, right?

Susan: Correct.

Dr. Miller: Now we need to find the image that we need to work on. You are coming up with the most shameful possible thoughts you could imagine, right?

Susan: Right.

Dr. Miller: There is nothing more shameful than the idea that you've molested a child, right?

Susan: Correct.

Dr. Miller: And the other thoughts, whatever they are, they're going to be equally shameful. Maybe even moreso. There is just this awful, awful shame, right?

Susan: Right.

Dr. Miller: What's happening is something very simple. You have this super, super, super intense feeling of shame. And what you do is you stick content on it.

ImTT Press, publisher

In other words, the feeling of shame is first. Then your mind wonders, "Well, what could I have done to feel this shame?" The answer of "Oh, I molested a child." Oh, I did this, oh, I did that, or "I'm going to kill" this person. Whatever it is, you're sticking thoughts on it as an adult of a reason why you would feel shame. In other words, shame gives rise to the thought, not the other way around.

You know, you think you did something and, therefore, you should feel shame, right?

Susan: Right.

Dr. Miller: That's not the way it works. You feel shame first and then you make up a thought to go with it. So the problem is your feeling of shame, not the thought.

Susan: Okay.

Dr. Miller: Does that make any sense?

Susan: Yeah.

Dr. Miller: If we eliminate the shame, you'll stop thinking those thoughts.

Susan: Okay.

Dr. Miller: Does that make sense?

Susan: Yeah, but then what am I feeling shameful about?

Dr. Miller: What does a three-year-old feel shameful about? What does a five-year-old feel shameful about?

Let me ask, are all the thoughts sexual, or are they just a variety of things?

Susan: Sexual, yeah.

Dr. Miller: Sexual. Okay. Look, I don't know what you originally felt shame about, but the original problem doesn't even have to be sexual.

Susan: Okay.

Dr. Miller: This has been going on for a long time, hasn't it?

Susan: Yeah.

Dr. Miller: Somewhere in your past, something you did and the interaction you had— probably with your mother or father maybe—I don't know—I'm not talking about abuse even. Maybe you were touching yourself and they said, "Don't do that!" in a shaming way.

Susan: Okay.

Dr. Miller: It could have been anything to which their response was intense and shaming to you as a child.

Susan: Okay.

Dr. Miller: Okay, think about what does a five-year-old feel shame about?

Susan: Yeah.

Dr. Miller: Okay.

Susan: It doesn't necessarily have to be my parents. It could be somebody else?

Dr. Miller: You're right. It could have been anybody. It could have been a teacher.

Susan: All right.

Dr. Miller: It's probably an adult, most likely, as opposed to another child.

Susan: Could it be because what happened when I was a little girl when I was four years old, like how I was sexually abused?

Dr. Miller: Yes. Okay. What kind of abuse was it?

Susan: It was he exposed himself to me.

Dr. Miller: Yeah, exactly.

Susan: Okay.

Dr. Miller: Okay. Now, my question would be, at that point, when did you actually feel shame about that? Did you tell your parents what happened?

Susan: Yeah, when I was sitting at the kitchen dinner table one night.

Dr. Miller: How old were you then? Was that right after that?

Susan: Yeah, it was the same age when that happened, four.

Dr. Miller: What were your parents' responses?

Susan: They were in complete shock.

Dr. Miller: Okay. That's probably when the shame occurred—their response to what happened. When it happened to you, what was your actual response?

Susan: I don't know. I think I was just a little girl trying to take a nap, you know, and this happened to me...

Dr. Miller: Right. But when you say it "happened" to you, when he exposed himself to you, can you remember what your response was?

Susan: No. But I knew it wasn't right. You know what I mean?

Dr. Miller: Right. But my guess is that, at four years old, your response might have been that it isn't right but that it's not that big of a deal. It became a big deal when your parents reacted so intensely.

Susan: Yeah.

Dr. Miller: That's when the shame really occurred.

Susan: Okay.

Dr. Miller: Does that make sense?

Susan: Yeah.

Dr. Miller: Because what does a four-year-old little girl know of what she's looking at?

Susan: Yeah.

Dr. Miller: Do you see what I'm saying? Yes, it's not right, but it's not that big of a deal. But your parents' responses made it a big deal.

Susan: Right, right.

Dr. Miller: When we're four years old, our whole idea of whether what we do is right or wrong and what we feel about ourselves depends entirely upon our parents' reactions. If you spill milk and your parent says, "Eh, clean it up, no big deal," there is no sense of shame. If your parent says, "You stupid kid. Can't you do anything right?" all of a sudden, it's shaming.

Susan: I didn't know how big a deal it was. My dad makes big deals out of little things. For instance, the night before Christmas Eve, my mom was making the egg bake for the morning and she spilled on the floor. How he reacted—my mom was like, "That's not normal, Will." He shouted at her, "You're nuts" and stuff.

Dr. Miller: So he went into a rage?

Susan: He didn't go into a rage. But he can make it a big deal when it's not a big deal.

Dr. Miller: Okay. But when he makes a big deal of it, what does that mean? He's very demeaning? He's contemptuous? He's hostile?

Susan: He said it in a louder voice. What is it like? It could be pretty scary and shaming.

Dr. Miller: Okay. It is very likely about your father. It could be that the sexual thing did originate from that event when you were four years old and that is why your thoughts contain that content. But the sense of shame—it sounds like your father has done a lot of shaming of you. Does that make sense?

Susan: Yeah. But do I blame him for that? Or maybe he didn't even know better. Maybe that's just the way he reacts to things.

Dr. Miller: You know something? This isn't about blame. It's about what he did and your reaction to what he did.

Susan: Okay.

Dr. Miller: This isn't about blame. Did he do it right? He did it wrong. He did it very wrong. I can't excuse that. It's not about excuse. It's about what he did and your reaction to feel shame. So then, because you have this intense feeling of shame, you then have to find some content to stick to it—namely, sexual content. So you start thinking of something, and your response to that is to tap your head to try and stop the thoughts.

Susan: Yeah. And I think that you should know, like when I...you know Penn State, right?

Dr. Miller: Sure.

Susan: Back in 2011, that fall, when the football coach molested all those kids, that's when all the sexual thoughts started and had to do with kids and stuff. So when that big Penn State scandal came out, it was like a big thing for my OCD.

Dr. Miller: Okay. Were you doing the tapping for other thoughts before then?

Susan: Yes.

Dr. Miller: So you're finding content to stick on the feeling of shame.

Susan: Yeah.

Dr. Miller: When the Penn State stuff came along, your mind found another area of content to put on the underlying feeling of shame.

Your father has very clearly shamed you very intensely. Okay?

Susan: Yeah.

Dr. Miller: We've got to be honest here, right? Your father's reactions—it's very easy to shame a child. For example, "You spilled the milk, and you're an awful, awful child. You're just a terrible person, and you'll never do anything good, and you're clumsy, and you're awful, and you're stupid." You can shame a child over nothing.

Susan: Yeah. But my dad is a good person. My dad is hardworking and stuff.

Dr. Miller: You clearly want to excuse your father. I'm not saying you don't love him. He may be a good person, and he also shamed you. These things don't come out of the blue. You don't have OCD out of the blue. This isn't something that you were born with.

Susan: This wasn't? Evironment?

Dr. Miller: This was developed psychologically. Environment, absolutely.

Susan: Okay.

Dr. Miller: Somebody with a different background might pick another way of dealing with it. But this isn't about excusing your father or blaming him, but he is responsible for that environment. He could be hardworking and have a lot of good intent, but his psychological problems came out in your childhood. And what he did was wrong.

When I say that, how does that make you feel?

Susan: I don't know. It's kind of harsh.

Dr. Miller: What he did to you was pretty harsh. Think about it. You have all those memories of him reacting out of control or just that kind of intensity. It doesn't take a super rage. You know, children are very attuned to their parents. If a parent has that kind of demeaning attitude towards their child, their child will pick it up.

Susan: Are you saying my OCD must have come from my dad, then?

Dr. Miller: Is it the only place? I don't know. All I do know is that what we're dealing with right now, this part where you're tapping your head and the shame, that's at least one very good place where it came from. What we'll have to do is clear that up, and then we will see where we go next. Okay?

See, when you're asking if all of it comes from your father, I have no idea. What I am saying is that this dynamic absolutely is related to your father because he is the one who shamed you.

Now, I'm not saying that somebody else didn't shame you too. Your mother was there too. Maybe there were other people as well. I don't know. But this dynamic is very clearly linked with your father.

Susan: Okay.

Dr. Miller: What we want to do is clear up the shame so that you don't need to stick content on it.

Susan: Okay.

Dr. Miller: Do you understand what I mean by that?

Susan: Yeah.

Dr. Miller: What happens is the mind tries to make it reasonable. When you feel something, the mind tries to make it reasonable. For example, "I feel all this shame; so I must have done something horrible to feel all this shame about. So I must have molested a child."

You come up with ideas. "What is the most shaming thing I could think of?" And that will change as you go through life.

It's kind of like with the Penn State thing. You found something else that everybody says is horrible, terrible, shameful, and it is. So you say, "Okay, that's what I feel. I feel the shame."

Susan: Yeah.

Dr. Miller: Your mind says, "I must have done that," "I must have done this."

Susan: Mm-hmm.

Dr. Miller: We all know it's nonsense, but the feelings are very powerful. The shame feelings are very, very powerful. That's why you have these thoughts that you did this.

Susan: Okay.

Dr. Miller: Am I making sense?

Susan: Yeah.

Dr. Miller: It's kind of hard to deal with it, huh?

Susan: I just never thought that. This is something new.

Dr. Miller: Well, it would be. That's why you still have your OCD.

Susan: Yeah.

Dr. Miller: [Laughs] Okay. So do you feel ready to clear it up?

Susan: Sure.

Dr. Miller: What I want you to do is give me an image that reflects shame. It's not going be realistic, but don't worry about it. Think of the most shameful thing you could possibly have done. Just make it up. It's just going be a nightmare shame. That's all it is.

Susan: That I molested a child. I mean it comes back to my head, molesting a child.

Dr. Miller: Okay, we will use that image. All right. Underlying shame is either pain or terror. Let me tell you where the terror comes from. Shame says, "I'm bad," right? "I'm a really bad person."

Susan: Yeah. Or I'm a horrible sexual person.

Dr. Miller: "Horrible sexual person," okay. If you are that horrible sexual person, then you don't really belong to the group, do you? You're an outcast. Does that make sense?

Susan: Yes. I don't belong to what group? My friends?

Dr. Miller: Any group. Think about it in tribal terms. You wouldn't belong to the tribe. If you're that awful of a person, do you even belong in a tribe? Are they going to cast you out?

Susan: They would cast, yeah.

Dr. Miller: Yeah. If you're cast out, that means you're abandoned, doesn't it?

Susan: Yeah.

Dr. Miller: If you're abandoned in a tribe and you're cast out from the tribe, what's going to happen to you?

Susan: You're going to be lonely.

Dr. Miller: You're going to be more than lonely. How are you going to survive?

Susan: You won't because you won't have anyone there for you.

Dr. Miller: Precisely my point. Underlying shame is a terror of dying.

Susan: Mm-hmm.

　　　　　　　　　　　　　　ImTT Press, publisher

Dr. Miller: What we're going to do is release the terror of dying from the shame.

Susan: Okay. What's the "dying" part?

Dr. Miller: If you're outcast and you can't survive, you'll die.

Susan: Yeah. That makes sense.

Dr. Miller: If you're abandoned by the tribe and you're outcast—whether, as a baby, you're placed on a rock and everybody leaves you or whether you're an adult and you have to go out and nobody is there to help you at all—you're going to die, right?

Susan: Mm-hmm.

Dr. Miller: Let me explain a little bit more about this kind of shame and what powers shame. The purpose of the feelings of guilt and shame is to reestablish a relationship.

Have you ever seen a dog who is in shame?

Susan: Yeah, that gets into like the garbage.

Dr. Miller: They put their head down.

Susan: Yeah.

Dr. Miller: "I am bad." The purpose of that is to say, "Yes, I'm bad, but please don't kick me out of the group."

Susan: Yeah.

Dr. Miller: "Yes, I'll accept my low status." You notice they have their head low, right?

Susan: Right.

Dr. Miller: "I'll accept my low status. Just don't kick me out so that I don't die."

Susan: Okay.

Dr. Miller: The reason why we feel shame is to tell the other people in the group, "Don't kick me out so I'll die."

If you weren't worried about dying, you wouldn't feel shame. Does that make sense?

Susan: If you weren't worried about dying, you're not worried about shame.

Dr. Miller: You just won't feel shame. The feeling just won't be there.

Susan: Right.

Dr. Miller: The only reason you feel shame is to allow you to reestablish your place in the group. If you're not worried about being in the group, you just don't feel shame.

Susan: Okay.

Dr. Miller: I know this sounds a little weird, doesn't it?

Susan: Yeah, kind of.

Dr. Miller: When we release the terror underlying the shame, the shame just goes away.

Susan: Just goes away?

Dr. Miller: Just goes away.

Susan: Okay.

Dr. Miller: Once the terror is gone, your mind just won't feel shame because it doesn't need to. You are no longer afraid of being kicked out of the group; so there's no reason to feel shame.

Susan: Okay.

Dr. Miller: It just goes away. That's why what we are going to do is release the terror underlying the shame.

Susan: Okay.

Dr. Miller: Just like we did last week when we did the other.

Susan: Okay.

Dr. Miller: We're going to do the same technique, just as easy as we did last week. Okay?

Susan: Okay.

Dr. Miller: It's not going be any more difficult than what we did.

Susan: Okay.

Dr. Miller: Okay? Again, just to reemphasize, once we start focusing on the color, forget everything else. Don't think about the terror, don't think about the event, don't think about the shame, don't think about anything—just the color once we identify it. Okay?

Susan: Okay.

Dr. Miller: All right. Start off with the image of you molesting a child. Just note the shame. I don't want you to really get into it very much, just very lightly. There is a shame about it, right?

Susan: Okay.

Dr. Miller: What color is the terror underlying the shame?

Susan: Blue.

Dr. Miller: Where is it located on your body?

Susan: My pelvis.

Dr. Miller: Now, we're just going to focus on the blue. That's it, right? See the blue as composed of tiny little particles. Just tell me when you've got it.

Susan: All right.

Dr. Miller: Breathe into these tiny little blue particles and see them going directly away from your pelvis, right away from your body.

Susan releases the terror with the P/TRP.

Dr. Miller: Okay. Now, when you think of that image, does it feel as charged as it was?

Susan: No.

Dr. Miller: What's your reaction now?

Susan: I'm more calm.

Dr. Miller: Okay. Now we're going to deconstruct the image just like we did last time.

Susan: All right.

Dr. Miller: See the image as being composed of tiny, tiny particles just like pixels in a TV screen.

Susan: Okay.

Dr. Miller: Drop all those pixel-particles to the ground and let them be absorbed into the earth.

Susan: Okay.

Dr. Miller: Re-image it again and tell me what you've got. Is it as intense as it was? Is it starting to fall apart, fade, or is it just as intense as it was?

Susan: It fades.

Dr. Miller: Okay. See the image that you have left as being composed of tiny, tiny little pixel-particles?

Susan: Okay.

Dr. Miller: Drop all the particles to the ground.

Susan: Okay.

Dr. Miller: Re-image it again and tell me what you've got.

Susan: It faded some more.

Dr. Miller: All right. So you've composed the tiny, tiny little pixel particles.

Susan: All right.

Dr. Miller: Then drop them all to the ground.

Susan: Okay.

Dr. Miller: Re-image it again and tell me what you've got.

Susan: It's still there, but it's unclear.

Dr. Miller: Okay. See even that composed of tiny little pixel-particles.

Susan: Okay.

Dr. Miller: Then drop them to the ground.

Susan: All right.

Dr. Miller: Re-image it again and tell me what you've got.

Susan: It's unclear.

Dr. Miller: Okay. Is there anything left of it?

Susan: Just like a little bit.

Dr. Miller: Okay. We're still not finished then. I know this is hard work.

Susan: Yeah.

Dr. Miller: See it as being composed of tiny, little pixel-particles.

Susan: Mm-hmm.

Dr. Miller: Drop them to the ground.

Susan: Okay.

Dr. Miller: Re-image it and tell me what you've got.

Susan: It's not in my head.

Dr. Miller: Is there no image left?

Susan: Like, I don't want to picture it. Yeah.

Dr. Miller: Well, but if you try to picture it, what do you get?

Susan: It's still not as in detail or clear or stuff like that.

Dr. Miller: Is there still some image left if you try to picture it?

Susan: Just a little bit.

Dr. Miller: Okay, then we're not quite finished. We want to really clear this up. Okay?

Susan: Okay.

Dr. Miller: See it composed of tiny, little pixel-particles again, and this time, instead of dropping the pixel-particles, take a hammer to it and just shatter the whole thing.
Then drop all the shards to the ground.

Susan: Okay.

Dr. Miller: Re-image it again and tell me what you've got.

Susan: It's gone.

Dr. Miller: Good. Okay. Now, we're going to finish this off by clearing out the pixel-particles of the image from your body.

Susan: Okay.

Susan releases the particles of the image from her body.

Dr. Miller: Okay. How do you feel?

Susan: Well.

Dr. Miller: When you think of that image, what's your reaction?

Susan: It's just an image.

Dr. Miller: Okay. Now, what I want you to do right now is think of several of the thoughts that you don't want to think that always make you tap your head. Just think and tell me what your reaction is.

Susan: Susan nods.

Dr. Miller: Okay. What I want you to do is, actually, take your time right now, and go through each thought for about 10 seconds and let yourself think about each negative thought for about 10 seconds, just focus on it, and then move to another thought. Don't try to stop it. Don't do anything. Just think the thought for about 10 seconds. Okay?

Susan: Okay.

Dr. Miller: Okay. What was your reaction to those thoughts now?

Susan: I didn't want to think them, but I just thought them and then let them go in 10 seconds.

Dr. Miller: Did it seem to be intense for about the first couple seconds and then the energy charge just went away?

                                                                 ImTT Press, publisher

Susan: Yes.

Dr. Miller: How does this feel now?

Susan: All right. I did get a lot done.

Susan OCD Session # 3

Dr. Miller: Just to re-evaluate, the tapping—is it the same level that it was last week?

Susan: I think it's less.

Dr. Miller: Even less than last week?

Susan: Yeah.

Dr. Miller: What percentage would you say it's down now?

Susan: That's hard to put, but I was in the car with my mother today, and she said, "Yeah, you are not doing, as much as last week, the reassurance like you were, the OCD thoughts—so it's working.

Dr. Miller: That's interesting. Those areas that we worked on two weeks ago are continuing to improve even though we didn't actually do therapy last week.

Susan: Yeah.

Dr. Miller: That's interesting. There are two different behavior changes. You're tapping less, and you're confessing less.

Susan: Yeah.

Dr. Miller: Okay.

Susan: Maybe not fixating on it super long, like I used to.

Dr. Miller: Tell me more about that. What do you mean by "fixating"?

Susan: I got a thought yesterday, but it wasn't an intense thought; so I just let it go.

Dr. Miller: You didn't need to do any of your OCD behavior to deal with it?

Susan: I did tell my mom, but it wasn't as intense as it used to be in the past.

Dr. Miller: When you say that you did tell your mother, in the past would you have told your mother a lot, many times?

Susan: Yeah, and asked for reassurance.

Dr. Miller: And how long would that go on for?

Susan: A minute.

Dr. Miller: Yesterday, when you did it with your mother, how long did it go on for?

Susan: Probably—I just told her, and I asked her if that was OCD, and that was the end of it.

Dr. Miller: Seconds, then.

Susan: But I moved on.

Dr. Miller: Well, this is good. What do you think about it?

Susan: I think it's good.

Dr. Miller: All right. Do you remember the phrase you used last time?

Susan: "I did something wrong."

Dr. Miller: "I did something wrong." Okay, good.

Right. So we want to work on your current stuff. What we want to work on is that feeling that you did something wrong. Now come up with an image of what you did wrong.

Susan: Oh.

Dr. Miller: Make it really, really wrong. [Laughs]

Susan: Okay. I am trying to think. Can it be the same one as we did last time?

Dr. Miller: Sure.

Susan: Or should it be something else?

Dr. Miller: No. I want it to epitomize what you did wrong. It could be totally made up.

Susan: It could be, like, a child, not me?

Dr. Miller: Yeah, like the worst of the worst, the absolute worst thing that you could do wrong? It doesn't have to be a real thing or anything you've done. So let your imagination think up something.

Susan: That's scary. [Laughs]

Dr. Miller: Yeah, but that's what in your head.

Susan: Yeah.

Dr. Miller: What we are processing is not what's real. None of this is ever real.

Susan: Right.

Dr. Miller: It's just in your head. That's what we are doing. It is working because we are clearing out your images you've imagined, what you've created out of your imagination.

Susan: I guess it would be doing something like doing oral sex with a child.

Dr. Miller: A child that you know?

Susan: Yeah, like a known child.

Dr. Miller: Somebody you know, in other words.

Susan: Can we do two rounds today?

Dr. Miller: Sure, if you want to. Absolutely.

Susan: The next one would be about my dog.

Dr. Miller: We'll see what we need to do afterwards. Those are content of your fear. Those are things you just stick in there. You may only need one round. Remember what we are doing. The feeling you have that you've done something wrong is the problem, not the made-up content. You can have five different images of doing something wrong, and the content of the images doesn't count. The only thing that really counts is the feeling that you've done something wrong.

Susan: Okay.

Dr. Miller: What may happen is that you don't even need to do any other one once we clear the first one.

Susan: Okay.

Dr. Miller: We'll see. If you've done something so awfully wrong, doesn't that mean you're a really horrible person?

Susan: Yeah, a horrible sexual person.

Dr. Miller: A horrible sexual person. If you're a horrible sexual person, nobody is going want you around, are they?

Susan: Right.

Dr. Miller: You're going to be an outcast, right?

Susan: Yeah. How could I do that?

Dr. Miller: What word would you use? abandoned? outcast? What image? If you're doing that, what is the image of yourself? What's going to happen?

Susan: People will ostracize me.

Dr. Miller: People are going to ostracize you. Nobody's going to ever want to have anything to do with you, right?

Susan: Right.

Dr. Miller: That sounds pretty terrifying. Is that terrifying to you?

Susan: Yeah.

Dr. Miller: What we are going to do is we are going to clear out the terror. What does being ostracized look like? Are you out in a desert and you're all alone? Give me an image of what it looks like to be ostracized.

Susan: Like me being in jail or prison.

Dr. Miller: That's what's going to happen. The image that you have whenever you think of these thoughts is you're going to be put in prison. And it's terrifying, right?

Susan: Right.

Dr. Miller: We are not actually going to work on the image anymore about the child, the sexual stuff. That's not even relevant. What's important is your image that you're going to be ostracized. That's terrifying, right?

Susan: Yeah.

Dr. Miller: What color is the terror?

Susan: Red.

Dr. Miller: Where is that color located in your body?

Susan: My shoulder.

Dr. Miller: See that red as being composed of tiny, little particles.

Susan: Do I close my eyes and image it?

Dr. Miller: Yeah. Just like we did last time. Okay?

Susan: Okay.

Dr. Miller: Just see the red as being composed of tiny, little red particles. Just nod your head when you get it. All right. Breathe into the tiny, tiny, little red particles and breathe them directly away from your body.

Susan: Okay.

Dr. Miller: Breathe into the center of your brain and see the tiny red particles go out of your forehead.

Susan: Okay.

Dr. Miller: Breathe into the center of your brain and see the tiny red particles go out your eyes.

Susan: Okay.

Susan does the P/TRT on the red particles.

Dr. Miller: Now, let's re-evaluate. When you think of going to prison, being ostracized, does it feel as charged as it was?

Susan: No. That might be because that's just a thought right now. It could come like tonight at nine o'clock and it could be really intense.

Dr. Miller: Well, we'll see. We're not finished. What I want you to do now is take that image of being in prison, being ostracized, right?

Susan: Mm-hmm.

Dr. Miller: See it composed of tiny, little particles.

Susan: Mm-hmm.

Dr. Miller: Drop all the particles to the ground.

Susan: Okay. I should try that one more time actually. What do I have to do?

Dr. Miller: Just re-image it again. Tell me what you've got. Is it the same as it was?

Susan: Yeah.

Dr. Miller: Okay. See it composed of tiny, little particles.

Susan: Okay.

Dr. Miller: Drop the image to the ground.

Susan: Okay.

Dr. Miller: Re-image it again, and tell me what you've got.

Susan: Not as intense.

Dr. Miller: Okay. See it composed of tiny, little particles.

Susan: Okay.

Dr. Miller: Drop all the particles to the ground.

Susan: Okay.

Dr. Miller: Re-image it again and tell me what you've got.

Susan: Just a little picture. That's all.

Dr. Miller: Okay. See that little picture as being composed of tiny, little particles.

Susan: Okay.

Dr. Miller: Drop all the particles to the ground.

Susan: Okay.

Dr. Miller: Re-image it again, and tell me what you've got.

Susan: I don't want to really think of it.

Dr. Miller: If you do think of it, what do you get?

Susan: Nothing, really.

Dr. Miller: Good, all right. Now we are going to release the particles of the image from your body just like we've done before.

Susan: Okay.

Dr. Miller: Breathe into the center of your brain and see the particles of the image go out of your forehead.

Susan: Okay.

Susan releases the particles of the image.

Dr. Miller: All right. When you think of that image, what's your response now?

Susan: Being like in prison?

Dr. Miller: Yes.

Susan: Nothing, nothing big.

Dr. Miller: Now I want you to think of what we started with. How does that feel to you now?

Susan: Yeah.

Dr. Miller: What's your response to you being a bad sexual being?

Susan: Nothing, really.

Dr. Miller: Okay.

Susan: I forgot the thought.

Dr. Miller: [Laughs] Okay. Think about the original image we started with.

Susan: Yeah.

Dr. Miller: What's your response to that now? Do you remember?

Susan: Yeah, I remember the thought, yeah. It's nothing really.

Dr. Miller: Right. Because it was always ridiculous, wasn't it?

Susan: Yeah.

Dr. Miller: You were thinking about another one. What was the other one?

Susan: The dog.

Dr. Miller: The dog. Think about that. Is there any charge left in that?

Susan: A little bit.

Dr. Miller: Okay. All right. Do you want to do another set? Do you feel tired?

Susan: No, let's finish off Archie.

Dr. Miller: Archie? Okay. What's the image with Archie?

Susan: Like I have been abusing him all his life.

Dr. Miller: Now, does it have the same feeling that you've done something wrong?

Susan: Yes. I guess. I don't know. Okay, so it would be like I'm a terrible person.

Dr. Miller: Okay. And was this a sexual thing too?

Susan: Yeah.

Dr. Miller: Okay, all right. We would do exactly the same thing. If you are a terrible person, what's going to happen to you?

Susan: People ostracize me.

Dr. Miller: Okay, what does that look like now?

Susan: Nothing, really. I mean I think I'll be—like Archie is my everything. So I feel like, "How could you do this to a dog?"

Dr. Miller: Okay. Is somebody is saying that to you, "How could you do this to the dog"?

Susan: In life?

Dr. Miller: No, in your imagination.

Susan: I was going to say, no one in my life. [Laughter]

   Yeah, I think it is just a thought.

Dr. Miller: "How could you do this to a dog?" Okay.

Susan: To an innocent dog.

Dr. Miller: To an innocent dog. Okay. And what you are doing again is a sexual thing?

Susan: Yeah, like touching him inappropriately or me pulling him on his ears or...

 ImTT Press, publisher

Dr. Miller: Okay.

Susan: Pinching him.

Dr. Miller: Hurting him in some way.

Susan: Yeah.

Dr. Miller: Okay, And so you imagine somebody who does that is a terrible person?

Susan: Yeah.

Dr. Miller: Okay. What's going to happen to you if you are a terrible person?

Susan: No one will be with me.

Dr. Miller: "No one will be with me."

Susan: Yes.

Dr. Miller: What does it look like that no one will be with you?

Susan: No one will like me.

Dr. Miller: No one will like you. So what does the image look like, no one liking you?

Susan: I don't know.

Dr. Miller: Okay. I mean, has everybody turned their backs on you? Are they pointing their fingers at you? Are you trying to talk to them and nobody is listening? Nobody is liking you—are you sitting all alone in the room?

Susan: Yeah. And Archie would be taken away from me.

Dr. Miller: Oh, okay. Archie would be taken away from you.

Susan: Yeah, he would be taken from me.

Dr. Miller: Okay. And would that be painful or terrifying?

Susan: Both.

Dr. Miller: Which one is stronger?

Susan: Painful.

Dr. Miller: Painful. Okay. What we are going to do now is release the pain of that image. So the image is that Archie is going to be taken away from you. And what is the color of that pain?

Susan: Blue came to my head

Dr. Miller: Okay. Where is it located?

Susan: My chest came to me.

Dr. Miller: Okay. So let's begin. See the blue in your chest being composed of tiny little particles.

Susan: Okay.

Dr. Miller: Breathe into those tiny little particles and breathe them directly away from your chest.

Susan: All right.

Dr. Miller: Breathe into the center of your brain and see the tiny blue particles go out through your forehead.

Susan: Okay.

Susan does the P/TRP on the blue particles.

Dr. Miller: Now, when you think of that image of Archie being taken away from you, is it as charged as it was?

Susan: No. It's dumb.

Dr. Miller: Okay. So now what we are going to do is deconstruct that image like we have done before.

Susan: Mm-hmm.

Dr. Miller: Right, the image is Archie being taken away from you, whatever that looks like.

Susan: Okay.

Dr. Miller: Okay. See that image.

Susan: Even though it started with me, like, abusing him.

Dr. Miller: Yeah, that's not the end part; that's not what we need to deal with.

Susan: Okay.

Dr. Miller: Okay. See image of him being taken away from you.

Susan: Okay.

Dr. Miller: See it as being composed of tiny little particles.

Susan: Okay.

Dr. Miller: And drop the particles to the floor.

Susan: Okay.

Dr. Miller: Re-image it again and tell me what you've got.

Susan: The same thought that he is being taken away.

Dr. Miller: Okay. Is it as intense as it was?

Susan: No.

Dr. Miller: Okay, good. So see the image as being composed of tiny little particles.

Susan: Mm-hmm.

Dr. Miller: Drop them to the ground.

Susan: Okay.

Dr. Miller: Re-image again and tell me what you've got.

Susan: Nothing, really. Like, him being taken away but not as scary.

Dr. Miller: Okay. We're still not finished. See that image being composed of tiny little particles.

Susan: Okay.

Dr. Miller: Drop them all to the ground.

Susan: Okay.

Dr. Miller: Re-image it again and tell me what you've got.

Susan: I don't really want to think of it because it's dumb.

Dr. Miller: It's dumb. Okay. Now we're going to go through and clear out the particles of the image out of the body again. Okay?

Breathe into the center of your brain and see the particles of the image go out your forehead.

Susan releases the particles of the image from her body.

Dr. Miller: All right now. So when you think of Archie being taken from you, how does that seem to you now?

Susan: Not that big of a deal.

Dr. Miller: Okay. And when you think of doing something inappropriate with him, how does that seem?

Susan: Like whatever. Because I know I don't do that; my mind just tells me that.

Dr. Miller: Okay. Very good. Well done today.

Jason: Developing Boundaries

Dr. Miller: Tell me more.

Jason: My father wasn't really there to act as a buffer, or to take control or to take charge. There's a fair amount of disappointment on that front.

Dr. Miller: What are you disappointed about?

Jason: I think if he had participated in the parenting area as an active participant, the learning could have been much faster and much more conducive, I think.

Dr. Miller: What do you think is missing in you as a result of your father not participating?

Jason: I would say a couple of things would have been a little different, I'm thinking. The biggest one is I would have probably learned the ability to deal with conflict and face it, rather than flee from it, perhaps. number one. And number two, be able to share, express, because there was no safe zone, right? So I think that would've made a huge difference in my development.

Dr. Miller: What is missing in you, that you can't do that?

Jason: I guess what's missing is that it takes me a little bit longer to forcefully address— or not forcefully—but to take things head on. I think that's sort of a—it's like a terrible lag. What I have is a terrible lag, just in general, across the board, in that sense.

Dr. Miller: It shows up both in work and in your relationships?

Jason: It shows up definitely in my relationships. There's no doubt about that. Work is probably more—yeah, I would say it shows up at work, probably. I never really looked at it that way. But I'd say until—yeah, I'm sure it showed up in my career.

Dr. Miller: You're talking about your behavior. What is missing in you that makes that behavior? What would you imagine would have to be inside of you in order to do the kind of behavior you want to do?

Jason: I don't know. It's hard to put words to it. It's hard to sort of articulate what it is that's missing. Well, at times, I feel, that's just me, that's my personality. If a person is sensitive, then you're sensitive. If a person is easygoing, "let it go," then the person is easygoing. But I think what's missing is more striking that balance or striking a consistent balance. That's what's missing.

Dr. Miller: Between what?

Jason: Striking a consistent balance.of sort of grasping the relationship aspect or just grasping that kind of stuff in general—interpersonal, for example—grasping that.

Dr. Miller: What you're missing is having psychological boundaries. Your mother was very intrusive, right?

Jason: Right.

Dr. Miller: When the mother is very intrusive or any parent is very intrusive, you don't have the psychological space you need in order to think.

When somebody is really intrusive in your psychological space, you learn you can't look at people's behavior and just think about it. It's like they're already in your psychological space.

Think about it like this: Let's say your psychological space goes out two feet. And that you need that two feet of space for thinking, that you need that kind of thinking. When you really don't have that, it's like your boundary gets pulled in right here. You have to think in this small space.

You just stay inside your little small space, but you can't really think, you can't really observe them out there. Is this making any sense at all?

Jason: I would say the closed space, yes. I would relate that to me—I was working too hard; I was overeating when I was younger, working too hard, in terms of—and up to, perhaps, well into my 30s or 40s. Until I was able to strike and sort of step back a little bit, that's when I was able to then manage things better. But until then, I was working way too hard. I was just overeating, so to speak.

Dr. Miller: People overeat when they feel intruded on. It's like the only defense you have is to overeat. You're kind of stuffing it down. Whereas, if you had your psychological space, you can actually think out there. You don't feel invaded. You can look at other people's thoughts and feelings objectively.

Instead of feeling overwhelmed by them, you go, "Okay, they're feeling this, they're thinking that. What do I think about that?" If you don't have psychological space, you can't ask yourself, "What do I think about what they're doing?"

They're just kind of in your face. You'd overeat because you can't think about anything. All you feel is the stress of everybody in your face. Does that sound right?

Jason: Yeah, I can relate to not being able to have that dialogue; that dialogue is missing.

Dr. Miller: Right. You can't have a dialogue if you don't have psychological space. In order to have a dialogue, you have to have your own thoughts. In order to have your own thoughts, you have to have psychological space. Is that making sense?

Jason: Yes.

ImTT Press, publisher

Dr. Miller: What would be your image of somebody always inside your boundaries? Who would it be? or how many people would it be? What would that image be, of people in your space?

Jason: It would be a magnified image of somebody, magnified figure or magnified space. Just something large like a mass, a huge mass. Inside that mass would be some attributes such as there would be fear, and something more fear related, something frightening. I do remember, as a child, I got a fair amount of nightmares.

Dr. Miller: A mass, and in that mass is something that's very threatening. Let's take this mass, and let's deconstruct it. Is it terrifying?

Jason: It's fearful, yes.

Dr. Miller: What color is the terror?

Jason: Black.

Dr. Miller: Black. Where is it located?

Jason: Just above my head somewhere. In front of me, in my eyes.

Dr. Miller: See that black as composed of tiny, little black particles, and breathe into those particles, and breathe them directly away from your body.

Jason releases the black particles of terror with the P/TRP.

Dr. Miller: How do you feel?

Jason: I could visualize it. I could definitely see its decomposition.

Dr. Miller: When you think of the mass, what's your reaction to it now?

Jason: The fear is gone. The color vaguely exists out there, but the fear part of it is gone.

Dr. Miller: Let's clear up the rest of the image. Pixelate the image and deconstruct it.

Jason deconstructs the image with the IDP.

Dr. Miller: How does that feel?

Jason: It feels good.

Dr. Miller: When you think of the image, what comes up for you?

Jason: I don't see it right now.

Dr. Miller: When you think of your father, what comes up for you?

Jason: I think what comes up for me when I think about him is—I mean he is a sweet person, but I see his weakness too. That's what I see.

Dr. Miller: How does that feel in terms of being disappointed?

Jason: I think I am more—how should I say it? I think I can accept it now.

Dr. Miller: Now, think of your wife. Just think of your wife for about 20 seconds. [Silence] And how does that feel now?

Jason: I think she is in a good space.

Dr. Miller: [Laughs]

Jason: I mean, I feel good about her.

Dr. Miller: Does this make sense, why these changes occurred?

Jason: Explain, please. Elaborate.

Dr. Miller: When you don't have the psychological space to think, everything is just kind of personal. It's kind of all about you in a certain kind of way. It's kind of overwhelming, and you really can't see other people.

You can see your father's weakness, and it's not impacting you, and so if it's not impacting you, it's easier to accept. With your wife, you need that psychological space in order to feel comfortable with her.

Otherwise, they're too much in your own thought patterns, in your own psychological space. When somebody is in your space too much, it's irritating; you want to get away from them some of the time, that kind of stuff.

People need their psychological space, they need their place to be, to think, to feel. One way to get that psychological space is to withdraw.

The trick in a relationship, the goal in a relationship is to be yourself while you're also connected with someone else. You can only do that if you have your own psychological space.

Jason: Yes, I see it.

Dr. Miller: Okay?

Jason: Yes.

Dr. Miller: All right. For whatever reason, that image you had represented all the intrusions on your psychological space. You started having nightmares from an early age, you said, right?

Jason: Yes.

Dr. Miller: That may have been part of what was going on—that you did not have your psychological space as a child. Okay?

Jason: Yes.

Dr. Miller: Very good. Good work today.

Appendix

ImTT Press, publisher

General Instructions and Protocols

General Instructions for the Image Transformation Therapy Protocols

The following protocols provide a thorough release of the images creating dysfunctional feelings and behaviors. However, developing the appropriate targets is essential. This requires a deeper understanding of ImTT and the Survival Model of Psychological Dynamics. For more specific scripts targeting different issues, see the manual, Image Transformation Therapy Scripts for Therapists by Robert Miller (2015).

The Pain/Terror Release Protocol

The P/TRP utilizes a breathing/visualization technique. This process works best if, when the color is visualized, it is thought of as an actual physical substance being removed from the body. Breathing the color out (releasing the color) is easier if the color is visualized as composed of tiny, tiny, tiniest particles of a size that easily flows out of the body. Alternately, if the person conceives of the P/T as a sound, the sound should be thought of as being composed of tiny units that somehow diminish. Whether you use a visual or auditory mode of identifying the P/T, it is very important to think of the color or sounds as an actual substance that is being released from the body. The more intensely this process can be visualized or represented in a sensory modality, the more complete the release of the P/T will be. The more complete the release, the more complete the transformation of the memories, feelings, and behaviors.

IMPORTANT!

Ideally, the process of the P/TRP moves seamlessly from identifying the event to identifying the feeling about the event to identifying the color (sound) of the P/T. Once the color of the P/T has been identified, it is no longer necessary to pay any attention to the event, the feeling, or the P/T. Instead, the focus is to hone in on the color (or sound) of the P/T that has been identified, functionally ignoring the P/T's roots.

The Pain/Terror Release Protocol Instructions

The Pain/Terror Release Protocol (P/TRP) releases the pain/terror (P/T) associated with disturbing memories or negative feelings and thoughts. If you are using sound as a way to identify the P/T, substitute the word 'sound' for the word 'color.'

The parts of the body chosen in this protocol for the release have been generally found to be effective. As you become more adept at this process, you may find that the colors are mostly focused in certain parts of the body and not others. Therefore, you may want to emphasize those areas. However, you can never really know ahead of time when a release from one area of the body will be useful. Therefore, the entire protocol should be performed every time

Another important part of the protocol is to see the color as composed of very tiny, tiny, tiny particles. Visualizing the color in this way appears to make the release easier. If the client uses sound instead of color, find an image in which the general image is composed of very small units such as small units of sound. The image does not have to be reasonable. The image just has to make sense to the client.

While this protocol can be done at home by the client, the problem is that a person's mind tends to lose focus on releasing the particles. A recording of a person's voice can be made to help overcome this wandering-mind problem. Listening to a recording of the protocol can be very useful for keeping your mind focused on releasing the color. Most people's minds tend to lose focus and drift off. A recording of the protocol can keep the client focused so that the particles can be completely released from all parts of the body.

The only purpose of the P/TRP is to release the P/T and transform the behavior and feelings. If the client finds focusing on different areas of the body or visualizing the color in different ways is more effective, go with what works for the client. Sometimes you just might have to get creative in order to get the P/T to release. How will you know if what you're doing is right? If the client's attitude and feelings toward the original memory or feeling undergo a permanent transformation, you're doing the protocol correctly.

Summary of Important Points:

1. The person is only to lightly acknowledge the presence of the pain or terror. Make sure the person understands that she is not to intensely connect with the feelings.

2. Process only one formative event in a session.

3. Do the entire protocol every time if the person can maintain psychological stability.

4. Visualize the color/sound as being composed of small units.

5. If the client becomes stuck in the release, be creative in finding a method of release.

224   ImTT Press, publisher

Learning the P/TRP

It is easiest to learn the P/TRP using an event that the client remembers as painful. So for the client's first processing with the P/TRP, pick an event that is obviously emotionally painful. This approach makes it easy to identify the pain and allows the client to focus on learning the basics of the protocol.

The following is a script of the instructions for the P/TRP. The script is in italics. The words in brackets are instructions for the therapist. For each part of the body, allow time for at least 3 breaths, though more time can be given as needed.

Some people have difficulty visualizing the color and/or the release of the particles. Sometimes the problem occurs because the person has unrealistic expectations about what he should be "seeing." A simple way around this difficulty is to have the person pretend or imagine the color, the location, and the release. Pretending to "see" the color removes the anxiety of having to visualize.

Non-visualizing approaches to releasing the P/T

Even the pretending-to-see technique does not always work. In this situation, it is important to work with the person to find some approach that will work for them. Instead of color, a sound or a tactile representation of the P/T can be utilized. Work with the person until he can find a way to represent the P/T and release it. The goal is to release the P/T. Exactly how the person releases the P/T is not important. Whatever method works is good.

Releasing the Pain from a Painful Event   (General Instructions)

The following is a general script of the instructions for using the P/TRP.
The script is in *italics*. The words in [brackets] are instructions for the therapist.

Script: *Before we begin, I want you to be very clear about something that is very important for making the treatment easy and gentle. When I ask you about what you feel, I don't want you to get into the feelings. I just want you to kind of notice the feelings from a distance. Okay? If you experience the feelings too much, it actually slows down the release process. Does that make sense to you? Just kind of notice the feelings from a distance. Once I ask you about the color of the feeling, I don't even want you to think of the event, image, or feeling again until we have finished processing and we evaluate the change. Okay? With that in mind, let's begin.*

1. *I'm going to ask you to lightly describe that painful memory. Again, I don't want you to get deeply into the pain. Feeling the pain is not necessary. Just be aware that the pain is there. Once the color of the pain is identified, just focus on the color. Don't think of the event or the feeling or the pain again–just the color.*

2. *Now lightly describe the painful memory.*

3. *What color is the pain?*

4. *From now on, I don't want you to think of anything but the color. Forget everything else. Just focus on the color, okay?*

5. *Where is the* [state color] *located in your body?*

6. *Visualize the* [state color] *as being composed of tiny, tiny, little* [state color] *particles.*

7. *Take a slow breath and visualize breathing into the* [state color] *particles.*

8. *As you breathe out, see the tiny* [state color] *particles moving directly out of your body.*

9. *Breathe into the center of your brain and release the tiny* [state color] *particles out the center of your forehead.*

10. *Breathe into the center of your brain and release the tiny* [state color] *particles out your eyes.*

11. *Breathe into your chest and release the tiny* [state color] *particles down your arms and out the palms of your open hands.*

12. *See your spine as being composed of guitar strings that go from the bottom of your spine to the top of your head. Breathe into the guitar strings; and as you breathe out, release the tension on the guitar strings and see the tiny, tiny* [state color] *particles radiate out in all directions as you release the tension on the lower guitar strings.*

13. *See the tiny* [state color] *particles radiate out in all directions as you release the tension on the middle guitar strings.*

14. *See the tiny* [state color] *particles radiate out in all directions as you release the tension on the upper guitar strings.*

15. *Breathe into your abdomen and release the tiny* [state color] *particles out your navel area.*

16. *Breathe into your abdomen and release the tiny* [state color] *particles down your legs and out the bottoms of your feet.*

17. *See a spot 6 inches below your feet, between your feet…breathe into that spot… and see the tiny* [state color] *particles drain down your body, go through the spot, and be absorbed into the earth…see the* [state color] *particles drain down your body, go through that spot, and be absorbed…absorbed…absorbed into the earth.*

18. *Place your feet flat against the floor. See a six-inch sphere 18 inches beneath your feet. Breathe into the sphere…breathe into the sphere and see the tiny* [state color] *particles release from the sphere…see the tiny, tiny* [state color] *particles releasing from the sphere.*

19. *Breathe into your heart...breathe into your heart and release the tiny, tiny* [state color] *particles out your heart...releasing the tiny* [state color] *particles out of your heart.*

20. *Breathe into the depths of your heart…breathe into the deep, deep depths of your heart and release the tiny, tiny* [state color] *particles from the depths of your heart... releasing the tiny* [state color] *particles from the deep depths of your heart.*

21. *Breathe into your throat…breathe into your throat and release the tiny* [state color] *particles out your throat…releasing the tiny* [state color] *particles out of your throat.*

22. *Breathe into your voice…breathe into the depths of your voice and release the tiny* [state color] *particles from your voice…releasing the tiny* [state color] *particles from the deep depths of your voice.*

23. *Breathe into the right side of your brain...breathe into the right side of your brain and release the tiny, tiny* [state color] *particles out the right side of your brain... releasing the tiny* [state color] *particles out the right side of your brain.*

24. *Breathe into the left side of your brain...breathe into the left side of your brain and release the tiny, tiny* [state color] *particles out the left side of your brain...releasing the tiny* [state color] *particles out the left side of your brain.*

25. *Breathe into the front of your brain...breathe into the front of your brain and release the tiny, tiny* [state color] *particles out the front of your brain...releasing the tiny* [state color] *particles out the front of your brain.*

26. *Breathe into the back of your brain...breathe into the back of your brain and release the tiny, tiny* [state color] *particles out the back of your brain...releasing the tiny* [state color] *particles out the back of your brain.*

27. *Breathe into the center of your brain...breathe into the center of your brain and see the tiny, tiny* [state color] *particles, releasing, radiating out in all directions from the center of your brain...see the tiny* [state color] *particles releasing, radiating out in all directions from the center of your brain.*

28. *Breathe into your mind...breathe into the deep depths of your mind and release the tiny* [state color] *particles from your mind...releasing the tiny* [state color] *particles from the deep depths of your mind.*

29. *Breathe into the core of your self...breathe into what you think of as the core of your self...and release the tiny, tiny* [state color] *particles out the core of your self... releasing the tiny* [state color] *particles out the core of your self.*

30. *Imagine that you are about to yawn. Imagine that you are yawning a deep, wide yawn. As you yawn, see the* [state color] *particles release from the core of your self...as you feel the yawn throughout your whole body...as you feel the yawn throughout your whole body, see the tiny* [state color] *particles releasing from the core of your self.*

31. *Let's re-evaluate the pain of the memory. Does it feel less charged when you think of the event again?*

32. [If the emotional reaction is acutely painful, if another feeling has surfaced, or if the color has changed, re-evaluate what the person is feeling. If another feeling has surfaced, the P/TRP for that feeling may need to be done.]

33. [If the memory is less charged, do the Image De-Construction Protocol.]

Image De-Construction Protocol

(General Instructions)

Once the P/T has been removed from the image, most of the energy has been released from the image. The image, thought, or feeling still exists but without the power it used to have. Deconstructing the image is the second stage in the process of transformation.

The following is a general script of the instructions for using the IDP.
The script is in *italics*. The words in [brackets] are instructions for the therapist.

Shaded areas indicate instructions to be repeated as needed.

1. *Visualize the image.* [Or whatever method the client has used to represent the image.]

2. *Now visualize the image as being composed of tiny, tiny particles like pixels on a TV screen.* [Client indicates when this is done.]

3. *Now we are going to deconstruct the image. You can deconstruct the image by dropping the particles to the ground, using a hammer to break up the image, washing the image away, or by using any other method that works for you. Pick a method you like and deconstruct the image. Tell me when you're finished.*
[Client indicates when this is done.]

4. *Now re-image it again, and tell me how it looks. Is the image as vivid as it was, starting to blur, falling apart, or changing in some way?* [Client describes the image.]

5. *Now pixelate the image again.* [Client indicates when this is done.]

6. *Okay, now deconstruct the image again.* [Client indicates when this is done.]

7. *Now re-image it again, and tell me how it looks.* [Client describes the image.]

8. [Continue with steps 5, 6, and 7 until the image cannot be re-created.]

9. [Once either the image cannot be re-created or a positive image emerges, release the pixel-particles of the image from the body. Allow about 3 breaths per part of the body, though more time can be given as needed.]

10. *Breathe into the center of your brain and release the tiny pixel-particles out the center of your forehead.*

11. *Breathe into the center of your brain and release the tiny pixel-particles out your eyes.*

12. *Breathe into your chest and release the tiny pixel-particles down your arms and out the palms of your open hands.*

13. *See your spine as being composed of guitar strings that go from the bottom of your spine to the top of your head. Breathe into the guitar strings; and as you breathe out, release the tension on the guitar strings and see the tiny pixel-particles radiate out in all directions as you release the tension on the lower guitar strings.*

14. *See the tiny pixel-particles radiate out in all directions as you release the tension on the middle guitar strings.*

15. *See the tiny pixel-particles radiate out in all directions as you release the tension on the upper guitar strings.*

16. *Breathe into your abdomen and release the tiny pixel-particles out your navel area.*

17. *Breathe into your abdomen and release the tiny pixel-particles down your legs and out the bottoms of your feet.*

18. *See a spot 6 inches below your feet, between your feet…breathe into that spot… and see the tiny pixel-particles drain down your body, go through the spot, and be absorbed into the earth…see the tiny pixel-particles drain down your body, go through that spot, and be absorbed…absorbed…absorbed into the earth.*

19. *Place your feet flat against the floor. See a six-inch sphere 18 inches beneath your feet. Breathe into the sphere…breathe into the sphere and see the tiny pixel-particles release from the sphere…see the tiny, tiny pixel-particles releasing from the sphere.*

20. *Breathe into your heart...breathe into your heart and release the tiny pixel-particles out your heart...releasing the tiny pixel-particles out of your heart.*

21. *Breathe into the depths of your heart…breathe into the deep, deep depths of your heart, and release the tiny, tiny pixel-particles from the deep depths of your heart... releasing the tiny pixel-particles from the deep depths of your heart.*

22. *Breathe into your throat…breathe into your throat and release the tiny pixel-particles out your throat…releasing the tiny pixel-particles out of your throat.*

23. *Breathe into your voice…breathe into the depths of your voice and release the tiny pixel-particles from your voice…releasing the tiny pixel-particles from the deep depths of your voice.*

24. *Breathe into the right side of your brain...breathe into the right side of your brain and release the tiny, tiny pixel-particles out the right side of your brain...releasing the tiny pixel-particles out the right side of your brain.*

25. *Breathe into the left side of your brain...breathe into the left side of your brain and release the tiny, tiny pixel-particles out the left side of your brain...releasing the tiny pixel-particles out the left side of your brain.*

ImTT Press, publisher

26. *Breathe into the front of your brain...breathe into the front of your brain and release the tiny, tiny pixel-particles out the front of your brain...releasing the tiny pixel-particles out the front of your brain.*

27. *Breathe into the back of your brain...breathe into the back of your brain and release the tiny, tiny pixel-particles out the back of your brain...releasing the tiny pixel-particles out the back of your brain.*

28. *Breathe into the center of your brain…breathe into the center of your brain and see the tiny, tiny pixel-particles, releasing, radiating out in all directions from the center of your brain...see the tiny pixel-particles, releasing, radiating out in all directions from the center of your brain.*

29. *Breathe into your mind…breathe into the deep depths of your mind and release the tiny pixel-particles from your mind…releasing the tiny pixel-particles from the deep depths of your mind.*

30. *Breathe into the core of your self...breathe into what you think of as the core of your self and release the tiny pixel-particles from the core of your self…releasing the tiny pixel-particles from the core of your self.*

31. *Imagine that you are about to yawn. Imagine that you are yawning a deep, wide yawn. As you yawn, see the tiny pixel-particles release from the core of your self...as you feel the yawn throughout your whole body...as you feel the yawn throughout your whole body, see the tiny pixel-particles releasing from the core of your self.*

32. *Scan your body to see if there are any particles remaining in your body. If there are, breathe into that part of your body and then breathe the tiny pixel-particles out the pores of your skin in that area.*

33. *Let's re-evaluate the image. What is your reaction to the image now?*
    [There should be some change in attitude toward the image even if some charge remains.]

34. [If the reaction is intensely charged, re-evaluate the situation. There may be another feeling related to the image.]

When there are multiple feelings related to an image or a memory, the image may become less charged or altered in some way without being completely released after one complete processing with the IDP. This may not be noticed until the next session. Then repeat both the P/TRP and the IDP on the memory or image.

Techniques for Deconstructing the image

There is no one best technique for deconstructing the image. Different people will find specific techniques that work best for them. For some people, allowing the pixel-particles to drop to the ground works best; for others, pixelating and scrambling the image (developed by Joseph Nicolosi) works best. Other techniques include turning the image inside out, allowing the pixels-particles to float away; changing the color of the pixel-particles and then scrambling them are all possible techniques for deconstructing the image. I do not recommend any one technique. Even for the same person, different techniques are useful for different images. If a person has difficulty using one technique, try a different one.

Sometimes when the the person has difficulty deconstructing the image, instructing the client to allow the pixel-particles to be absorbed into the earth after a deconstruction set is performed is useful.

When the Negative Image Changes into a Positive Image

During the Image De-Construction Protocol, negative images appear to transform into positive images. The person's mind is now capable of creating a positive image because the negative image is no longer as intense as previously. What this means, however, is that the positive image is now overriding the negative image—but the negative is still there.

When the person states that there is a positive image, ask the person to return to the original negative image. Continue processing the original negative image until that image has been completely deconstructed. Once the negative image has been completely deconstructed, no positive image is necessary.

Changing Patterns Protocol

Having released the P/T, the person's psychological dynamics are now different. He will have a different attitude toward previous memories, feelings, and behavior. However, the old psychological patterns created by the P/T still need to be transformed. This transformation is accomplished by focusing for a short time on significant memories and daily behaviors. When the person focuses on the old patterns, his mind will automatically begin to transform the old thoughts and patterns. Even without doing this Protocol, the mind would begin this process, but the Changing Patterns Protocol will accelerate the transformation and make the inner shift smoother.

The areas to best focus on are the areas of the person's life that the P/T has most affected. For example, if the P/T of an underlying anger was processed, focusing on the person's interactions with certain people who have often triggered that anger is likely a good place to begin.

Chronic Pain Protocol

The P/TRP can help reduce the intensity of chronic pain. When a person experiences pain for a long time, the sensation of pain builds up in the body. The effect is that the experience of pain is more intense. Releasing the built-up pain will reduce the sensation of pain. Often, the sensation of pain will reduce by half or more. However, because the physical pain is being constantly created, the release of the physical pain sensation will have to be done every day to prevent a buildup of the pain sensation.

A problem that occurs more with physical pain than with a psychological P/T is a difficulty releasing the color. Often a person will sense that the color seems to get "stuck" or won't move through a part of their body. The solution is to think of the tiny pain particles as a physical substance that is trying to move through and out the body. Thinking in terms of "How can I drain those particles out of the body?" or "Why are the particles getting stuck?" can guide you to resolving the problems.

Example: Gentry's chronic pain is in his hips. He has been trying to move the particles down his leg, but the particles seem to get stuck in his knee. A solution may be to visualize the particles leaving out the front of the knee instead of moving down the body. Another possibility is for the person to visualize the particles dissolving and then flowing out. The goal is to creatively find a solution to the blockage.

It is often useful for the person to come up with their own creative ways to release the color. When Jerry visualized his pain, he saw it as "compressed." His method of release was to visualize the black color as being made of small particles and then that an "avalanche" released the particles. Ruth visualized the pain around her spine as a black rubber band. She released the rubber band by seeing it being composed of small particles and the rubber band falling apart. Working with the person to find a creative solution to release the pain will also give them the experience and confidence to utilize the technique at home.

233

The Chronic Pain Protocol Script

1. *Identify the area of the body that is painful.*

2. *On a 1 - 10 scale, how intense is the pain?*

3. *What color is the pain?*

4. *From now on, I don't want you to think of anything but the color.*

5. *Forget everything else. Just focus on the color, okay?*

6. *See the color as being composed of tiny, tiny little* [state color] *particles.*

7. *Take a slow breath and visualize the breath going into the color particles.*

8. *Now breathe the* [state color] *particles directly out of your body through the pores of your skin. Visualize the tiny, tiny, tiny* [state color] *particles flowing out of your body. Take your time and find a way to release the* [state color] *particles out that part of your body.*

9. [At this point, have the client release the color particles from whatever exit point is closest to the pain. If the pain is in the shoulder, begin by releasing the particles from the hand. Then release the particles from the elbow down to the arm. This pattern of release clears the path for releasing the color particles from the painful part of the body. Use this same pattern if the pain is located in the hip: begin releasing with the foot and work up the leg.]

10. *Now we are going to release the* [state color] *particles from the closest easy exit point. We are going to start at that exit point so that we can clear the channels; otherwise, some of the particles might get stuck. So breathe into your* [name the exit point–e.g., foot] *and see the tiny* [state color] *particles flow out your* [name the exit point].

11. *Breathe into your* [name a part of the body further from the exit point] *and visualize the* [state color] *particles flowing down your* [name limb–e.g., leg].

12. [Continue with step 10 until you reach the area of the pain.]

13. [After releasing the color particles from the specific area where the pain is experienced, release the color particles from the other parts of the body.]

14. *As the sensation of pain often builds up in other parts of the body, we are going to release these particles from other parts of your body.*

15. *Breathe into the center of your brain and release the tiny* [state color] *particles out the center of your forehead.*

16. *Breathe into the center of your brain and release the tiny* [state color] *particles out your eyes.*

17. *Breathe into your chest and release the tiny* [state color] *particles down your arms and out the palms of your open hands.*

234

18. See your spine as being composed of guitar strings that go from the bottom of your spine to the top of your head. Breathe into the guitar strings; and as you breathe out, release the tension on the guitar strings and see the tiny [state color] particles radiate out in all directions as you release the tension on the lower guitar strings.

19. See the tiny [state color] particles radiate out in all directions as you release the tension on the middle guitar strings.

20. See the tiny [state color] particles radiate out in all directions as you release the tension on the upper guitar strings.

21. Breathe into your abdomen and release the tiny [state color] particles out your navel area.

22. Breathe into your abdomen and release the tiny [state color] particles down your legs and out the bottoms of your feet.

23. See a spot 6 inches below your feet, between your feet...breathe into that spot...and see the tiny [state color] particles drain down your body, go through the spot, and be absorbed into the earth...see the tiny [state color] particles drain down your body, go through that spot, and be absorbed...absorbed...absorbed into the earth.

24. Place your feet flat against the floor. See a six-inch sphere 18 inches beneath your feet. Breathe into the sphere...breathe into the sphere and see the tiny [state color] particles release from the sphere...see the tiny, tiny [state color] particles releasing from the sphere.

25. Breathe into your heart...breathe into your heart and release the tiny [state color] particles out your heart...releasing the tiny [state color] particles out your heart.

26. Breathe into the depths of your heart...breathe into the deep, deep, depths of your heart and release the tiny, tiny [state color] particles from the deep depths of your heart...releasing the tiny [state color] particles from the deep depths of your heart.

27. Breathe into your throat...breathe into your throat and release the tiny [state color] particles out your throat...releasing the tiny [state color] particles out of your throat.

28. Breathe into your voice...breathe into the depths of your voice and release the tiny [state color] particles from your voice...releasing the tiny [state color] particles from the deep depths of your voice.

29. Breathe into the right side of your brain...breathe into the right side of your brain and release the tiny, tiny [state color] particles out the right side of your brain...releasing the tiny [state color] particles out the right side of your brain.

30. Breathe into the left side of your brain...breathe into the left side of your brain and release the tiny, tiny [state color] particles out the left side of your brain...releasing the tiny [state color] particles out the left side of your brain.

31. *Breathe into the front of your brain...breathe into the front of your brain and release the tiny, tiny* [state color] *particles out the front of your brain...releasing the tiny* [state color] *particles out the front of your brain.*

32. *Breathe into the back of your brain...breathe into the back of your brain and release the tiny, tiny* [state color] *particles out the back of your brain...releasing the tiny* [state color] *particles out the back of your brain.*

33. *Breathe into the center of your brain...breathe into the center of your brain and see the tiny, tiny* [state color] *particles, releasing, radiating out in all directions from the center of your brain...see the tiny* [state color] *particles, releasing, radiating out in all directions from the center of your brain.*

34. *Breathe into your mind…breathe into the deep depths of your mind and release the tiny* [state color] *particles from your mind…releasing the tiny* [state color] *particles from the deep depths of your mind.*

35. *Breathe into the core of your self… breathe into what you think of as the core of your self and release the tiny* [state color] *particles from the core of your self...releasing the tiny* [state color] *particles from the core of your self.*

36. *Imagine that you are about to yawn. Imagine that you are yawning a deep, wide yawn. As you yawn, see the tiny* [state color] *particles release from the core of your self...as you feel the yawn throughout your whole body...as you feel the yawn throughout your whole body, see the tiny* [state color] *particles releasing from the core of your self.*

37. *Scan your body to see if there are any color particles left in your body. If there are, breathe into that part of your body and then breathe the tiny* [state color] *particles out the pores of your skin in that area.*

38. *Let's re-evaluate the pain level. On a scale of 1 – 10, how intense is your pain now?*

39. *Is there another color? What is the color?*

40. [Evaluate for other emotions and images that may need to be processed.]

Deconstructing the Image of Being in Pain

When a person has been in pain a long time, the person often begins to constantly see themselves as a "person in pain." That kind of image adds to the problem. After reducing the pain with the P/TRP, deconstruct the image of being in pain.

The image may not disappear but be altered in some way. If the image is still present when the IDP has been completed, check for feelings such as depression, despair, a feeling of helplessness, hopelessness, or any negative cognitions that the person may have developed from the chronic pain condition. Process those feelings with ImTT.

                                       ImTT Press, publisher

Image De-Construction Protocol

Script: *When a person has been in pain a long time, the person often begins to constantly see themselves as a person in pain, which adds to the problem. So what we're going to do is release that image.*

1. *Visualize an image of yourself being in pain.*

2. *Now visualize the image as being composed of tiny, tiny particles like pixels on a TV screen.* [Client indicates when this is done.]

3. *Now we are going to deconstruct the image. You can deconstruct the image by dropping the particles to the ground, using a hammer to break up the image, washing the image away, or by using any other method that works for you. So pick a method you like and deconstruct the image. Tell me when you're finished.* [Client indicates when this is done.]

4. *Now re-image it again, and tell me how it looks. Is it just as intense, beginning to fade, or are parts of the image dropping out?* [Client describes the image.]

5. *Now pixelate the image again.* [Client indicates when this is done.]

6. *Okay, now deconstruct the image again.* [Client indicates when this is done.]

7. *Let's re-evaluate. Now re-image it again, and tell me how it looks.* [Client describes the image.]

8. [Continue with steps 5, 6, and 7 until the image cannot be re-created.]

9. [Once either the image cannot be re-created or a positive image emerges, release the pixel-particles of the image from the body. Allow about 3 breaths per part of the body, though more time can be given as needed.]

10. *Breathe into the center of your brain and release the tiny pixel-particles out the center of your forehead.*

11. *Breathe into the center of your brain and release the tiny pixel-particles out your eyes.*

12. *Breathe into your chest and release the tiny pixel-particles down your arms and out the palms of your open hands.*

13. *See your spine as being composed of guitar strings that go from the bottom of your spine to the top of your head. Breathe into the guitar strings; and as you breathe out, release the tension on the guitar strings and see the tiny pixel-particles radiate out in all directions as you release the tension on the lower guitar strings.*

14. *See the tiny pixel-particles radiate out in all directions as you release the tension on the middle guitar strings.*

15. *See the tiny pixel-particles radiate out in all directions as you release the tension on the upper guitar strings.*

16. Breathe into your abdomen and release the tiny pixel-particles out your navel area.

17. Breathe into your abdomen and release the tiny pixel-particles down your legs and out the bottoms of your feet.

18. See a spot 6 inches below your feet, between your feet…breathe into that spot… and see the tiny pixel-particles drain down your body, go through the spot, and be absorbed into the earth…see the tiny pixel-particles drain down your body, go through that spot, and be absorbed…absorbed…absorbed into the earth.

19. Place your feet flat against the floor. See a six-inch sphere 18 inches beneath your feet. Breathe into the sphere…breathe into the sphere and see the tiny pixel-particles release from the sphere…see the tiny, tiny pixel-particles releasing from the sphere.

20. Breathe into your heart...breathe into your heart and release the tiny pixel-particles out your heart...releasing the tiny pixel-particles out of your heart.

21. Breathe into the depths of your heart…breathe into the deep, deep depths of your heart, and release the tiny, tiny pixel-particles from the deep depths of your heart… releasing the tiny pixel-particles from the deep depths of your heart.

22. Breathe into your throat…breathe into your throat and release the tiny pixel-particles out your throat…releasing the tiny pixel-particles out of your throat.

23. Breathe into your voice…breathe into the depths of your voice and release the tiny pixel-particles from your voice…releasing the tiny pixel-particles from the deep depths of your voice.

24. Breathe into the right side of your brain...breathe into the right side of your brain and release the tiny, tiny pixel-particles out the right side of your brain...releasing the tiny pixel-particles out the right side of your brain.

25. Breathe into the left side of your brain...breathe into the left side of your brain and release the tiny, tiny pixel-particles out the left side of your brain...releasing the tiny pixel-particles out the left side of your brain.

26. Breathe into the front of your brain...breathe into the front of your brain and release the tiny, tiny pixel-particles out the front of your brain...releasing the tiny pixel-particles out the front of your brain.

27. Breathe into the back of your brain...breathe into the back of your brain and release the tiny, tiny pixel-particles out the back of your brain...releasing the tiny pixel-particles out the back of your brain.

28. Breathe into the center of your brain...breathe into the center of your brain and see the tiny, tiny pixel-particles, releasing, radiating out in all directions from the center of your brain…see the tiny pixel-particles, releasing, radiating out in all directions from the center of your brain.

29. Breathe into your mind…breathe into the deep depths of your mind and release the tiny pixel-particles from your mind…releasing the tiny pixel-particles from the deep depths of your mind.

30. Breathe into the core of your self...breathe into what you think of as the core of your self and release the tiny pixel-particles from the core of your self…releasing the tiny pixel-particles from the core of your self.

31. Imagine that you are about to yawn. Imagine that you are yawning a deep, wide yawn. As you yawn, see the tiny pixel-particles release from the core of your self...as you feel the yawn throughout your whole body...as you feel the yawn throughout your whole body, see the tiny pixel-particles releasing from the core of your self.

32. Scan your body to see if there are any particles remaining in your body. If there are, breathe into that part of your body and then breathe the tiny pixel-particles out the pores of your skin in that area.

33. Let's re-evaluate the image. What is your emotional reaction to the image now?

34. [At this point, the person's attitude toward the image should have altered. If the person's attitude has not changed, re-evaluate the situation for additional emotions.]

The Feeling-State Image Protocol

The FSIP Flow Chart

The FSIP flow chart illustrates the different steps of the FSIP. The FSIP processes the addictive behavior in the reverse direction in which it was created.

Starting with the addictive behavior, the FSIP processes the FS first. Then the trauma or negative event that created the intense desire for the ASF is processed.

Processing the FS first before processing the trauma ensures that the negative cognition and trauma targeted for processing are directly related to the addiction.

People have many different negative cognitions and traumas. Discerning which trauma is related to the addiction before processing the FS would be both extremely difficult and unnecessary.

Processing the FS prior to processing the NC allows the underlying trauma to easily surface to awareness. In fact, sometimes the trauma begins to emerge before the FS is even completely processed.

FSIP Flow Chart

Identify the addictive behavior

Identify the intensified ASF driving the behavior

Process the FS

(Created by the intensified ASF)

Identify the negative cognition (NC)

that blocks experiencing the ASF

Either float back to the event creating the NC or

create an image resonating with the NC

Process the negative memory or image

The Feeling-State Image Protocol

The words in italics are a script for questions the therapist might ask the client.

Phase 1: History and Evaluation

1. Obtain history, frequency, and context of the addictive behavior.

2. Evaluate the person for having adequate coping skills to manage negative feelings if the person is no longer using substances to cope. If the person is too fragile for releasing the addictive behavior, process the pain, terror, and traumas until the person is capable of coping without the addictive behavior.

Phase 2: Preparation

3. Explain the FSIP including the Feeling-State Theory and how fixated memories cause behavioral and substance addictions.

4. Explain how addictive behavior can also be used to avoid memories and feelings.

5. Prepare the client for trauma processing by explaining Image Transformation Therapy and the link between trauma and feeling-states.

6. Release an emotional pain utilizing the P/TRP so that the person has an experience of the protocol and can understand the basic process.

Phase 3: Processing the FS

7. Identify the specific aspect of the addictive behavior that has the most intensity associated with it. If the addiction is to a stimulant drug, then the rush/euphoria memory is processed first. However, if some other memory is more intense, process that first. The starting memory may be the first time or the most recent—whichever is most potent.

8. Identify the specific self-referential positive feeling (ASF) linked with the addictive behavior.

9. Instruct the client to combine 1) visualizing, <u>as if from a distance</u>, doing the addictive behavior and 2) <u>lightly experiencing</u> the positive feeling.

10. Eliminate the image with the Image De-Construction Protocol.

11. If the ASF is a drug-induced Sensation-FS of rush or euphoria, release the reduced feeling-sensation using the Euphoric Sensation Release Protocol (ESRP). If the ASF is not a drug-induced Sensation-FS, go to step 14 without doing the ESRP.

12. After releasing the FS with the ESRP, obtain PFS level. If the PFS is greater than 1, either repeat the IDP or eliminate other Sensation-FSs related to the drug, as necessary, by repeating Steps 7-11.

13. After eliminating the Sensation-FSs, use the Changing Patterns Protocol focusing on different events related to the FS.

Phase 4: Process the NC and Image Underlying the FS

14. Identify the NC linked with the wanted feeling. (*What's the negative belief you have about yourself that makes you feel you can't belong? connect? aren't important? et cetera.*)

15. Identify the image or memory linked with the NC.
    (*Can you remember an event that made you feel that way?*)

16. Process the NC or memory/image with ImTT.

17. Give homework to facilitate an evaluation of the progress of therapy and to elicit any other feelings related to the addictive behavior.

18. During the next session, reevaluate the addictive behavior for the feeling-state identified in the last session. If that FS is still active, continue processing. If the FS has been eliminated, evaluate for other FSs.

19. Steps 7-15 are performed again as necessary.

Phase 5: Process Negative Images and Cognitions Caused by the FS-created Behavior

20. Use memories or a fantasy to identify the negative image that was created as a result of the addictive behavior.

21. Process the image with ImTT. Intense feelings of guilt or shame may need to be processed first if there is resistance to releasing the image.

Phase 6: Process the Memories and Images that May Cause Anxiety about Relapsing

22. Identify the image or memories related to expectations or anxiety about relapsing. Process the identified image or memory with ImTT.

ImTT Press, publisher

Image Transformation Therapy for Children

Created by Dana Tennison, MA, LMFT
© Copyright 2015 Dana Tennison

This intervention was created for use with children and is based on the adult Image Transformation Therapy, the theory and protocols, created by Dr. Robert Miller.

Use of ImTT for Children assumes the following:

- The clinician has trained with Dr. Miller in ImTT for adults.
- The clinician is experienced and proficient in using ImTT with adults.
- The clinician has substantial experience working with children in general and is proficient in treating childhood disorders.
- The child client is between ages 5 and 11 years. Pre-adolescent and adolescent clients can usually follow ImTT for Adults, though clinicians may need to implement parts of ImTT for Children if teen client is emotionally immature or developmentally delayed.
- For children with extensive trauma and/or significant attachment injuries, clinicians are advised to use this intervention conservatively. These children can easily flood and shut down, therefore using this intervention on one body part (e.g., just the head or just the heart) vs. the whole body is advised.

ImTT for Children follows the basic format of the Adult ImTT:

- Pain/Terror Release Protocol
- Image Deconstruction Protocol
- Changing Patterns Technique

ImTT for Children differs from adult version in that:

- Children have shorter attention spans than adult clients; clinician needs to guide children through ImTT protocols faster than with adults.
- Children need concrete pictures to work with vs. abstract images; the younger the child is, the more important this point becomes, the more concrete they will need each step to be.
- Children generally use the words "icky/hurt feelings" for psychological pain and "fear/scary feelings" for terror.
- Because children need concrete steps and experiences, I use a stuffed owl and owl pot (ceramic container with lid) as a depository for both released feelings and pieces of the image during the deconstruction phase.

ImTT Press, publisher

Prior to starting ImTT with a child client, it is assumed the clinician has attended to the following:

- Rapport and trust have been established between clinician and child.

- Clinician has discussed ImTT with parents, as with any modality used, to provide parent education and explanation of treatment.

- Child's sense of safety is established and affect tolerance has been assessed by clinician as sufficient for this intervention.

- Clinician has assessed child's ability to be checked into his/her body and has co-created language with the child for purposes of grounding and age-appropriate self-awareness.

- Child has working knowledge of emotions and language to articulate his/her emotional experiences.

- Child and clinician have worked on basic breathing skills (diaphragmatic breathing) and have created language around this specific skill, for example, "in-breath, out-breath."

- Child can identify unwanted pain or terror, has an understanding of his/her emotional experience involving pain or terror and the target event.

- Child is willing and motivated (enough) to release the pain or terror.

Preparation Phase is critical:

Awareness and adherence to the above criteria are critical to the success of ImTT with children. As with any intervention, it is important to assess the child's baseline functioning and do "the work before the work" to avoid compromising the child's sense of safety or therapeutic trust and rapport. The gentleness of ImTT is one of its most valuable features, yet does not exempt clinicians from the preparation phase of therapy. Once the clinician feels the child is ready, it is important to explain ImTT and gain agreement from the child that he/she is ready and willing to proceed.

Sample explanation to child: *"You know how you wash your hands to clean them? Or brush your teeth to get rid of the icky stuff on them? We need to do the same thing with icky feelings that are inside our bodies. Sometimes feelings get big, uncomfortable and stuck in your body. They might make it hard to do things you really want to do – like play with your friends, go to school, eat, or sleep. Big feelings are a normal part of life AND they can make life hard. It takes a lot of energy to carry those big feelings around all the time. We all have icky feelings – that is normal.*

So it is important to clean our insides, just like we clean our outsides. We are going to do an activity that lets you get rid of any icky feelings that are too big. This activity lets you get rid of whatever big feelings you don't want anymore, the ones that bug you the most. You can get rid of as much or as little as you want (reinforcing the notion that they are in control). I will do this with you and tell you exactly what you need to do. Your job is to breathe and notice what is going on in your body. The first thing we need to do is make a picture of [event]. I know it can be hard to think about [event]: so let me know if it gets too scary and we will stop. We don't have to talk about it too much, just enough to figure out the scariest part and make a picture of that part."

       ImTT Press, publisher

Pain/Terror Release Protocol

Important Points:

- The child need only identify the disturbing event and does not need to intensely connect with the associated feelings.
- Process only one formative event per session.
- Have the child draw the disturbing event, specifically the worst part of it.
- Children need to concretely see the fear in their bodies as opposed to adults who can imagine it and assign it a color. Use of a white board and pom-poms (described below) helps children visualize the feeling and see it composed of particles.
- Depending upon age of child, do your best to help him/her identify necessary points outlined below. As with child therapy in general, sometimes "close enough" is good enough to move forward; be flexible and allow the child's natural creative process to help in the release.

Tools Referenced in Child Protocol:

Owl and owl pot for IDP.

Potential helpers and magnifying glass for P/TRP.

Whiteboard and pom-poms for P/TRP.

Protocol Steps:

1. Have the child describe the disturbing event (past or future) and create an image of the event through drawing or sand tray. Help child identify the most disturbing part of the event: i.e., if they identify "going to the dentist" as the disturbing event, ask them about the worst part of going to the dentist. (The smell? A particular sound? Getting a shot?) Make sure their picture accurately captures this worst part of the event.

2. Help child identify the most disturbing feeling associated with the event – "icky/hurt feelings" or "scared/scary feelings." If child says "both, icky and scary," have them identify which is the bigger of the two, if they can, and concentrate on that.

3. Help child identify a color that goes with the feeling and where the feeling (color) is in the body. Make this more concrete by drawing an outline of their body on a separate piece of paper and have them color in where the pain/terror is located. I use a white board (24 inches x 36 inches) and pom-poms in a variety of colors and sizes. I draw a gingerbread outline on the white board and children use dry erase markers and/or pom-poms to concretely identify where the disturbing feelings are in the body. Use of pom-poms also helps the child see the color as composed of tiny particles, making the release portion easier to complete. The younger the child, the more they tend to identify with the quantity of pom-poms rather than the actual color.

                                       ImTT Press, publisher

4. Have the child stand and conduct a practice release on just one hand. Because this portion of the therapy is so abstract, it is helpful to conduct a practice release to assess the child's understanding of the instructions.

    "Okay, let's get rid of the scary feelings. Remember, you can decide how much you want to get rid of. You can also tell me to stop at any time and we will. Let's practice on your hand first. I want you to take in a deep breath, send it down your arm, into your hand and out through your fingertips. Can you feel it move through your hand?"

    Continue to practice with the child until clinician is assured of the child's understanding of the directions. Also at this stage, encourage the child to select a helper (see photo above) in case child wants assistance with the release.

5. Lead child through the release, moving head to toe, regardless of where he/she identified the feeling is in the body. Have children close their eyes and keep them closed during the release if they can. Most children have no trouble keeping their eyes closed. They also seem more adept than adults at opening and closing them if needed, without interrupting the rhythm of the release. Younger children seem more adept at using a full body breath to clear the entire body instead of breathing into each separate body part. Older children seem better able to take more time and breathe through each body part. For younger children, I encourage them to exhale the unwanted feelings right into the owl pot. As they clear pom-poms, children seem to delight in placing them into the owl pot. As well, if they have drawn on the gingerbread outline, children will erase those markings as they are cleared.

6. Double check that you got all of the feeling/color released. Most kids will be able to tell you along the way if it is stuck as well as if it is all cleared by this point. If it gets stuck, encourage them to use any tool or resource their imagination can provide for assistance, just like with adult clients. Children often organically generate whatever tool they need to help them with this process. For younger children, I hand a magnifying glass to the parent and ask him/her to check the child's body, see if any unwanted feelings are left inside. Children seem very excited to use the magnifying glass and will often tell the parent how much is left and where it is located. If additional feelings are identified, repeat Step 5 until the child endorses the body as completely clear.

7. Most children clear the white board as they release the feelings. If so, proceed to Step 8. If they have not, complete Step 7. Return to the body outline (on white board) and ask the child, *"I wonder how much you got rid of? When you think of* [event] *how many icky feelings are in your body now?"* Encourage the child to remove pom-poms to reflect what was released and what remains. I encourage younger children to put the released pom-poms into the owl pot.

8. **Magic Water procedure**: Once the child confirms the unwanted feelings have been cleared, use this procedure to provide closure on the release portion. You can use a parent, if present, to "pour" the water into the child's head.

   Sample language: "*Great job. Now I want you to picture a small opening in the top of your head and I am going to pour magic water into that opening* [lightly touch top of child's head] *just so it fills up your head. This is magical water and it's kind of sparkly and glittery. It cleans out your body to make sure all the unwanted feelings are gone. The water is just going to fill up your head; when I count to three, you get to release it and let it flow through the rest of your body. Are you ready?* [build anticipation] *Here comes the magic water* [touch head again]. *I want you to feel it slowly fill your head and just your head…* [keep pouring, making water sounds if you like]*…your head is slowly filling with special water, almost to the top* [stop pouring, some kids will tell you when their head is full].

   Follow your in-breath and slowly move your head to the side, bringing your right ear to your right shoulder. Do this as slowly as you can. Do you feel how heavy your head is with all that magic water in it? I want you to notice how the water feels sloshing around. [Depending on age, some kids will say they can feel it sloshing, some will just be able to see it in their imagination] *And then bring your head back to the middle… then move it to the other side, touching your left ear to your left shoulder. You might be able to feel the water sloshing side to side or maybe you can just see it – either way is okay.*

   When I count to three you are going to release the magic water and let it pour down the rest of your body to clean out any last bits of fear/red/pom-poms. Are you ready? [build anticipation again] *I'll count to three and then you let it go…one…two…three! Let the magic water go and feel it running down your neck, back, arms and out your hands…feel it go down your chest, belly, legs and out your toes! Now let's shake out your hands* [one at a time, shake out each hand] *for any last drops of water and then shake out your feet* [one at a time, stomping each foot on the floor] *for any last drops of water. Great job!*

Image Deconstruction Protocol

9. Return to the image he/she drew and instruct child to rip it into tiny pieces and place the pieces into the owl pot. Most children will eagerly use their hands to rip up the drawing, although scissors can be used if desired.

For younger children or those with more concrete thinking:

Instruct them to put the pieces into the owl jar along with the pom-poms. Explain to them that the owl's job is to deliver the contents of the owl pot to a place far away so that the icky feelings never bother them again. Help them determine where they want the owl to take the pieces so that these unwanted feelings are gone forever. Encourage them to whisper their request to the owl and put the lid back onto the pot.

For older children or those with the capacity to think more abstractly:

Have the child take some of the destroyed "pieces" in hand and, with eyes closed, encourage him/her to release the pieces wherever they want to; e.g., from a high place (many pick the tallest building in Dubai or outer space), or whatever place they can think of that will safely absorb/eat/take forever the pieces. Some children do this with eyes open, others prefer eyes closed. Encourage the child to take the time necessary to see the pieces disappear.

Sample script: *On the next in-breath, see yourself flying over to the building in Dubai and let me know when you get there…on the next in-breath I want you to release the pieces you have in your hand…just watch the pieces fly away in the wind…watch them disappear…keep following your breath until all the pieces are gone and you cannot see them anymore. Now I want you to try to re-imagine the imag. Can you see it? Has it changed? What do you notice about the image now?* Repeat this step as many times as needed until the child can no longer re-imagine the image or it is replaced with a positive image. Children often accomplish this step in one or two attempts; it goes much more quickly than when working with adults.

.Glossary of Terms with Acronyms

Assured-Survival Feeling (ASF): ASFs are the result of experiences that promote a person's survival. Examples of ASFs are feelings of belonging, being special, important, loved, or safe.

Bilateral Stimulation (BLS): The processing of a memory using alternating side-to-side stimulation, such as eye movements, sound, or tappers.

Changing Patterns Protocol (CPP): An ImTT protocol used to trigger changes in psychological patterns that were created as a result of a previous dysfunctional image.

Euphoric Sensation Release Protocol (ESRP): The ESRP reduces the intensity of the euphoric or rush sensation of a Sensation-FS.

Eye Movement Desensitization and Reprocessing (EMDR): A psychotherapy shown to be effective for processing traumatic memories, using BLS.

Feeling-State (FS): A fixated linkage between an ASF and a person, behavior, or object. The FS is postulated to be a cause of both behavioral and substance addictions.

Feeling-State Addiction Protocol (FSAP): The protocol for breaking the fixation of the FS. The FSAP utilizes a modified form of EMDR for processing the FS.

Feeling-State Image Protocol (FSIP): The protocol for breaking the fixation of the FS. The FSIP utilizes the protocols of Image Transformation Therapy for processing the FS.

Feeling-State Theory: The theory that explains how FSs create behavioral and substance addictions.

Feeling-State Therapy (FST): The therapy for processing substance and behavioral addiction based on Feeling-State Theory.

Image: In ImTT, the word "image" is defined as a psychologically powered mental representation. The image could be powered by feelings of pain, terror, ASFs, or culturally accepted images such as what is considered "manly."

Image Transformation Therapy (ImTT): A new therapy that utilizes different forms of breathing/visualization protocols to process trauma, OCD, anxiety, shock, depression, and phobias.

Image De-Construction Protocol (IDP): An ImTT protocol that eliminates traumatic or dysfunctional images. ImTT is often used in conjunction with the P/TRP.

Intergenerational Joining: An FS in which the person unconsciously mimics a behavior or quality of another person, often a parent. Using "parent" as an example, the person feels connected with the "parent" by taking on a characteristic of the "parent."

Pain/Terror Release Protocol (P/TRP): An ImTT protocol that releases pain and terror in such a way that it is not necessary for the person to experience the feeling in order to process it. ImTT is often used in the processing of trauma.

Positive Feeling Scale (PFS): A zero to 10 scale that measures the intensity of a person's experience of a positive feeling.

Psychologically Induced FS: An FS that is created because of an intensified need for an ASF.

Sensation-FS: An FS that is composed entirely of an intensely positive sensation, such as a euphoric high or the adrenaline excitement triggered by danger.

ImTT Press, publisher

Books by Robert Miller, PhD

Image Transformation Therapy

Image Transformation Therapy Scripts for Therapists

Feeling-State Theory & Protocols of

Behavioral and Substance Addictions

(available on Amazon)

Training

FOR INFORMATION ABOUT TRAINING WORKSHOPS

AND

certification in FSAP or ImTT, go to

www.fsaprotocol.com

www.imttherapy.com

79502039R00146

Made in the USA
Columbia, SC
03 November 2017